Remaking Communities and Adult Learning

Research on the Education and Learning of Adults

Series Editors

(*On behalf of the European Society for Research on the Education of Adults*)
Emilio Lucio-Villegas (*University of Seville, Spain*)
Barbara Merrill (*University of Warwick, United Kingdom*)
Henning Salling Olesen (*Roskilde University, Denmark*)
Cristina C. Vieira (*University of Coimbra, Portugal*)

Editorial Advisory Board

Michal Bron Jr. (*Södertörn University College, Sweden*)
Darlene Clover (*University of Victoria, Canada*)
Gökçe Guvercin (*Malpete University, Turkey*)
Anja Heikkinen (*University of Tampere, Finland*)
Licinio C. Lima (*University of Minho, Portugal*)
Adrianna Nizinska (*Goteborg University, Sweden*)
Joanna Ostrouch-Kamińska (*University of Warmia and Mazury in Olsztyn, Poland*)
Angela Pilch Ortega (*Graz University, Austria*)
Georgios Zarifis (*Aristotle University of Thessaloniki, Greece*)

VOLUME 11

The titles published in this series are listed at *brill.com/esre*

Remaking Communities and Adult Learning

Social and Community-based Learning, New Forms of Knowledge and Action for Change

Edited by

Rob Evans, Ewa Kurantowicz and Emilio Lucio-Villegas

BRILL

LEIDEN | BOSTON

This is an open access title distributed under the terms of the CC BY-NC 4.0 license, which permits any non-commercial use, distribution, and reproduction in any medium, provided the original author(s) and source are credited. Further information and the complete license text can be found at https://creativecommons.org/licenses/by-nc/4.0/

The terms of the CC license apply only to the original material. The use of material from other sources (indicated by a reference) such as diagrams, illustrations, photos and text samples may require further permission from the respective copyright holder.

Cover illustration: Artwork by Rob Evans

All chapters in this book have undergone peer review.

The Library of Congress Cataloging-in-Publication Data is available online at https://catalog.loc.gov

Typeface for the Latin, Greek, and Cyrillic scripts: "Brill". See and download: brill.com/brill-typeface.

ISSN 2542-9345
ISBN 978-90-04-51801-8 (paperback)
ISBN 978-90-04-51802-5 (hardback)
ISBN 978-90-04-51803-2 (e-book)

Copyright 2022 by Rob Evans, Ewa Kurantowicz and Emilio Lucio-Villegas. Published by Koninklijke Brill NV, Leiden, The Netherlands.
Koninklijke Brill NV incorporates the imprints Brill, Brill Nijhoff, Brill Hotei, Brill Schöningh, Brill Fink, Brill mentis, Vandenhoeck & Ruprecht, Böhlau and V&R unipress.
All rights reserved. No part of this publication may be reproduced, translated, stored in a retrieval system, or transmitted in any form or by any means, electronic, mechanical, photocopying, recording or otherwise, without prior written permission from the publisher. Requests for re-use and/or translations must be addressed to Koninklijke Brill NV via brill.com or copyright.com.

This book is printed on acid-free paper and produced in a sustainable manner.

Contents

The European Society for Research on the Education of
Adults (ESREA) IX
Acknowledgements XI
List of Figures XII
List of Acronyms XIII
Notes on Contributors XIV

Introduction: Remaking Communities and Adult Learning 1
   Rob Evans, Ewa Kurantowicz and Emilio Lucio-Villegas

PART 1
Popular Education Looking Back, Looking Forward

1 Adult Learning and Mainstream Education Discourse: Revisiting Freire's *Pedagogy of the Oppressed* 19
   Licínio C. Lima

2 Resisting Mainstream Lifelong Learning: The Contributions of Popular Education and Participatory Research 37
   Emilio Lucio-Villegas

3 Lifelong Education in Diverse Communities: Reading Ettore Gelpi and Leonardo Zanier on Complex Environments 'in Transition' 51
   Davide Zoletto

4 Is Active Citizenship a Forgotten Idea in Europe? Educational Interventions in Five European Countries 64
   Monika Noworolnik-Mastalska

PART 2
Knowledge Democracy, New Pedagogies, Creative Inclusion

5 Co-Constructing Knowledge and Communities: Community-University Research Partnerships and Participatory Research Training 79
   Walter Lepore, Yashvi Sharma, Budd L. Hall and Rajesh Tandon

6   Women's and Gender Museums: Feminist Pedagogies for Illumination, Imagination, Provocation, and Collaboration   94
    Darlene E. Clover

7   Living and Learning with Dementia: Implications for Re-Making Community Life   110
    Jocey Quinn

PART 3
Social Learning and Activism for Change

8   Regaining Lost Community Knowledge: The Impact of Individual and Collective Biographical Work   127
    Rozalia Ligus

9   Social Learning and Building Solidarity: Learning in the Context of a Natural Disaster   142
    Angela Pilch Ortega

10 The 'Pulsating Activism' of Polish Activists: Oscillation between the Mainstream and the Margins   156
    Anna Bilon-Piórko

11 Learning (for) Civil Disobedience in Poland: Extinction Rebellion as a New Form of Social Movement   170
    Marta Gontarska, Paweł Rudnicki and Piotr Zańko

PART 4
Re-Making Community

12 Changes in Community Life   191
    Marjorie Mayo

13 Learning to Make (and Remake) Society: Social Mediation and Mediators' Learning Biographies   205
    Rob Evans

14 Social Pedagogy and Community Networks: Global Coexistence in Pandemic Times   228
    José Antonio Caride, Rita Gradaílle and Laura Varela Crespo

15 Communities and Adult Learning in the Making and Remade   242
    Rob Evans, Ewa Kurantowicz and Emilio Lucio-Villegas

    Index   251

The European Society for Research on the Education of Adults (ESREA)

ESREA is a European scientific society. It was established in 1991 to provide a European-wide forum for all researchers engaged in research on adult education and learning and to promote and disseminate theoretical and empirical research in the field. Since 1991 the landscape of adult education and learning has changed to include more diverse learning contexts at formal and informal levels. At the same time there has been a policy push by the European Union, OECD, UNESCO and national governments to promote a policy of lifelong learning. ESREA provides an important space for these changes and (re)definition of adult education and learning in relation to research, theory, policy and practice to be reflected upon and discussed. This takes place at the triennial conference, network conferences and through the publication of books and a journal.

ESREA Research Networks

The major priority of ESREA is the encouragement of co-operation between active researchers in the form of thematic research networks which encourage inter-disciplinary research drawing on a broad range of the social sciences. These research networks hold annual/biennial seminars and conferences for the exchange of research results and to encourage publications.

The current active ESREA networks are:
- Access, Learning Careers and Identities
- Active Democratic Citizenship and Adult Learning
- Adult Educators, Trainers and Their Professional Development
- Between Global and Local: Adult Learning and Communities
- Education and Learning of Older Adults
- Gender and Adult Learning
- History of Adult Education and Training in Europe
- Interrogating Transformative Processes in Learning: An International Exchange
- Life-history and Biographical Research
- Migration, Ethnicity, Racism and Xenophobia
- Policy Studies in Adult Education
- Working Life and Learning

ESREA Triennial European Research Conference

In order to encourage the widest possible forum for the exchange of ongoing research activities ESREA holds a triennial European Research Conference. The conferences have been held in Strobl (1995), Bruxelles (1998), Lisbon (2001), Wrocław (2004), Seville (2007), Linköping (2010), Berlin (2013), Maynooth (2016) and Belgrade (2019).

ESREA Journal

ESREA publishes a scientific open access journal entitled *The European Journal for Research on the Education and Learning of Adults* (RELA). All issues of the journal can be read at www.rela.ep.liu.se. You can also find more information about call for papers and submission procedures on this website.

ESREA Books

ESREA's research networks and conferences have led to the publication of over forty books. A full list, giving details of the various publishers, and the books' availability, is on the ESREA website. ESREA's current book series is published in co-operation with Brill.

Further information on ESREA is available at www.esrea.org

Emilio Lucio-Villegas
Barbara Merrill
Henning Salling Olesen
Cristina C. Vieira

Acknowledgements

In many ways thanks have to go to all the people who over the years have contributed to the patient construction of a body of ideas and to the desire to give these ideas expression in the form of publications. This first declaration of gratitude therefore goes to all who have participated – routine and one-off – to the work of this research network.

The editors wish of course to thank above all the authors of the chapters in this volume for their energy, their enthusiasm, their interest, and of course, for their intellectual and emotional contribution to a book that wants to talk about the future and wishes to face up to the difficulties of the present, too. Above all, their graciousness in accepting the repeated requests for more here, less there, and for their skill and speed in executing what we hope were just and judicious requests.

Our thanks go naturally to ESREA for providing the Between Global and Local – Adult Learning and Community Research Network with a friendly roof for the last 16 years, under which discussions and encounters of the best kind have been experienced. Particular recognition is owed to the Editorial Board of the series in which this volume appears. Thanks go to them for suggestions at an early stage of the work on this book, and in particular we wish to thank Cristina Vieira and Barbara Merrill for taking on the closer task of editorial guides should we run into difficulties. It is to the readers of this to judge how well we made good use of the excellent help offered us.

Finally, sincere thanks must go to Anna Andrejów-Kubów of the University of Lower Silesia in Wrocław who took on the task of going through the whole book upon near-completion to control the work of the editors. Anna possesses solid knowledge of the sometimes arcane intricacies of APA and she worked methodically, precisely and with both judgement and comprehension for the often maddening irregularities even the most experienced writers succeed in introducing into texts. The editors thank her for doing a vital job with aplomb and authority.

Figures

9.1   A church in the centre of Juchitán (© Pilch Ortega, 2017).   144
9.2   The town hall of the city (© Pilch Ortega, 2017).   145
9.3   A residential building (© Pilch Ortega, 2017).   145
9.4   A residential building (© Pilch Ortega, 2017).   146
9.5   Emergency shelters (© Pilch Ortega, 2017).   146
9.6   Temporary marketplace in Juchitán (© Pilch Ortega, 2017).   146
9.7   "La señora anciana" (© NVI Noticias, 2018).   151
9.8   Mural by the artist group "Colectivo Chiquitraca" (© Pilch Ortega, 2018).   152
9.9   "Señora de las iguanas" by Demian Flores (© Pilch Ortega, 2018).   153
9.10   "El relato del sismo en Juchitán 8.2" (© Santiago Noriega, 2017).   153
9.11   "El Corrido del Terremoto de 7 Septiembre" (© El Tío Memero Vlogs, 2017).   154

Acronyms

CBPR	Community-Based Participatory Research
CBR-SR	Community-Based Research and Social Responsibility
COVID-19	Corona Virus Disease 2019 (year of first description)
CSO	Civil Society Organisation
CUE	Community-University Engagement
CURP	Community-University Research Partnership
DC	Democratic Camp
DLE	Democratic Learning Environments
ELEF	European Learning Environment Formats
HEI	Higher Education Institution
IDA	Investigating Democratic Action
IRWMM	Iranian Women's Movement Museum
LOMCE	Law for the Improvement of Educational Quality (Spain)
MML	Marx Memorial Library (London)
NCCPE	National Coordinating Centre for Public Engagement (UK)
OECD	Organisation for Economic Cooperation and Development
PRIA	Participatory Research in Asia
SE	Street Education
TWT	The World Transformed
UBA	Unnat Bharat Abhiyan (India)
WAM	Women's Active Museum on War and Peace (Japan)
WHO	World Health Organisation
WWHRM	War and Women's Human Rights Museum (Korea)

Notes on Contributors

Anna Bilon-Piórko
(PhD) works at the University of Lower Silesia in Wroclaw, Poland. She graduated in education and philosophy. Her research interests lie primarily in the areas of adult education and critical pedagogy. Therefore, she is currently involved in the research projects related to the relationships between social justice, activism, labour markets and social inequalities. She is focused on strengthening individuals' agency through learning and education, career guidance, and social activity and activism.

José Antonio Caride
is Full Professor of Social Pedagogy at the University of Santiago de Compostela (USC), Spain. He heads the group of investigation "Social Pedagogy and Environmental Education" (SEPA-interea) and the network for research in Education and Formation for the Citizenship and the Knowledge Company (RINEF-CISOC). His lines of investigation and publications are Social Pedagogy, Community Development and Civic Initiative, Educational and Social Times, Social Education, Citizenship and Human Rights, Environmental Education, Culture of Sustainability and Human Development. In 2004, he was awarded the Order of Institutional Merit of the World Council for Curriculum and Instruction.

Darlene E. Clover
is Professor of adult education and leadership studies, University of Victoria, Canada. Her areas of research and teaching include cultural leadership and education, feminist adult education and leadership, and arts-based adult education and research methods. Darlene's current international research focuses on art galleries and museums. Her most recent edited volumes include *Feminist Critique and the Museum: Educating for a Critical Consciousness* (2020) and *Adult Education and Museums: Animating Social, Cultural and Institutional Change* (2016). Darlene is currently President of the Board of the Society of Friends of St Ann's Academy, a heritage site that facilitates critical feminist conversations and arts-based workshops on women's and gender issues.

Rob Evans
born in London, studied Russian and History at Leeds and Tübingen. After working in adult, further and higher education at universities in Italy, Germany and Egypt and as a freelance adult and management trainer for many years, he taught Academic English Writing at the University of Magdeburg, Germany

until 2019. His main research interests include biography research methods, the language of narrative, conversation analysis and discourses of learning. Publications include chapters, journal articles, and edited books, including (with Ewa Kurantowicz and Emilio Lucio-Villegas) *Researching and Transforming Adult Learning and Communities* (Brill Sense, 2016).

Marta Gontarska
is a PhD candidate at the Faculty of Applied Studies, University of Lower Silesia in Wrocław, Poland. She has 15 years of experience cooperating with civil society organisations and movements on global education and sustainable development both at a national and European level.

Rita Gradaílle
is Doctor in Philosophy and Educational Sciences (awarded special Prize for Doctorate and Degree) at the University of Santiago de Compostela, Spain. She completed her academic training with a Master in Gender and Social Education, as well as different national and international exchanges. She works as a lecturer and researcher at the Faculty of Education Sciences and has been part – since 1999 – of the SEPA research team of the USC. She is Secretary of the Ibero-American Society of Social Pedagogy (SIPS) since 2005. Her main research lines are: pedagogy of social education, education and community development, social and leisure times, gender and equity, and socio-educational policies and human rights.

Budd L. Hall
shares the UNESCO Chair in Community Based Research and Social Responsibility in Higher Education with Rajesh Tandon. Budd has worked in Nigeria, Tanzania, Venezuela, Brazil, Chile, Germany, Thailand, Yemen, Uganda, England, and the United States. He has done both theoretical and practical work for almost 50 years in various aspects of community-based adult education and learning and participatory research. His most recent books include *Learning and Education for a Better World: The Role of Social Movements* (Sense); *Knowledge, Democracy and Action: Community University Research Partnerships in Global Perspectives* (Manchester University Press); and *Strengthening Community University Research Partnerships: Global Perspectives* (UVic and PRIA).

Ewa Kurantowicz
is a researcher in Adult and Community Learning and is Rector of the University of Lower Silesia, Wrocław, Poland. Her main research interests are

civil society and its organisations, local community development, community learning, non-traditional students and graduates at the universities, recognition of prior learning in Higher Education Institutions and cultural heritage in the context of the third mission of the European universities. She mainly prefers the approach of narrative and critical research around adult learning and communities.

Walter Lepore
is an Assistant Professor in the School of Public Administration at the University of Victoria, Canada, and a co-founder of the Salish Sea Training Hub that provides training in community-based research. Before joining the University of Victoria, he was an Associate Professor in the Division of Public Administration at Centro de Investigación y Docencia Económicas (CIDE), Mexico, and the Research Coordinator for the UNESCO Chair in Community-Based Research and Social Responsibility in Higher Education. Walter's research is currently focused on the incorporation of traditional and scientific knowledge systems for environmental protection, and on decision making on wicked sustainability problems.

Rozalia Ligus
is an Associate Professor in Adult Education and Cultural Studies, Institute of Pedagogy, University of Wrocław. Her main interest is focused on socio-cultural aspects of adult learning, biographical (re)construction of identity, collective memory, and the development of local community. She is the author of the book *Teachers' Biographical Identity* (2009) and articles published in Polish and English. Since 2004 she has been a member of ESREA (European Society for Research on Education of Adults), and since 2018 a member of the Polish Sociological Association.

Licínio C. Lima
is Full Professor of Sociology of Education and Educational Administration at the Department of Social Sciences of Education, Institute of Education – University of Minho, Portugal. At UMinho he was Head of the Unit for Adult Education (1984–2004), Director of the Research Centre for Education and Psychology (1994–1997), Head of Department (1998–2004) and Director of the PhD in Education (2011–2013). He is guest professor in various universities in Europe, Africa, Asia and Latin America. He has been in charge of a large number of research and international co-operation projects, and he is the author of academic works published in eighteen countries and seven languages, including more than thirty books.

Emilio Lucio-Villegas

is Full Professor of Adult Education at the University of Seville, Spain. He is the author or co-author of articles, chapters and books in Spanish, English and Portuguese. From 2008 to 2013 he was Head of The Paulo Freire Chair at the University of Seville. He has participated in research at national and international level. He was a member of the Steering Committee of the European Society for Research on the Education of the Adults (ESREA) from 2008 to 2019 and has been convenor of the Network: 'Between Global and Local: Adult Learning and Communities' since 2006. *Adult Education and Communities: Approaches from a Participatory Perspective* was published by Sense Publishers in 2015.

Marjorie Mayo

is Emeritus Professor of Community Development in the Department of Social, Therapeutic and Community Studies, Goldsmiths, University of London. Main research interests: Community Education and Development, Community Cohesion and Social Solidarity, Participation, Active Citizenship, Global citizenship. Publications include: *Access to Justice for Disadvantaged Communities* (Mayo et al., Policy Press, 2015); *Global Citizens: Social Movements and the Challenge of Globalization* (Zed Books, 2005).

Monika Noworolnik-Mastalska

is a Ph.D. in Education, and a PhD student in the Department of People and Technology (IMT) at the Roskilde University, Denmark. Her research explores adults learning in organisations and their cultural, economic, administrative, political and global contexts. Most recently she has been conducting research on participation and learning in local cultures of organisations that practice the global idea of Corporate Social Responsibility (CSR) in Denmark, employing a Habermasian perspective.

Angela Pilch Ortega

(Dr. phil.) is Associate Professor in Learning World Research and University Didactics at the Department of Education, University of Graz, Austria. Her research focuses on biographical and learning world research, social movements and societal learning, transnationalism and postcolonialism.

Jocey Quinn

is Professor of Education at Plymouth Institute of Education, Plymouth University UK. She has published widely in the field of higher education and lifelong learning and led many research projects funded by research councils, government bodies, major charities, and international organisations. Her current research focuses on the informal learning of marginalised people: ranging from young people to people with dementia.

Paweł Rudnicki
is Associate Professor at the Faculty of Applied Studies, University of Lower Silesia in Wrocław, Poland. He is head of the ULS Doctoral School. His areas of interest and research are critical education, alternative schooling, and educational practices in the activity of nonformal groups.

Yashvi Sharma
serves as Training Specialist in Participatory Research In Asia (PRIA). With more than 7 years of experience, she is engaged in developing training designs, training materials (written and audio-visual) and training support across PRIA's thematic areas. She specialises in participatory training, capacity building, community mobilisation and programme implementation. She has been evolving various creative learning methodologies to engage adolescents, youth, and women on issues of gender-based violence, sexual health and hygiene and livelihoods. Yashvi's work history includes managing programmes focusing on building youth-leadership to end gender-based violence and ending sexual harassment at the workplace.

Rajesh Tandon
shares the UNESCO Chair in Community Based Research and Social Responsibility in Higher Education with Budd Hall. They have worked together since creating the International Participatory Research Network in 1978. Rajesh started his career in the development sector in rural areas of India. He founded the Society for Participatory Research in Asia PRIA to strengthen learning opportunities at grassroots level and to articulate knowledge for wider social influence, in 1982. His contributions revolve around issues of participatory research, people centred development, policy reform and networking in India, South-Asia and beyond. The UN named him a significant social leader of our times. He has published more than 100 articles and more than 30 books.

Laura Varela Crespo
is Doctor in Educational Sciences (awarded Extraordinary Prize from the University of Santiago de Compostela USC for Doctorate and Degree). She has carried out predoctoral and postdoctoral research stays in Spanish and foreign universities (Brazil, Chile, etc.). She works as a professor and researcher at the Faculty of Science Education (USC) and has been part of the SEPA-interea

research team, of university excellence in the Autonomous Community of Galicia (Spain). Her main lines of research and publication are: social education in public welfare policies; pedagogy of social education; social and leisure times; education and community development.

Piotr Zańko
is Assistant Professor at the Faculty of Education at the University of Warsaw. His primary area of interest and research are educational contexts of cultural resistance. His most recently published book is entitled *Pedagogie oporu* (*Pedagogies of Resistance*).

Davide Zoletto
is an Associate Professor in General and Social Education at the Department of Languages and Literatures, Communication, Education and Society (DILL) at the University of Udine in Italy. His primary areas of research are educational theory and research in diverse learning environments and communities, which also encompass a focus on cultural and postcolonial studies in education.

INTRODUCTION

Remaking Communities and Adult Learning

Rob Evans, Ewa Kurantowicz and Emilio Lucio-Villegas

1   Framing a Critical Response

As a critical response to the contemporary mainstream discourses of adult education and learning – which habitually forget adult education and all too often only focus on education and skills for the labour market – it would seem to be urgently necessary to develop counter-hegemonic research to recuperate the ideas of emancipation and personal and social development that were born from the ideas of authors such as Paulo Freire, Shirley Walters, Raymond Williams, and others, in the past century. These ideas were linked with decolonising processes around the world and the emergence of post-colonial theory and produced powerful concepts such as critical democracy and popular culture, popular education, and literacy movements worldwide. These ideas also promoted methodologies that embodied practices of democratic participation and critical reflexivity, such as participatory research, feminist research and ecological research activism, to name only some.

At the present time, much of adult education is not providing any response to the great social problems: environmental issues, populism and the return of authoritarian practices, racism, gender inequality, xenophobia, precariousness, and so on. The COVID-19 pandemic, which erupted in the first months of work on this book and has accompanied its development, has added even greater urgency to finding answers to these global issues, as well as sharpening our awareness of other originally less obvious problems.

It seems important, then, to recuperate what was at the heart of adult education and learning in their connection with people living in communities. Communities, with all their contradictions, remain privileged spaces for the organisation of social relationships and, however they may be structured, they are the natural place where people live. In the pandemic they have proven time and again to be the places where problems are felt most sharply, and where some of the most creative responses are born.

We invited contributions to a book that should explore and discuss these questions. Contributors were asked to explore critical approaches to adult learning and adult education that enable people living in communities to defy

© ROB EVANS, EWA KURANTOWICZ AND EMILIO LUCIO-VILLEGAS, 2022
DOI:10.1163/9789004518032_001
This is an open access chapter distributed under the terms of the CC BY-NC 4.0 License.

the challenges that people have to face in their daily life and that affect them not only at a local level but also on a global scale.

By undertaking this effort to explore learning in communities in the early 21st century, it should be possible, we thought, to uncover in the present and for the future what is still rich and vigorous in the tradition of community-based adult learning and to work towards recognition of new developments and new directions that learning communities can take today to confront the challenges coming from the global mainstream and facing the global margins. In addition, we wanted to ask to what extent the margins – traditionally despised and discriminated – are the unequivocal avant-garde in the creation of new concepts for globally-connected communities.

2   Between Global and Local

This book is the work of the research network Between Global and Local – Adult Learning and Community which comes together and discusses under the friendly roof of the European Society for the Research on the Education of Adults (ESREA). Since 2006 the network has pitched its tents in Spain and Portugal, Poland and Slovenia, Germany and Croatia, Hungary and Belgium and Turkey. The most recent conference, 2021 in Seville, Spain, inevitably took place because of the pandemic via zoom, a development that no-one previously expected and one which, most no doubt hope, will not become the only norm for the future, despite certain interesting aspects of distance-conferences. Costs are an obvious factor, though it must be said that the notion of the conference-for-nothing is a dangerous fallacy: high-value conference organisation in zoom times has significant costs, too. More salient are the considerations around reduced CO_2 footprints and environmental effects generally. However, as an international network operating within a bundle of other internationally operating institutions and activities, the pitching of tents will remain an important moment of *communitas* – or as this book will have it, of *vivencia* – of physical exchange and dialogue in the spaces in which we respectively work and are active and from which we draw much of our research energy and the desire to go on.

In the spirit of moving ahead, the editors agreed back in 2019 on the idea of a further publication from the network. After Kurantowicz (2008), Evans (2009, 2010), Lucio-Villegas (2010), Ünlühisarcikli et al. (2011, 2013), Guimaraes et al. (2014), Evans, Kurantowicz and Lucio-Villegas (2016), Evans and Kurantowicz (2018) and Evans (2019) the consensus was that it was a good time to look back in order to know where to look forward. The Call for the book was distributed widely in our networks and was taken up by an interesting mix of researchers who in different ways reflect the 15-year history of the network. As a network that wrote global and local on its sails, we came from the 'margins' of EU Europe – Poland, Spain and Portugal – and have constantly welcomed the opportunity to collaborate with colleagues from far beyond the EU club of states. The European reality of the network remained from the start porous to a much larger global community where fundamental experiences in research and action are grounded, springing as they do from knowledge of the field in a wide variety of local contexts of adult learning as well as of the social movements that have arisen to fight for social justice and equality and that lead individuals and communities to access new forms of knowledge, acquire new types of social capital and, in the process, change the life worlds of people. Thus, we are encouraged to keep on going on by the response to the Call from a mix of younger and more senior researchers, from individuals and teams, from voices and research hitherto unknown in the network to old friends of the road, from seven EU countries as well as from Canada and India.

The single chapters of this volume reflect the research in the field of adult education and learning in and with communities and represent the important consensus of direction, purpose and conviction that characterises the activity of the network and its participants. The individual contributions give proof of the range of practice, the varieties in methodology and theory as well as the scope of research experience they demonstrate in their papers.

3   Part 1: Popular Education Looking Back, Looking Forward

The first part of the book concentrates on the central concern of this volume: a pause to look back and forward reflexively to take stock of the powerful contribution to adult learning and community development played by forms of participatory research in diverse communities, that start from a post-colonial, egalitarian, dialogic approach to the making and remaking of community and society.

The first three authors in this first part – Licínio Lima (Braga), Emilio Lucio-Villegas (Seville), and Davide Zoletto (Udine) employ re-readings of seminal texts (Freire, Illich, Fals Borda, Gelpi, Zanier) in order to reassess the developing discourses around lifelong education/lifelong learning and the stark choice between instrumentalistic and democratic, participatory forms of learning and living together. The fourth chapter by Monika Noworolnik-Mastalska (Roskilde) takes up the theme of 'useful knowledge' as proffered by EU programmes and considers the difficulties facing citizenship education in a European project.

Licínio Lima: "Adult Learning and Mainstream Education Discourse"
The importance of a critical reflection on the sources of the mainstream discourses governing not only the market economies but more importantly, also the fora of global educational policy discussion and formulation, is the rationale for the finely calibrated analysis offered us by Licínio Lima of positions taken up on the one hand by successive official documents produced, for example, by the EU or UNESCO, while on the other hand he traces Paolo Freire's thought to trace a trenchant critique of neo-liberal skills regimes and 'qualificationism'.

Lima's critique of neo-liberal and liberal social thinking is grounded in a reappraisal of the concept of dialogue. For him, dialogue and dialogic learning are tools of enormous value in combatting the hegemonies of misinformation and manipulation which confront us in the oppressive pedagogism demanding the need for the honing of individual skills as the main solution for economic competitiveness. Dialogical action, on the contrary, aims to create and strengthen cultures of openness, democracy, and participation, favouring sustainable development over instrumental, expansionist modernisation.

Arguing from the perspective of Freire's major work Pedagogy of the Oppressed (Freire, 2020), Lima points out that adult learning and education take place in diverse communities, where difference – cultural, linguistic, religious, gender, ethnical, class or economic – can be lived as causes of discrimination or 'cultural invasion'. Difference, however, can also be the foundation of democratic dialogue and conviviality, 'dialogical action' for liberation and for adult learning and education environments grounded in active citizenship, solidarity, and cooperation.

This critical reflection leads us to question – as was done under different circumstances, from a radical position, 50–60 years ago as countries began moving away from their colonial pasts – the purposes of education and learning, above all learning for all and for lives together, living together. Lucio-Villegas and Zoletto draw out for us the critical heritage of radical movements promoting learning for change.

Emilio Lucio-Villegas: "Resisting Mainstream Lifelong Learning"
Emilio Lucio-Villegas cites three major areas that have shaped popular education and have grounded its critique of mainstream discourses within lifelong learning. These are Paulo Freire's work and, overall, his notion of dialogue as the main methodology to organise educational processes, then theories of deschooling as a revolt against the colonised school, and finally participatory research as a way of creating knowledge from people's experiences. The author proposes to focus on the second and third aspects and concentrates on the fertile ground offered by the social laboratory of middle and southern America

in the second half of the 20th century, drawing into the discussion the work of that close fellow-traveller of Freire, Ivan Illich. Lucio-Villegas is interested in Illich and others' notion of deschooling as it challenges discourses of "endless progress and unlimited growth" as well as the utility of knowledge provided by a (global) school system that continues to represent colonial and hegemonic interpretations of society.

In similar vein, Lucio-Villegas presents participatory research not only as a methodology for working with adult learners but as an instrument to decolonise knowledge and create new knowledge. Citing Orlando Fals Borda, he proposes participatory research as an engine of new knowledge – 'popular science'. While the enduring dependence on positivistic notions of science can be heard here, Lucio-Villegas' point is that such knowledge is "practical, empirical and common-sense knowledge, the ancestral possession of common people, that enabled them to create, work and understand mainly with the resources that nature gave to people" (Fals Borda, 1990, p. 70, author's translation).

Emphasising that popular education sees the group as a space for learning, while communities and people remain the ultimate resource for learning, the author presents two experiences which he considers exemplary of popular education.

Davide Zoletto: "Lifelong Education in Diverse Communities"

Zoletto also offers us a review of a well-known figure of adult education, Ettore Gelpi, and sketches in Gelpi's prescience in seeing the centrality of notions of diversity in a plural society. Zoletto looks at Gelpi's understanding of the element of multi-diversity as a central factor of change emerging particularly within urban environments. Attention is directed towards the 'new cultural values' that are seen as emerging in these contexts and he links Gelpi's understanding of popular and social culture with Raymond Williams' definition that 'culture' is a whole way of life, that is, a way to interpret everyday experiences (Williams, 1958). Zoletto shows that the close collaboration of Gelpi with the Friulian poet and educator Leonardo Zanier in the 1970s must be seen in this approach to lifelong education. Both Gelpi and Zanier worked to build on the histories, expectations, and resources (including the linguistic resources) of people – in this concrete case, the Italian emigrants in Switzerland and Germany in the 1960s and 70s – in favour of a perspective embracing the whole community in which diverse communities live together.

Monika Noworolnik-Mastalska: "Is Active Citizenship a Forgotten Idea in Europe?"

Monika Noworolnik-Mastalska discusses the difficulties within neo-liberal discourses of resurrecting and filling with new meaning the notion of being a citizen, with all the trappings of life experience, knowledge, and desires. Describing educational programmes implemented in 5 EU countries in an EU-funded project employing participatory teaching methods which focused on the learning of civic competencies by disadvantaged young learners, the author finds that economic roll-backs in educational funding, markedly conservative discourses of lifelong learning in some countries, and a general incomprehension of the global context of active citizenship and learning were serious brakes on the achievement of the project's modest goals.

Despite the accumulation of experience and achievements in the broadening of inclusive practices in democratic societies, the real practice of inclusion and participation remains to be realised everywhere. Such practice would entail the respect for the rights of the socially vulnerable, the readiness of society to engage in a fundamental manner with otherness through the opening towards other epistemologies, which would mean learning to embrace a re-drawing of histories and a real remaking of knowledge in order to remake communities of people and whole societies. The next part looks more closely at these questions.

4   Part 2: Knowledge Democracy, New Pedagogies, Creative Inclusion

Thus, in the second part of the book, the focus shifts to pedagogies of possibility and change. Each of the chapters discusses a different aspect of knowledge creation and the transformation of pedagogies of inclusion. The notion of "pedagogies of possibility" (Manicom & Walters, 2012) seems particularly relevant to the three following discussions of different but connected "ways of understanding 'the world' and self that identify, demystify, and challenge prevailing relations of domination to open up new possibilities for engagement and incite collective action for change" (p. 3).

> *Walter Lepore, Yashvi Sharma, Budd Hall & Rajesh Tandon:*
> *"Co-Constructing Knowledge and Communities"*

The authors state at the outset that community and belief in community as a fundamental source of transformation and change is under attack as the role of the individual and their function in globalised supply chains comes more and more to replace the notion of society and the social good. The challenge to the idea and practice of community goes hand in hand with structural inequality and social injustice and these have, in turn, come under greater pressure as a result of the COVID-19 pandemic. The authors see the attack on community and its knowledge driven by depredation of the environment, genocide of vulnerable Indigenous peoples, and justified by Euro-centric epistemicide of alternative knowledge.

Lepore, Sharma, Hall and Tandon report on the findings of two surveys used in studies which provide a global overview of how higher education institutions and civil society organisations contribute to engaged research processes and knowledge democracy through the creation of Community-University Research Partnerships or CURPs. They show that change has taken place in the approach to, and practice of, knowledge production, reflected in the idea of 'engaged research'. This must be taken up, especially as a response to the siren songs of 'build back better' in the pandemic. The authors call, instead, for 'build back equal', as a start.

Darlene Clover: "Women's and Gender Museums"

The feminist pedagogies moving the creation and development of women's and gender museums which are actively questioning presences and absences in mainstream pedagogies of lifelong learning around the world – currently in 96 countries – are the subject of Darlene Clover's contribution. Women's and gender museums, she argues, have the responsibility to present, to see and to know the world differently. They confront in their physical or virtual forms xenophobia and religious intolerance, they explore issues critically from feminism to food insecurity, fascism to fashion.

Operating as spaces of feminist adult education, working to (re)historicise (herstory), (re)represent, (re)imagine and (re)educate the past and the present, women's and gender museums share an epistemological mandate to disrupt the problematic gendered representations and narratives that proliferate in most of the world's museums and art galleries, as well as across society. Clover argues forcibly and with the confidence her recognised authority in this field lends her arguments, that the pedagogical contributions women's and gender museums are making to the struggle for socio-gender justice and change makes them valuable resources for feminist adult educators around the world. As vital and vibrant sources of an historical feminist imaginary, these institutions look back to move forward, wielding the powers of imagination and representation through animation, theatre, artefacts and artefiction as pedagogies of epistemic responsibility, the responsibility to present, to see and to know the world differently, in ways that can change the imagination of change.

Jocey Quinn: "Living and Learning with Dementia"

People living with dementia have been largely absent in debates on adult learning and positioned on the margins of communities. This chapter presents an alternative vision of people living with dementia. People namely who are open to the possibilities of learning, as vital parts of communities and, as Quinn emphasises, as avant-garde agents of change.

In terms of andragogy, both as adult education theory and didactics, research with people living with dementia helps to illustrate that bodies are an active part of learning, not just as shells for the mind but fundamentally imbricated in the process. Thus, Quinn argues for what she terms 'the corporeality of learning' stressing that we must understand learning as an embodied process. The pleasures and pains of the body help to shape what is learnt and how that happens, not just when considering disability issues. but for everyone. Researching with people with dementia highlights and accentuates this.

The chapter wishes to generate the following discussions: the extent to which people living with dementia are already active community members; how they free up non-humanistic ontologies and generate visions of 'more than human and more than social mutuality', which contribute to moves towards decolonisation; and finally, how they help to highlight hopes for the future, not nostalgia for the past, and help to further an andragogy of inclusion that is both more corporeal and creative.

The chapter provides positive answers to these questions and hopeful examples of how people living with dementia are remaking communities and understandings of what learning might be. The role of adult learning as a site of resistance is an ever more urgent one, but the terms need to be rewritten to move beyond limited humanistic visions of what humans are and what they can do. Moreover, as this chapter illustrates, thinking through their role in remaking community life opens some key debates and visions.

5   Part 3: Social Learning and Activism for Change

The third part, on activism and change turns its attention to the motivations for activism and their forms of expression and how they are lived, by individuals, political groups, and whole communities. The scope of the part is wide, stretching from intergenerational knowledge in Polish communities 'with migratory background' (with all the contradictions and lived experiences sealed into this easy phrase), to communities struggling to stand up in dignity and solidarity after (another) natural disaster, to different generations of social activism and their diverse or not so diverse pedagogies of action. Alongside the case study from the Mexican reality of Juchitán, we have here three contributions from Polish authors, who reflect in different ways on the transition of Polish communities since World War II across the fault-lines of ethnic, geo-political and ideological-systemic spaces into post-national and global activism. All four contributions are based on field research employing biographical narrative methods and two (Pilch Ortega and Gontarska et al.) employ a mix of data alongside the qualitative interview.

Rozalia Ligus: "Regaining Lost Community Knowledge"
Rozalia Ligus offers us an example of capillary community knowledge retrieval and re-evaluation. In connection with a community of families of former emigrants from Polish Galizia to Bosnia who were resettled in Poland, she shows how the post-1989 political transformation in Poland strongly influenced the current shape of local communities, some of which, like the formerly named 'Western and Northern Territories' which only became part of Poland after 1945, were themselves the result of profound experiences of war and resettlement. The shaping of post-war Poland had an enduring impact on local/regional images of localism and collective memories, identities and learning processes within communities. In this context, the process of individual and collective identity formation in intergenerational transmission is constantly reinterpreted, providing a rich source of knowledge, often recovered in the process of social dialogue and informal learning.

As part of an ongoing project (*'Migrating biographies'*) Ligus interviewed members of the Polish-Yugoslavian community. A particular feature of Ligus' work is, in fact, her close attention to her interviewees' words. Rather than allowing the all-too-often employed brief authored summary of the interview talk, she delves into the modes of expression of individual authors, and this brings the speakers to the fore in their individuality and their authority and dignity as representatives of an important example of popular knowledge.

Ligus' chapter demonstrates the durability of intergenerational transmission. Changes in attitudes take place generationally, she observes, in which different forms of memory are activated – nostalgic, mnemonic experience and historical memory, to the experiences of the youngest community members who draw on cultural and communicative memory with an awareness of their origin and orientation towards the future.

Angela Pilch Ortega: "Social Learning and Building Solidarity"
Angela Pilch Ortega has contributed a number of stimulating papers around her Mexican fieldwork to the publications of this network in the last decade and more, and this chapter continues to unfold the fruits and insights of her very particular research undertaking. Here she discusses opportunities for social learning in a context characterised by distribution conflicts, social vulnerability and solidarity building after a natural disaster in the Istmo de

Tehuantepec region of Mexico. The paper draws on an empirical study conducted in Juchitán, six months after a strong earthquake affected the region. The study explores the impacts of a natural disaster on community life and the transformative potential that lies in such a social crisis. Alongside biographical interviews, initiatives of regional artist groups and video documentaries related to the earthquake were analysed. The research findings reveal the way people structure and frame the experience of the natural disaster and the consequences that such crises bear for their social lives.

Pilch Ortega finds that people's socio-cultural heritage becomes a useful potential resource in order to overcome the conditions of vulnerability in which the people find themselves. Processes of solidarity building as well as waves of social disintegration and an erosion of solidarity were observed. Collaborative social practises observed show, however, that the disruption of community and society led people to question social rules and power relationships in their locality. Social reflexivity, despite a situation of acute vulnerability and need can enable people to analyse social structures and create new forms of social solidarity.

Anna Bilon-Piórko: "The 'Pulsating' Activism of Polish Activists"

Anna Bilon-Piórko's investigation with the aid of biographical-narrative interviews with long-term and lifelong Polish activists spans the history of Polish society in the last 70 years. She argues that the complexity of social engagement and activism has important implications for adult learning and work in and with communities. Issues of learning and education surfaced in the activists' narratives as significant factors both in becoming engaged in social activity and in withdrawing from it. In fact, it is this 'oscillation' between periods of extreme activism and periods of withdrawal into private life that is central to Bilon-Piórko's analysis. The subjects of her research demonstrate a 'pulsating' rhythm of engagement and disengagement and this in turn determines identity and participation in civil society.

The wish to re-make society has its costs, of course. The role and significance of negative emotions and frustrations need to be understood, she argues, and both the detail of these very extensive in-depth interviews and the space given to the individual narratives of two very different protagonists, who are very much products of their generations, genders and educations, demonstrate the author's conviction that the study of individual meanings and lifetime trajectories is essential to understand better the members of community action groups and to know the individual motivations for social engagement. Positive and negative experiences acquired in the course of a life of political commitment to remaking society are worked through with the biographical resources that activists acquire in the course of the shifts demanded of them in a pulsating career of social activism.

> *Marta Gontarska, Paweł Rudnicki & Piotr Zańko: "Learning (for) Civil Disobedience in Poland"*

This chapter looks at the significance of individual and collective counter-hegemonic practices of the Extinction Rebellion (XR) movement in Poland. Founded on the idea of civil disobedience, the practice of XR is seen by the authors as contesting the passive attitude of political decision-makers vis-à-vis the dramatic threats posed by the global climate crisis. The three authors explore the dimensions of learning (for) civil disobedience in the recruitment and educational activities inside the local groups of XR and show the relevance of this commitment to collective learning for the civic awareness of XR activists and as a differentiator for the movement as a whole.

Gontarska, Rudnicki and Zańko's research is based on narrative interviews with selected XR activists from Warsaw and Wrocław and serves as a critical exploratory study. Importantly, the authors also see their work as a tool of pedagogical intervention which aims to demonstrate and strengthen the voice of young people concerned about the fate of the planet in the real context of the hegemony of the neoliberal, neoconservative, populist state.

The pedagogical strengths of the XR movement in Poland, whose significance they rightly see in contrast both to the prevailing reactionary government of the PiS party but more importantly as an important addition to the political landscape of post-Solidarnosc EU Poland, are found in XR's principled bottom-up process of creating and learning democracy in action, which, the authors argue, allows them to see XR as a new social movement with a glocal orientation, creating a new quality of social participation that through mass action fights for the survival of our planet.

6 Part 4: Remaking Society

The final part of the volume is to do with the move to re-make society and community with particular relevance, of course, to the consequences to date of the COVID-19 pandemic. Marjorie Mayo writes with the confidence of her long experience and tallies the damages done particularly in the UK to society and civil society by the obvious alliance of Far Right populism and neoliberal globalisation. Her conclusions are nonetheless hopeful. Rob Evans examines the motivations of social mediators to work in vulnerable communities, and Spanish researchers José Caride, Rita Gradaílle and Laura Varela Crespo consider the fertile link between social pedagogy and the many initiatives experimented in the COVID-19 pandemic.

Marjorie Mayo: "Changes in Community Life"
The impact of neoliberal globalisation has resulted in increasing polarisation in societies everywhere, and this, coupled with austerity policies, notably in the years after the world financial crisis of 2008, leading to cuts in social services or the running-down of health services, is the world which was confronted with the COVID-19 pandemic. Mayo sets popular education against polarisation and exclusion as it works with communities to explore in their own right their real anxieties and concerns. This approach can permit strategies for social change to emerge. Community-based learning and mutual support networks, developing shared strategies for responding to the challenges of COVID-19 are more important than ever in the contemporary context, Mayo argues.

She points to how the lockdown – an experience unknown for generations in many societies that have been free of war or civil war and therefore unprepared for physically and psychologically – has caused adult educators to respond in innovative ways, reaching out to communities, to the vulnerable and those without advocates or voice, and that this has potentially significant implications for post pandemic times. The value of dialogue and critical thinking so central to Freirian approaches, are tools that can facilitate the mobilisation of communities to question the global significance of what they are coping with locally, and what is valid for the pandemic is valid, too, Mayo underlines, for climate change, arguments for sustainability, human-nature relations, and so on. Indeed, citing Veronique Tadjo's tales from the Ebola outbreak in West Africa (Tadjo, 2021), Mayo echoes Jocey Quinn's concerns (see Chapter 7) that our pedagogies should embrace the post-human and more than human if they are to overcome the limits of historically fuelled colonial epistemologies. Ultimately, Mayo sees in the efforts of people at the grassroots to overcome the pandemic experiences of "prefigurative forms, sketching out alternative ways of living and relating to each other in more mutually supportive ways". There *are* other, more hopeful – and more sustainable – possibilities ahead of us.

Rob Evans: "Learning to Make (and Remake) Society"
In this chapter, Rob Evans looks at the life histories driving the professional and personal development of social mediators and proposes that there is a clear link between these personal trajectories and the role many social mediators played around Europe during the pandemic, and that this has importance for the role of mediation in remaking society.

Social mediation and the culture associated with it, characterised by the respect towards the other, focusing on dialogue, the enhancement of citizenship, the importance given to individuals and to the development of their skills in the process of change, would seem to constitute an important factor in any process of 're-sewing' social ties under threat of rupture or loss. The research is based on biographical-narrative interviews with social mediators in a European Erasmus+ project. The detail of the interview talk, Evans maintains, documents significantly how professional trajectories are defined, and how this is affected by group belonging, ethnic or cultural discourses, as well as gender, age, professional and educational relationships. The biographical narratives show that the creation of a common space of experience – a space of learning in diversity – can be heard as it emerges in talk.

In their respective narratives, the social mediators heard in this chapter map out this space of learning in diversity – a space where, in the words of one mediator, *"everyone can be a friend to everyone else"*, a space from it is argued they make their contribution to the making and remaking of solidarity and inclusivity in communities.

> *José Caride, Rita Gradaílle & Laura Varela Crespo: "Social Pedagogy and Community Networks"*

José Caride, Rita Gradaílle and Laura Varela Crespo of the University of Santiago de Compostela start from the principal tensions between the global and the local, the universal, and the particular identified in the now distant 1996 report prepared by Jacques Delors for UNESCO *"The Treasure Within"* (Delors, 1996). In its proposals, 'learning to live together' was one of the four basic pillars of contemporary education along with 'learning to be', 'learning to do', and 'learning to learn'. Learning to live together has been an area thrown very much into question in recent years by the growth of xenophobic populism, but also by increasing economic and social inequalities globally. Ironically, it is the COVID-19 pandemic that has galvanised people's efforts to find new ways of making communities and the authors see how it has revitalised experiences that already had a long history of collaboration in local communities. Given their importance, they argue, it is important to recognise the community networks created in neighbourhoods and districts, which emerged in strength during the lockdowns, and also the virtual communities whose role in generating and maintaining social ties beyond physical boundaries was fundamental. Seen in this way, they suggest that the response to the pandemic has attempted in many places to raise up a system of shared obligations and responsibilities, put at the service of the common good.

The authors are of the opinion that a return to community solidarities acquires news meanings for knowledge and social action-intervention. Adverse situations, such as those caused by the COVID-19 pandemic, require a social pedagogy that criticises inequalities and is committed to development that is more just and more inclusive and which is able to create alliances for the common good, promoting dialogue and a community focus when tackling the social challenges that it has posed.

References

Delors, J. (1996). *Learning: The treasure within.* Report to UNESCO of the International Commission on Education for the twenty-first century. http://hdl.voced.edu.au/10707/114597

Evans, R. (Ed.). (2009). *Local development, community, and adult learning – Learning landscapes between the mainstream and the margins* (Vol. 1). nisaba verlag.

Evans, R. (Ed.). (2010). *Local development, community, and adult learning – Learning landscapes between the mainstream and the margins* (Vol. 2). nisaba verlag.

Evans, R. (Ed.). (2019). Education 2030 and adult learning: Global perspectives and local communities – Bridges or gaps? *Andragoška Spoznanja, 25*(3).

Evans, R., & Kurantowicz, E. (Eds.). (2018). Adult learning & communities in a world on the move (Vol. 24). *Andragoska Spoznanja, 24*(1). https://doi.org/https://doi.org/10.4312/as.24.1

Evans, R., Kurantowicz, E., & Lucio-Villegas, E. (Eds.). (2016). *Researching and transforming adult learning and communities: The local/global context.* Sense.

Fals Borda, O. (1990). La ciencia y el pueblo: Nuevas reflexiones. In M. C. Salazar (Ed.), *La investigación acción participative: Inicios y desarrollo* (pp. 65–84). Popular.

Freire, P. (2020). *Pedagogia do oprimido* (75th ed.). Paz & Terra.

Guimarães, P., Cavaco, C., Marrocos, L., Paulos, C., Bruno, A., Rodrigues, S., & Marques, M. (Eds.). (2014). *Local change, social actions and adult learning: Challenges and responses.* University of Lisbon.

Kurantowicz, E. (Ed.). (2008). *Local in global. Adult learning and community development.* Wydawnictwo Naukowe.

Lucio-Villegas, E. (Ed.). (2010). *Transforming/researching communities.* dialogos.red.

Manicom, L., & Walters, S. (2012). Introduction: Feminist popular education. In L. Manicom & S. Walters (Eds.), *Feminist popular education in transnational debates: Building pedagogies of possibility* (pp. 1–23). Palgrave Macmillan.

Tadjo, V. (2021). *In the company of men.* Hope Road Small Axes.

Ünlühisarcıklı, Ö., Gökce, G., Seçkin, O., & Sabırlı, I. (Eds.). (2011). *Positioning and conceptualising adult education and learning within local development* (Vol. 1). Boğaziçi University Press.

Ünlühisarcıklı, Ö., Gökce, G., Seçkin, O., & Sabırlı, I. (Eds.). (2013). *Positioning and conceptualising adult education and learning within local development* (Vol. 2). Boğaziçi University Press.

Williams, R. (1958). *Culture and society*. Chatto and Windus.

PART 1

Popular Education Looking Back, Looking Forward

CHAPTER 1

Adult Learning and Mainstream Education Discourse

Revisiting Freire's Pedagogy of the Oppressed

Licínio C. Lima

Abstract

At different scales and involving various dimensions, adult learning and education take place in diverse communities. Cultural, linguistic, religious, gender, ethnical, class and economic differences, among many others, may be sources of discrimination or of democratic dialogue and conviviality in political and social terms, also including adult learning and education environments.

Based on a Freirean perspective, and especially on his major work *Pedagogy of the Oppressed*, a critical analysis of adult learning and education policies and practices as "cultural invasion" for discrimination or as "dialogical action" for liberation is presented. Observing global and local policies based on rational-instrumental conceptions of adult learning which stress in a hyperbolic manner the promotion of individual skills as the main solution for economic competitiveness – which may be considered as a sort of oppressive pedagogism – possible impacts on communities and societies will be discussed in terms of democracy and active citizenship, solidarity and cooperation, the process of humanization of human beings and their capacity to live together in diverse communities.

Keywords

adult education – adult learning policies – community education – qualificationism – pedagogism – European Union – Paulo Freire – dialogical action – pedagogy of the oppressed – cultural invasion

1   Introduction: Monocultural Policies for Diverse Communities?

As human communities become increasingly diverse and heterogeneous as a result of migratory flows, the recognition of political and social rights and freedom of religion, active gender equality policies, and a whole range of social policies aiming to combat discrimination in all of its forms, adult learning and education clearly face new challenges. The challenge is not simply to adapt to changes to contemporary society, but rather to participate in the processes of cultural and educational transformation. In diverse and pluralistic communities that seek peaceful coexistence and dialogue between cultures and subcultures, cooperation and solidarity and the ability to live and learn together, adult learning and education policy and practice cannot be driven by monocultural agendas and narrow political and economic interests, or exclusionary processes of modernisation and competition. Education policies that promote dialogical action, active democracy and citizen participation, participatory research methods, reflexive community work and practical experience of organisation, self-governance, and sustainable development, are essential to the democratisation of adult learning and education policy and practice. Moreover, both historically and today, there is a significant connection between popular and community education and the promotion of democracy and citizenship (see Walters & Kotze, 2018).

Although the declarations of principles of the major international and supranational organisations frequently allude to the relationship between adult learning and education and human rights, democracy, citizenship and social inclusion, business has increasingly encroached on the world of education, calling for "entrepreneurial spirit" and managerialist approaches, human resource management and policies that focus on the qualification of human capital. In the specific case of the European Union, the subordination of adult learning and education to employability targets, economic competitiveness and increasing workforce productivity places greater stress on adaptation, competitiveness and rivalry between citizens than on the values of social transformation, solidarity, dialogue and cooperation. The hegemonic approach of learning for economic competitiveness tends to adopt a monocultural perspective in which capitalist business assumes institutional centrality, disseminating a pedagogy of entrepreneurialism and competition, which undervalues cultural diversity, dialogue and action.

Half a century after its publication, against this backdrop of instrumentalist educational policy, Paulo Freire's masterpiece, *Pedagogy of the Oppressed*, a seminal work in the field of Critical Pedagogy written in Chile between 1967 and 1968 and published in English for the first time in 1970, remains a powerful resource for criticising technicist, instrumentalist approaches to education, training and learning, as opposed to education as a means of constant problem-posing and an active practice of freedom, proposed by the same author in his previous book *Education as the Practice of Freedom* (Freire, 1967).

Political pedagogy and the concepts presented in *Pedagogy of the Oppressed* and revisited and developed in the following decades can serve as a basis for analysing many of today's prevalent education policy documents, particularly European Union texts, but also those produced by other bodies such as the *Organisation for Economic Cooperation and Development* (OECD), and debating the shifting definition of education under an agenda driven by skills, the strengthening of human capital and the promotion of employability and competitiveness.

In what I will refer to as an entrepreneurialist pedagogy – one based on promotion of *entrepreneurial spirit*, with the purported aim of filling gaps, scarcities and shortages of skills and qualifications – by nature tailored to the new capitalist economy, the promotion of employment and social inclusion, this chapter will interrogate the focus on qualifications as a phenomenon of "cultural invasion", "accommodation" and "deproblematisation of the future" (Freire, 1975a).[1] In more general terms, the frequently depoliticised and socially atomised stress placed on *the right skills*, purportedly *tailored to the job market*, presents an inherent risk of becoming an oppressive pedagogy. If we declare the other to be uncompetitive and unsuited to the world – even to the "world of oppression" which today presents many facets and forms – it becomes necessary for them to be *immersed* in programmes, often "extensionalist" or charitable by nature, transforming them into a "pure object of their actions" (1975a, p. 186). This conditioning – though presented as the result of a free choice without rational alternatives – is based on the reification of the subject, transforming him or her into an essentially passive target, the object of economic and managerialist dictates that claim to guarantee employability and inclusion of all individuals capable of managing their individual learning and strengthening their skills as "a core strategic asset for growth" (European Union, 2012, p. 2). As such, it breaks with the problem-posing, participative and discursive approach of liberation pedagogy, which, according to Freire (1975a, p. 78), cannot result from donation or from pseudo-participation, but only from "true organisation", in other words, non-oligarchic organisation "in which individuals are subjects in the act of organising themselves" (p. 207) and where the exercise of leadership is incompatible with acts of managerialism and vanguardism.

2   Education as a Process of Humanisation

According to Freire, education is, ultimately, an ongoing process of humanisation and liberation of human beings. Therefore, the pedagogy he proposed was a pedagogy *of* the oppressed and not a pedagogy *for* the oppressed. The central idea of this work is that if the oppressed 'host' the oppressor within themselves, it is through the process of becoming aware that they may free themselves from the oppressor while, simultaneously, freeing the oppressor from their condition.

The key ideas of the work include criticism of "banking education", "cultural invasion" and the "slogan", and present the concepts of "problem-posing education", "dialogical education", "critical consciousness", "generative themes", "freedom" and "authority", "immersion/emersion", "lifting the veil", and "the viable unknown" (or *untested feasibility*), among others. Criticisms of "banking education", oligarchic and bureaucratic structures, vanguardist and managerialist leadership, dogmatism and propaganda, the "objectification" of the masses and "populism" and "elitism", as forms of sectarianism, are among the key principles of Freire's radical democratic pedagogy. The epistemological and pedagogical consequences of this radical nature are a common thread in much of his work, associated with notions of radical, participatory democracy, participation, citizenship, permanent education, etc.

However, Freire does not stop at denouncing oppression and the reproduction of injustice. He proposes alternatives, presenting a world of possibilities for transformation, and, through words and acts, proclaims the power of dream and utopia.

Freire presents an alternative to what he calls "humanitarianist", "paternalist" and "assistentialist" approaches, refusing to adopt a view based on the salvation of the oppressed and, by extension, the unqualified, those with low levels of education, or with few skills. As Freire (1975a) wrote, "Attempting to liberate the oppressed without their reflective participation in the act of liberation is to treat them as objects which must be saved from a burning building" (p. 72).

Therefore, *Pedagogy of the Oppressed* has great potential for criticising the technocratic, modernising, and normalising positions that dominate today the theory of skills gaps, and the approach that reduces lifelong education – from birth to death – to a matter of continuous training and human resource management, subject to the fetishisation of "narrowly defined" skills, supposedly capable of attracting investment in an increasingly competitive market (Mayo, 2014, p. 9). Freire is notable for his political and educational clarity and his epistemological and pedagogical approach to permanent education, currently neglected or underappreciated, and his rejection of the vocational and technicist approaches which have, conversely, become dominant. As he later wrote, in *Under the Shade of This Mango Tree*,

> The technicist view of education, which reduces it to pure, and moreover neutral, technique, works towards the instrumental *training* of the

learner, in the belief that there is no longer any conflict of interests, that everything is more or less the same. From this view, what is important is purely technical training, the standardisation of content, the transmission of a well-behaved *knowledge of results.* (Freire, 1995, p. 79)

In his final book, *Pedagogy of Freedom* (Freire, 1996, p. 15), he was yet more emphatic: "I insist once again that education (or 'formation' as I sometimes call it) is much more than a question of training a student to be dexterous or competent".

However, the Freirean approach to permanent education finds no place in the political rationale of lifelong acquisition of skills and qualifications, which gave rise to the creation of a European space for the promotion of "entrepreneurial skills and competences", aimed at tackling the problems of "skills shortages" and the "need to upgrade skills for employability", in order to increase economic productivity and growth (European Union, 2012, pp. 2, 6, 16).

In archetypal "human capital theory" and "human resource management" approaches, and according to the logic of clients and consumers of educational products and services, traded in a global "learning market", the subjects of training are viewed as "raw materials" – objects to be shaped, adapted and accommodated. They are often viewed, in the words of Freire, as "patients", undergoing "treatment" or "therapy", through the provision of commodified services capable of offering the required training solutions (Lima, 2018).

Therefore, contrary to a long tradition of thought, particularly in the fields of adult education and popular and community education, it is based on a negative; on the perceived deficiencies or limitations of the "recipients" or "target groups", which it attempts to overcome, rather than building on participants' culture, lived experience and "reading of the world", with a view to revitalisation and critical problem-posing. It fixates on vocational approaches and functional modernisation, exogenous and hierarchical in nature, either through training service provision and the learning experience market, or through assistentialist public programmes. In both cases, it creates a significant risk of a return to "extensionism", and its *antidialogical* dimensions of "domestication" and "normalisation", analysed by Freire (1975b), for example in his work *Extension or Communication?* Such approaches are typical of the technocratic view of learning for employment and ignore the fact that not all forms of technical and vocational education can be considered to be decent and fair, with democratic and social qualities, necessarily incorporating participative decision-making processes and discussion of the values, objectives, content, processes, organisation and assessment of the professional training by the learners themselves.

The view of permanent education as a means of humanisation and transformation is founded on drastically different reasoning, which Paulo Freire justifies in the following terms:

> Education is permanent not because it is required by a given ideological approach or political position or economic interest. Education is permanent because of, on the one hand, the finitude of human beings, and, on the other, the awareness human beings have of their own finitude. (Freire, 1993, p. 20)

As the author makes clear, human beings are not simply unfinished beings; they are also the only beings to be aware of their own unfinished nature:

> This means that humans, as historical beings, are finite, limited, unfinished beings, but conscious of their own unfinishedness. Therefore, they are beings in constant search, naturally in a process, beings that, having humanisation as their vocation, are, however, faced with the incessant threat of dehumanisation, as a historical distortion of this vocation. (Freire, 1993, p. 18)

According to Freire, over and above providing social skills, qualities and abilities that prepare learners for the labour market, permanent education makes an essential contribution to the humanisation of human beings and the fulfilment of their intellectual vocation, through critical interpretation of the world and active participation in the process of transforming it. The unfinished nature of human beings, and not the rationale of shortages and gaps in the skills needed for growth and employment, provides substantive justification for permanent education. Therefore, it is not founded on a negative, but rather on hope, without which "there is no human existence, and therefore no history" (Freire, 2017, p. 1).

As we will see, the focus of education policy in the European Union and other international bodies stands in stark contrast, and often in opposition, to this view, replacing the ongoing quest to "make history" in a world of possibilities with truisms about the "inexorability of the future", almost always "considered to be a given", in the terms used by Freire (1992, pp. 92, 101–102) in *Pedagogy of Hope: Reliving Pedagogy of the Oppressed*. This is why the European Union, adopting an imperative and at times slightly dramatic tone, constantly urges us to adapt or risk perishing. This applies, in particular, to individuals classified as lacking in "key competencies" or belonging to "target groups identified as priorities in the national, regional and/or local contexts, such as individuals needing to update their skills" (European Union, 2006a, p. 11) and reinforce their employability, defined as "the capacity to secure and keep employment" (European Union, 2000, p. 5).

3 Qualificationism as Cultural Invasion, Accommodation and Deproblematisation of the Future

Since the Memorandum on Lifelong Learning (European Union, 2000) at the latest, there has been strong insistence that "lifelong learning must accompany a successful transition to a knowledge-based economy and society" (2000, p. 3). Political discourse is centred on individuals, who are responsible for their decisions, since lifelong learning is defined as something that "[…] concerns everyone's future, in a uniquely individual way" (p. 3). "Levels of investment in human resources" must increase considerably (p. 4), an essential condition for increasing economic competitiveness and employment within the European Union. All education, and in particular professional and vocational education, is considered to be a motor for change, within which "teachers and trainers become guides, mentors and mediators", helping each learner to manage their own learning (p. 14). Social and community dimensions are erased by the competitive individualisation of learning proposed by the EU.

In addition to its instrumental, corporate and managerialist language, and despite prevailing generic allusions to the exercise of active citizenship occurring hand in hand with employability without notable tension, (European Union, 2000, p. 4), the general tone of this, and subsequent European documents, exhibits a degree of vanguardism and dirigisme, evident in its heavily prescriptive tone. The idea that the world has moved, and will, supposedly, continue to move in a certain direction is presented as irrefutable fact. Adaptation to this reality, to market demands, and new digital technologies is imperative in the technical determinist European Union approach to qualifications. To this end, its documents state that, "lifelong learning needs to build on strong collaboration and synergies between industry, education, training and learning settings. At the same time, education and training systems need to adapt to this reality" (European Union, 2018, p. 2). Adaptation is the keyword, just as private sector business is the institutional archetype and the legitimate source of social and personal attributes in pursuit of business-related qualifications, "essential skills and attitudes including creativity, initiative-taking, teamwork, understanding of risk and a sense of responsibility" (2018, p. 4).

Despite the complex, systematic consultations that the various European Union bodies claim to undertake, there is a clear political and institutional prevalence of economically-motivated, technocratic approaches, intrinsically aligned with various dimensions that Freire associated with the theory of anti-dialogical action, dividing, categorising, creating hierarchies and focusing on the accumulation of skills and qualifications that are, for the most part, pre-determined and constantly refer to a banking concept of education and training. What is more, the prevailing theory of deficits not only gives rise to a one sided, monocultural approach, but also appears to dispense with pluralist and open discussion with respect to the "unveiling" of reality and the low intensity of democratic debate. The great challenges facing the world have already been identified. They are not an issue under debate, but rather an apparently unanimously agreed starting point revealed to us by the texts, which invite us to "sign up" and act accordingly. They aim to conquer us, paradoxically claiming to mobilise us at the implementation phase, having demobilised us during the construction process. This leads to a form of conditioning – a narrowing of options that promotes accommodation, "de-problematisation of the future" and a rigid, culturally invasive agenda, which standardises and "rolls out" its modernising and normalising efforts.

The qualificationist ideology imposes a worldview and a culture that is presented as rationally superior from the technical and instrumental point of view, supposedly the only view capable of successfully rising to the (also supposedly universally acknowledged) challenges of adaptation "to the increasingly inevitable changes in the labour market", "employment and social inclusion", "the ongoing digital revolution", and "increasing productivity" (European Union, 2012, pp. 2, 4, 11). As one European Union document, entitled "Rethinking Education: Investing in skills for better socio-economic outcomes" concludes:

> Europe will only resume growth through higher productivity and the supply of highly skilled workers, and it is the reform of education and training systems which is essential to achieving this. (European Union, 2012, p. 17)

In its efforts to "Create a European Area for Skills and Qualifications" (European Union, 2012, p. 16) capable of harnessing "real world experience" – to be read as the world of business and economic competitiveness – which identifies the study of science, technology, engineering and mathematics (STEM subjects) as a "priority area of education" (pp. 4–5), the qualificationist ideology not only limits the understanding, scope and content of education but, more significantly, tends to abandon the very concept of education itself. It adopts a functional and adaptive approach, driven by the promotion of qualifications, skills, abilities and learning outcomes, all of which focus on tackling "skills shortages", "skills gaps and mismatches" and the resulting risks associated with "low-skilled people" (European Union, 2016a, p. 2). The same document, entitled "A new skills agenda for Europe: Working together to strengthen human capital, employability and competitiveness", states that in a context defined by "human capital" requirements, and faced with the current "global race for talent" (p. 2), it is essential to invest in skills that "are a pathway to employability and prosperity" (p. 2), as well as "entrepreneurial mindsets and skills needed to set up their own business" among young people (p. 2). Adopting a managerialist "just in time" strategy, the document adds that "The supply of the right skills at the right time is key for enabling competitiveness and innovation" (p. 11), thus serving "to help bridge the gap between education and training and the labour market" (p. 13). Curiously, there are constant references to pedagogy, which is considered to be innovative and flexible in spirit, or, in other words entrepreneurial:

> Particular attention will be given to innovation in pedagogy; this will include supporting flexible curricula, promoting interdisciplinary and collaborative approaches within institutions, and supporting professional development to enhance innovative teaching practice, including ways of using and bringing digital tools into the classroom and stimulating entrepreneurial mindsets. (p. 16)

"Education for entrepreneurship", from the primary level, "entrepreneurial education" and the "creation of an entrepreneurial culture" (European Union, 2016b, pp. 12–26), are at the heart of current European Union education policy, which considers it "[...] essential not only to shape the mind-sets of young people but also to provide the skills, knowledge and attitudes that are central to developing an entrepreneurial culture" (2016b, p. 9). The agenda presented is systematic, strongly prescriptive and employs arguments that aim to "persuade", to make people internalise its rhetoric and to dominate through "slogans" and what Freire (1993, p. 63) called the "acritical nature of clichés". It is part of a process of "conquest", and socialisation – sometimes showing traces of indoctrination – based on a qualificationist ideology that often makes promises it is unable to fulfil, thus constructing a world based on widely accepted myths.

The process of "*mythologising* the world", which Freire (1975a) refers to in *Pedagogy of the Oppressed*, encompasses a vast body of myths, in a constant process of production and reproduction. Those previously identified by Freire (1975a, pp. 195–197) include the myth that "we are all free to work where we want", reinforced today by freedom of movement within the European Union, and the myth that "anyone who is industrious can become an entrepreneur", today viewed as more a matter of entrepreneurial skills and the right combination of intelligence and effort, resulting in a fair, meritocratic reward. In both cases, the permeation of business in education and culture has fostered and strengthened other, more powerful, myths, such as the link between qualifications and employment/unemployment, the *right skills* as a *factor in attracting investment*, the association between competitiveness, prosperity and improved quality, or the idea that the key is to *bridge the gap between education and training and the world of work*, notably through dual education systems that will produce *returns for businesses*, as well as inviting business people into the classroom *in order to improve learning*.

4 Division, Hostility, and the Risks of an Oppressive Pedagogism

Despite the great educational, historical, and cultural diversity that profoundly marks each European Union member state, the last two decades have seen increased efforts at harmonisation and coordination, in particular through so-called 'soft' rules and the 'open method of coordination', integration schemes and the creation of common 'areas' within the Union, sometimes even including third countries. While it is true that official EU discourse focuses on the advantages of the 'European social model', social inclusion and cohesion policies and the fight against structural unemployment, in which lifelong learning plays a central role, these principles, as we have seen, are subordinated to targets for economic competitiveness on the global market. These targets exist against the backdrop of the European Union's repeatedly stated fears of an inability to successfully and rapidly transition to a knowledge-based economy, not only in comparison to the United States and Japan, but also relative to other emerging powers, particularly in Asia.

Indeed, in the major policy documents produced in the last two decades, references to training and learning are rarely absent, thought the extent of these varies according to the body issuing the text and its historical context. While such references are present, they rarely exist outside an economic context, stressing the need to train human capital in order to gain a competitive advantage. Education, referenced less frequently today and, more commonly, learning, are viewed as instruments; as essential tools for creating a "skilled, trained and adaptable workforce" (European Union, 2001, p. 6); a productive investment in terms of employability, productivity, and mobility, and therefore part of what is heralded as a "fundamentally new approach" (2001, p. 7) to lifelong education. This is a recurring theme, justified by a climate of economic instability and turbulence, leading to renewed emphasis of the importance of lifelong learning, since the acquisition of competitive advantages "is increasingly dependent on investment in human capital", transforming knowledge and skills into a "powerful engine for economic growth" (2001, p. 6).

In practice, however, the purported harmonisation and coordination often lead to increased uniformity and standardisation, notably through the creation of convergence mechanisms, common concepts and categories, shared standards and goals, the dissemination of "best practices", the imposition of assessment and monitoring methods, the identification of "benchmarks", etc. In all of these cases, the broad definition of "permanent education", developed in the 1950s, notably through the actions of the Council of Europe and various developments in France (Hake, 2018), is increasingly absent from political discourse, and its modern-day substitutes have heightened tensions between emancipation and the instrumentalisation of adult learning and education (Alheit & Hernández-Carrera, 2018).

Since the production of policy documents and, in particular communiqués, recommendations and orders, by the various European Union bodies is particularly intense, there is strong intertextuality between these documents, certain concepts, key ideas and expressions tend to become "slogans".

In its discursive output certain data is occasionally favoured as evidence in policy documents. However, in most cases, it is the realms of professional training, business, the economy and human resources management that shape the lifelong learning approaches, concepts and objectives established by the EU. There has also been a resurgence in certain scientific and rationalist pedagogies, which many believed to have been critically discredited, such as Benjamin Bloom et al.'s taxonomy of educational objectives (1977), with its omnipresent "qualifications", "skills" and "competences" becoming today's "learning outcomes". This lineage or evolution is clearly expressed in the study carried out by Cedefop (2009), which considers widespread reliance on "learning outcomes" to be part of an innovative approach to vocational education and training.

Within this approach the social dynamics of community education and local development tend to be ignored. Social and cultural diversity are seemingly absent or are implicitly regarded as a problem to be solved, given their potentially negative impact on global efforts to equip adults with skills, often presented as a monolithic project with no rational alternative. In the policy documents, human beings are considered in an atomized, divided, and fragmented manner, hierarchically ranked according to their possession or lack of skills. For these men and women, it is no longer enough to 'learn to be', in the sense in which this phrase is used in social-democratic approaches of a humanist or comprehensive nature, for example those of certain, vaguely Enlightenment-inspired, advocates of lifelong education in the 1970s (such as Lengrand, 1981; Faure et al., 1977). Today, however, the phrase "learning to be" may be considered overly generic and inadequate, even after the updates and additions made by Jacques Delors and his colleagues (1996) – learning to know, learning to do, learning to live together – as it is the subject of cumulative, and potentially endless additions: learning to be ... relevant, attractive, employable, entrepreneurial, well-adapted, flexible, competent, competitive, efficient, skilled, qualified, innovative, productive ... In other words, it focuses solely on what I have, in other papers, referred to as the "right hand" of lifelong education (Lima, 2007, 2012a), which Ettore Gelpi (1998, p. 134) has also associated with "education as training", as opposed to "education as culture" (see also Gomes & Monteiro, 2016).

The moulding of a young human learner is not viewed as part of the humanisation of human beings (see Lucio-Villegas, 2018), but is presented as an essential mechanism for survival and functional adaptation to a new, complex world that is beyond our control. An appropriate slogan would be *Learn to adapt and you may survive.* Should you fail to do so, you will fall victim to your lack, or scarcity, of key competitive skills, unequipped to face a hostile environment that will, ultimately, reject you as a human resource, instead viewing you as a social problem and enrolling you in compulsory second-tier integration projects, schemes for marginalised persons, or public assistance, rehabilitation and training programmes, or, as a last resort, a sort of palliative learning in which you will remain indefinitely, or cyclically "in training". Here, efforts are made to restructure the self of each unemployed, unqualified or marginalised person, managing their hopes and combating the desperation of individuals with a tendency to internalise personal failings and individual blame, without understanding the structural dimensions that condemn them to be defeated by life, "redundant" or "wasted" (Bauman, 2004), and therefore unable to make a mark, to take decisions, to act. Forgetting the potential of critical education and of utopian thinking in the context of long-term unemployment (e.g., Bonna, 2021) as well as of imagination in times of crisis (e.g., Rasmussen, 2021). In the conservative perspective, not only is lifelong learning for the purposes of cultural assimilation and functional and acquiescent adaption considered the civil and moral duty of each individual; it is also an institutional strategy for social control and combatting anomy, through the action of old and new specialist support agencies, and for fostering discipline and political passivity.

The current approach of training human capital, which is central to European Union texts, highlights the importance of seeking the right combination of knowledge, skills, and attitudes, in order to succeed in the labour market. In response to the objective and imperative needs of the labour market, each individual must identify their 'skills gaps', and make efforts to fill or compensate for them by accessing effective 'training products' to ensure employability, productivity and economic growth, thus simultaneously guaranteeing greater competitiveness and improved social cohesion. The protagonists are now individuals and their families, as well as companies and the training industry. The State plays a limited strategic role in regulation, establishing partnerships, contracts, and promoting competitive funding schemes. The workplace emerges as the site of learning *par excellence*, especially where cohesive corporate cultures of continuing professional development within a company socialise and develop staff in line with corporate objectives, in other words *moulding* employees. Considerations of divergent interests, power relationships, conflict and the social struggle for more and better democracy are residual and viewed as mere temporary difficulties – failings in communication and learning. Regular, active participation in continuing professional development programmes is a priority but, paradoxically, it is understood in depoliticised terms, disconnected from the exercise of democratic citizenship.

5   Final Remarks: Education and Learning as Cultures of Openness and Dialogical Action

Subordinated to market interests and the creation of value, lifelong learning and continuing professional development have been transformed into merchandise and subjected to the principle of maximising profit. Professional training is big business, and today encompasses a powerful and growing learning market, arising, for the most part, from the globalisation of the economy, which "[...] seems to have blinded those responsible for education, who cannot see beyond the professional dimension" (Gelpi, 2009, p. 144). The "EdTech" global market, reinforced during the COVID-19 pandemic crisis, comprises "learning solutions" that are not only industrial and market products, but also relevant educational actors, changing the character and the meaning of education, and the learning experiences (Grimaldi & Ball, 2020).

The new professional training market adopts a blinkered logic of business, marketing, publicity and the conquest of new markets and learner-customers. It diligently pursues profit, disseminating the ideology of skills gaps, producing entrepreneurial pedagogies, training kits and franchise-based teaching systems within a market that produces and trains the humans of the future: flexible, competitive, and useful technico-rational resources.

The usefulness of training is measured only in its exchange value – its capacity to provide what is considered a positive response to gaps or deficits in the training of the other, in a global context where the other constantly reveals his or her own incompetence and, consequently his or her skills gaps and learning needs. This is yet another form of social differentiation that discriminates against the other, sometimes offering conversion or acculturation programmes, while denying them recognition "as subjects with rights, knowledge, culture, identities, dignity" (Arroyo, 2017, p. 49).

In a society of constant competition, of ceaseless, merciless rivalry, there is no option but to acquire stronger skills in order to compete and win (Lima, 2012b). Training therefore becomes central to a new "art of war", with learning as its most effective weapon, in the wider context of a pedagogy that, by producing winners must also, necessarily, produce losers, and normalise their existence. In other words, based on a "naive optimism regarding the practice of education", which Freire (Escobar et al., 1994, p. 30) critically labelled "pedagogism" and which, according to the latter, in conversation with Ivan Illich, once "disconnected from power" is at risk of being considered "a lever that transforms reality" (Freire, 2013, p. 41), we face the risk of an oppressive pedagogism, aimed, in particular, at individuals considered "unskilled", at the masses considered reluctant, mediocre and static – the classic argument of all forms of oppression and elitism. As Freire (1975a, pp. 131, 150, 153) wrote, this would be typical of oppressive education, based on the "absolutisation of ignorance", the "intrinsic inferiority" of culturally invaded people, the "uncultured nature of the people", the "proclamation" of the ignorance of the masses. The dominant terms associated with "high quality education" today are qualifications and marketable skills, competitiveness, and entrepreneurialism, hyperbolically claimed to be capable of providing "the starting point for a successful professional career and the best protection against unemployment and poverty" (European Union, 2017, p. 2).

In any eventuality, the vanguardist utilitarianism afflicting adult education impedes critical distancing required to recognise new emerging "situations of oppression" (Morollón del Rio, 2018, p. 9), the imposition of accommodative models, and the normalisation of oppressive pedagogical solutions and cultural actions. As Gadotti (1998, p. 118) observed in his interpretation of Freire, neoliberal pedagogy "limits the pedagogical to the strictly pedagogical". But oppression runs far deeper than marginalisation or exclusion by the education and training system. Carnoy and Tarlau (2018, p. 87) conclude that Pedagogy of the Oppressed includes efforts to liberate adults belonging to different social classes from various forms of oppression. Even in settings considered democratic, these forces subordinate education to new capitalism and its objectives of domination, adaptation and socialisation, and can, therefore, give rise to a new pedagogy of oppression. In such contexts, Paulo Freire's Pedagogy of the Oppressed remains an essential critical resource and an ethical and political call for "dialogical and problem-posing education" (Freire, 1975a, p. 261). It treats adult learning and training as a democratic and liberating force, rejecting processes of cultural invasion and monocultural, technocratic policies, blinkered by the logic of exogenous economic and corporate modernisation and detached from the local sociocultural fabric and its rich diversity. Dialogical action, on the contrary, aims to create and strengthen cultures of openness, democracy, and participation, favouring sustainable development over instrumental, expansionist modernisation. It aims to prevent social structures undergoing transformation from being objects, shaped solely by the hierarchical external actions of those holding power or certain types of knowledge, instead making them the subject of their own transformative process, seeking to create what Freire calls "cultural synthesis" in communities viewed as complete in their own right and, simultaneously part of other larger and more complex wholes. In such communities, cultural, linguistic, religious, gender, ethnic, class and economic differences, among many others, may be sources of discrimination or of democratic dialogue and conviviality in political and social terms, also including adult learning and education environments. The latter perspective, which views education as a process of humanisation and liberation of human beings is particularly indebted to the work of several authors, including John Dewey, Ivan Illich, Ettore Gelpi, among others, namely the authors associated with critical pedagogy today. In this field, Paulo Freire remains an essential author, and, half a century after its publication, his work *Pedagogy of the Oppressed* still exhibits the relevance and critical force of a magnum opus.

Note

1   This work is funded by CIEd – Research Centre on Education, project UID/CED/01661/2019, Institute of Education, University of Minho, through national funds of FCT/MCTES-PT.

References

Alheit, P., & Hernández-Carrera, R. M. (2018). La doble visión de la educación permanente: Dos perspectivas analíticas. *Linhas Críticas, 24*, 555–581. https://doi.org/10.26512/lc.v24i0.19170

Arroyo, M. G. (2017). *Passageiros da noite: do trabalho para a EJA. Itinerários pelo direito a uma vida justa.* Vozes.

Bauman, Z. (2004). *Wasted lives: Modernity and its outcasts.* Polity Press.

Bloom, B. S. (1977). *Taxonomía de los objetivos de la educación: La classificación de las metas educacionales*. Editorial El Ateneo.

Bonna, F. (2021). Creating connections for expansive learning in crisis-laden times of long-term unemployment. *European Journal for Research on the Education and Learning of Adults*, 12(3), 251–266. http://doi.org/10.3384/rela.2000-7426.3882

Carnoy, M., & Tarlau, R. (2018). Paulo Freire continua relevante para a educação nos EUA. In M. Gadotti & M. Carnoy (Eds.), *Reinventando Freire* (pp. 87–100). Instituto Paulo Freire e Lemann Center/Stanford Graduate School of Education.

Cedefop – European Centre for the Development of Vocational Training. (2009). *The shift to learning outcomes: Policies and practices in Europe*. Office for Official Publications of the European Communities. https://www.cedefop.europa.eu/en/publications/3054

Delors, J. (1996). *Learning: The treasure within*. Report to UNESCO of the International Commission on Education for the twenty-first century. http://hdl.voced.edu.au/10707/114597

Escobar, M., Fernández, A. L., & Guevara-Niebla, G. (with Freire, P.). (1994). *Paulo Freire on higher education: A dialogue at the National University of Mexico*. Suny Press.

European Union. (2000). *A memorandum on lifelong learning*. SEC(2000)1832. https://uil.unesco.org/document/european-communities-memorandum-lifelong-learning-issued-2000

European Union. (2001). *Making a European area of lifelong learning a reality*. COM(2001)678 final. https://eur-lex.europa.eu/LexUriServ/LexUriServ.do?uri=COM:2001:0678:FIN:EN:PDF

European Union. (2006a). *Recommendation of the European Parliament and of the council of 18 December 2006 on key competences for lifelong learning*. 2006/962/EC. https://eur-lex.europa.eu/LexUriServ/LexUriServ.do?uri=OJ:L:2006:394:0010:0018:en:PDF

European Union. (2012). *Rethinking education: Investing in skills for better socio-economic outcomes*. COM(2012) 669 final. https://eur-lex.europa.eu/legal-content/HR/TXT/?uri=CELEX:52012DC0669

European Union. (2016a). *Working together to strengthen human capital, employability and competitiveness*. COM(2016) 381 final. https://eur-lex.europa.eu/legal-content/EN/TXT/?uri=CELEX%3A52016DC0381

European Union. (2016b). *Entrepreneurship education at school in Europe. Eurydice report*. Publications Office of the European Union. https://eacea.ec.europa.eu/national-policies/eurydice/content/entrepreneurship-education-school-europe_en

European Union. (2017). *School development and excellent teaching for a great start in life*. COM(2017) 248 final. https://eur-lex.europa.eu/legal-content/EN/TXT/?uri=COM%3A2017%3A248%3AFIN

European Union. (2018). *Proposal for a council recommendation on key competences for lifelong learning*. COM(2018) 24 final. https://eur-lex.europa.eu/resource.html?uri=cellar:395443f6-fb6d-11e7-b8f5-01aa75ed71a1.0001.02/DOC_1&format=PDF

Faure, E., Herrera, F., Kaddoura, A.-R., Lopes, H., Petrovski A. V., Rahnema, M., & Champion Ward, F. (1977). *Aprender a ser*. Livraria Bertrand.

Freire, P. (1967). *Educação como prática da liberdade*. Paz e Terra.

Freire, P. (1975a). *Pedagogia do oprimido*. Afrontamento.

Freire, P. (1975b). *Extensão ou comunicação?* Paz e Terra.

Freire, P. (1992). *Pedagogia da esperança. Um reencontro com a pedagogia do oprimido*. Paz e Terra.

Freire, P. (1993). *Política e educação*. Cortez.

Freire, P. (1995). *À sombra desta mangueira*. Olho d'Água.

Freire, P. (1996). *Pedagogia da autonomia: Saberes necessários à prática educativa*. Paz e Terra.

Freire, P. (2013). Una invitación a la conscientización y a la desescolarización. In P. Freire & I. Illich, *Diálogo* (pp. 37–89). Instituto Paulo Freire de España e L'Ullal Edicions.

Freire, P. (2017). Discurso por ocasião do doutoramento honoris causa que lhe foi outorgado pela Universidade Complutense de Madrid em 16 de dezembro de 1991 [manuscrito]. *Rizoma Freireano, 23*, 1–4. http://www.rizoma-freireano.org/revista2323/discurso-paulo-freire-384-23

Gadotti, M. (1998). Lições de Freire. *Educação. Sociedade & Culturas, 10*, 111–122. https://www.fpce.up.pt/ciie/revistaesc/ESC10/10-5-gadotti.pdf

Gelpi, E. (1998). *Identidades, conflictos y educación de adultos*. Universitat de les Illes Balears y Diálogos.

Gelpi, E. (2009). *Formación de personas adultas: Inclusión y exclusión*. Edicions del CREC.

Gomes, I., & Monteiro, A. A. (2016). Why choose one hand over the other when we can use the best of two? Adult educators' perspectives on adult education. In R. Evans, E. Kurantowicz, & E. Lucio-Villegas (Eds.), *Researching and transforming adult learning and communities* (pp. 105–118). Sense Publishers.

Grimaldi, E., & Ball, S. J. (2020). Paradoxes of freedom. An archaeological analysis of educational online platforms interfaces. *Critical Studies in Education, 62*(1), 114–129. https://doi.org/10.1080/17508487.2020.1861043

Hake, B. J. (2018). Éducation permanente in France en route to 'permanent education' at the Council of Europe? Revisiting a projet social to create 'a long life of learning'. *History of Education, 47*(6), 779–805. https://doi.org/10.1080/0046760X.2018.1484182

Lengrand, P. (1981). *Introdução à educação permanente*. Livros Horizonte.

Lima, L. C. (2007). *Educação ao longo da vida. Entre a mão direita e a mão esquerda de Miró*. Cortez.

Lima, L. C. (2012a). On the right hand of lifelong education. In R. Arnold (Ed.), *Entgrenzungen des Lerners: Internationale Perspektiven für Erwachsenenbildung* (pp. 137–158). Bertelsmann Verlag.

Lima, L. C. (2012b). *Aprender para ganhar, conhecer para competir: Sobre a subordinação da educação na 'Sociedade da Aprendizagem'*. Cortez.

Lima, L. C. (2018). Adult and permanent education in times of crisis: A critical perspective based on Freire and Gelpi. *Studies in the Education of Adults, 50*(2), 219–238. https://doi.org/10.1080/02660830.2018.1523087

Lucio-Villegas, E. (2018). Revisiting Paulo Freire: Adult education for emancipation. In M. Milana, S. Webb, J. Holford, R. Waller, & P. Jarvis (Eds.), *The Palgrave international handbook on adult and lifelong education and learning* (pp. 151–168). Macmillan Publishers.

Mayo, P. (2014). Las competencias y el derecho a una educación permanente: Elementos para un discurso crítico alternativo. In *Laboratori d'iniciatives ciutadanes Ettore Gelpi, nº 10. Gelpi, Freire y el Aprendizaje Permanente* (pp. 7–10). Laboratori d'iniciatives ciutadanes Ettore Gelpi; Instituto Paulo Freire.

Morollón Del Rio, D. (2018). *Filosofía latinoamericana en la pedagogía de Paulo Freire: Influencias y relaciones hasta 1970*. L' Ullal Ediciones; Instituto Paulo Freire.

Rasmussen, P. (2021). Public reason, adult education and social imagination. *European Journal of Research on the Education and Learning of Adults, 12*(1), 15–29. http://doi.org/10.3384/rela.2000-7426.ojs3465

Walters, S., & von Kotze, A. (2018). "If you can't measure it, it doesn't exist"? Popular education in the shadows of global reporting on adult learning and education. *Studies in the Education of Adults, 51*(1), 3–14. https://doi.org/10.1080/02660830.2018.1522052

CHAPTER 2

Resisting Mainstream Lifelong Learning

The Contributions of Popular Education and Participatory Research

Emilio Lucio-Villegas

Abstract

Popular education as a way to organise the process of learning and teaching has a long tradition around the world. Usually, it is taken for granted that popular education was born in Latin America in the 1960s, with the primary representative of it being Paulo Reglus Neves Freire. In this chapter, I will explore the intellectual context that shapes the building of a different education. On the one hand, the theories, and practices of deschooling society. On the other, the building of a 'popular' knowledge through participatory research. I will also refer, very briefly, to methodologies, considering the dialogue as their central element. Finally, the chapter looks at two experiences that can be considered as exemplary of popular education.

Keywords

deschooling society – lifelong learning – non-formal adult education – Paulo Freire – popular education – participatory research

1   Introduction

Popular education as a way of organising the process of learning and teaching has a long international tradition. Sometimes it has been reduced to the field of adult education, but it is better considered as an educational approach for all rather than as an approach addressed to a specific group of people. Usually, it is taken for granted that popular education was born in Latin America in the 1960s, with the primary representative of it being Paulo Reglus Neves Freire.

In some ways, this is true. There is a consensus that considers Latin-America the geographic space and *Pedagogy of the Oppressed* (first published in 1970 in the USA) as the foundational work of popular education. As Kane (1999) stated:

> Throughout Latin America, popular education was inspired by the Brazilian experience of the early 1960s when, in the course of struggling to bring about social change, popular organisations themselves identified the need for an alternative education; one which was related to their experience and under their control. (p. 55)

But it could also be important to consider two major elements related to the concept of popular education. On the one hand, the geographical context that cannot only be reduced to Brazil or Latin America, but must also include other countries, regions and historical times. In this direction I will refer to the 'Misiones Pedagógicas' in Spain as an experience that can be presented as a practice of popular education.

There is also an important second element, which is how to define experiences of popular education? What experiences can be considered models for confronting the mainstream policies and practices of Lifelong Learning? To that end, I will later present a singular experience related to recovering the memory of people. Finally, how do we define popular education?

Martin (1999) stated that "the idea of popular education, [refers to] an education that is rooted in the interest, aspirations, and struggles of ordinary people" (p. 4).

In the same line, Turay argues that

> Popular education refers to a non-formal adult education approach that develops the capacity of learners to critically analyse the root causes of their socioeconomic, political, cultural, spiritual and religious struggles, with the ultimate goal of organising and taking collective action that will enhance social transformation. (2005, pp. 480–481)

In short, there are two major ideas regarding the understanding of popular education. First, the understanding that education is a process in which people reflect on their life, their experience, and about their community. Secondly, education is a powerful tool for helping people to imagine and build a different community and another world.

Popular education has an important methodological element too. It is an attempt to develop education in a t way which is more concerned with a collective than an individual approach. To Martin (1999), the methodological approach is based on three aspects: (1) the curriculum comes from the experience and interest of the people, (2) it is focused on group activities, and (3) "it attempts, wherever possible, to forge a direct link between education and social action" (p. 5). Finally, another methodological element is to focus more on people's lives and experiences that on transmitting the content of textbooks. In short, connections between the ideas of education and the way this education is developed are clearly related and the borders between theory and practice seem very diffuse.

In this chapter I shall develop all these aspects, starting from a brief look at the Latin American intellectual context.

2   The Intellectual Context

According to Osorio (2020), the birth of popular education in Latin America is related, among others, to three major intellectual influences: Paulo Freire's work and, overall, his notion of dialogue as the main methodology to organise educational processes, (2) the theories of unschooling as a revolt against the colonised school, and (3) participatory research as a way of creating knowledge from people's experiences. In this paper I am going to focus on the second and third aspects already mentioned and only refer to Freire's work when talking about dialogue as a methodology.

If I focus on these two and not others it is because both are strongly implicated in the resistance to, and confrontation of colonialism in the domains of school, education and the creation of knowledge. In some ways, these two influences on popular education can inspire us to challenge Lifelong Learning policies and practices.

Before this, however, I wish to refer briefly to another important intellectual influence: the Theology of Liberation. Kyrilo and Boyd (2017) have explored the relationships between Freire's thought and his Christian beliefs. They affirm that it is very important "to explore the connections between Freire's faith […] and its impact on his thought, practice and his overall work of fostering the humanisation of humanity" (p. XIX). On the other hand, in interview Kirkwood suggests that the major influence on Freire's ideas are the personalist thinkers – mainly Emanuel Mounier – and other Christian philosophers (Kirkwood & Lucio-Villegas, 2012).

Jeria (quoted in Kirylo & Boyd, 2017) sums up this aspect of Freire's thinking very well:

> These early experiences in Catholic Action led Freire to pursue his literacy work among the rural poor, and eventually led to his exile from Brazil […] Moreover, these experiences caused his spiritual sensitivities to become intricately and intimately related to a commitment to social change and a fight against oppression. (p. 5)

3   Deschooling Society

Even though the theories of deschooling have traditionally been focused on Ivan Illich and his book *Deschooling Society* (Illich, 1971), there are other important thinkers (for example, Reimer, 1976) that have reflected on this trend to build an educational system outside of the school. As Tort (2001) states, "Deschooling appears in a context of cultural and educational opposition. It is related to the crisis of the myth of endless progress and unlimited growth" (p. 271). But it is related also to increasing doubts concerning the utility of the knowledge provided by the school that represents the colonial and hegemonic views that maintain the system of social classes in a society. To Illich (1971), who lived and worked in Mexico, this system is derived, in the case of Latin America, from the colonial domination.

The idea of a school that reproduces unequal social relations is not only developed by deschooling authors. Sociologists such as Bourdieu and Passeron, in their classic work (1977), exposed how the school is an apparatus for reproducing the hegemonic view of society in each specific period. Apple (1986) explained how this transmission is not only explicit but is also done by means of the school organisation, norms and hierarchy, defined as the 'hidden curriculum'. Deriving from this, deschooling theorists consider that the school is an instrument of oppression – in colonial and social class terms – and must be replaced by the community. Illich saw the school as an apparatus whose major aim is to reproduce the unequal social relations in capitalist colonial society. This aim is achieved by acting in a double sense: (1) in an ideological direction reproducing hegemonic thought, and (2) not enabling people to aspire to social mobility. According to Illich (1971), the school guarantees neither the value of merit and effort, nor the development of individuals and communities. He stated:

> Neither learning nor justice is promoted by schooling because educators insist on packaging instructions with certification. Learning and the assignment of social roles are melted into schooling. Yet to learn means to acquire a new skill or insight, while promotion depends on an opinion which others have formed. [...] Instruction is the choice of circumstances which facilitate learning. Roles are assigned by setting a curriculum of conditions which the candidate must meet if he [sic] is to make the grade. School links instruction but no learning to these roles. (1971, p. 11)

Illich also argues that the organisation of the school gives the teacher unlimited power over the learners. And this is not only a power related to knowledge, but control over their entire lives, including moral judgement, or simply denigration, of the learners. This denigration is also present in the effort to exclude people's daily life from school, where they learn things that dismiss their experiential knowledge. Always very critical of the school, Dickens, notably, already in 1854 ridiculed this lifeless knowledge – taking the definition of a horse as his example – in the second chapter of *Hard Times* ([1854] 2008).

To confront this situation of inequality, Illich's proposal is to replace the school with the community. This also means to transfer the educational power and knowledge from the colonial and classist school to the community. Illich named this system 'learning webs', by affirming that people can learn in different places and with different methods.

The program of this proposal can be summarised as follows: (1) to guarantee full access to educational resources during the entire lifetime of the individuals, (2) the conviction that every person can share their knowledge with other people who are interested in it, and (3) that every person can present their own knowledge in public talks to the community.

This program takes shape in four different webs: (1) services related to educational objects that should facilitate the processes of learning. These objects can be stored in libraries, exhibition rooms, etc.; (2) skilled workshops that enable people to offer and share their skills with other people; (3) the search for learning partners as part of the entire process of teaching and learning; (4) finally, building a catalogue of people with any type of qualification.

I think that Illich's major contribution to popular education is to consider the community as a privileged space for teaching and learning, replacing the school by the community. And this is one of the features of popular education: the listening phase (Freire, 1970) is essential in order to look for generative themes derived from people living in communities. These generative themes organise the process of teaching and learning. In the learning webs, community is the foundation of the knowledge that is in the educational process.

4   Popular Knowledge and Participatory Research

A second significant element that helps to explore the contributions that give shape to popular education is related to participatory research. I want to approach it not only as a methodology for working with adult learners but as an instrument to decolonise knowledge and create new knowledge.

Even though the origins of participatory research can be first found in the work done by Kurt Lewin (1946), there is a certain agreement (see Hall, 2001) to consider the seminal work by Matja-Liisa Swantz (see Swantz et al., 2001) with women and unemployed people in Tanzania in the 1970s as a foundational experience, far removed from the more technical approach developed by Lewin (Fals Borda, 1998). This last author, Fals Borda, is important not only because of his contributions to participatory research and his work with peasants in Colombia, but because his work is in Latin America, the geographical context where I have situated one of the 'origins' of popular education.

Participatory research is thus closely related to the creation of knowledge in a different way and with different actors compared to the 'traditional' knowledge elaborated through academic research. In some ways it is also closely related to another Mexican thinker: Rodolfo Stavenhagen. In the early 1970s, Stavenhagen wrote an article on "Decolonizing social sciences" (1971) as an attempt to reflect on the limits of the traditional paths of creating knowledge.

Stavenhagen's first idea is that the most fruitful theory must be confirmed only if it enables people to resolve the problems that arise in their daily life. In this direction, social sciences must serve people by providing answers to their problems and by exploring new paths for creating and disseminating knowledge.

Summarising Stavenhagen's proposal, it can be said that he looked for a social science that focuses on researching people's daily lives so that individuals can understand and transform them. In doing that, social sciences become more scientific (Demo, 1988). On the other hand, this approach broke with the traditional differentiation between researchers and common people as objects of research. People become subjects and participants in the research process.

When talking about participatory research, Fals Borda tried to define what he called 'popular science':

> It is the practical, empirical and common-sense knowledge, the ancestral possession of common people, that enabled them to create, work and understand mainly with the resources that nature gave to people. (1980, p. 70, author's translation)

One of the pillars of popular education is this idea of a popular or quotidian knowledge. In fact, when Illich criticised the school, one of his major considerations is that the school is not an institution which creates knowledge but is only transmitting a specific type of it – the knowledge already created by the hegemonic powers in society.

To achieve what Hall (2011) has called 'knowledge democracy', it is very important to organise the 'socialisation' of knowledge in a way that Fals Borda (1986) named 'systematic return'. He differentiated four steps for this devolution. The first is related to the fact that speeches, resources, etc. must be organised and presented in a comprehensive language and in a format that enables individuals to read, to understand, to ask for and discuss the information. The second step is to organise the return of the knowledge created in an accessible language that allows and encourages people to participate in and share new knowledge. The third step is related to the origin of the research. The research themes arise from the curiosity, problems, desires, and interest of the people and are nearest to the environment of the community. In doing so, research and community establish a close collaboration whose main aim is to provide responses to the situation people are living in.

The last step of this process, according to Fals Borda (1986), is focused on the use of a certain methodological approach. Usually, participatory research uses a biographical approach that facilitates people's participation not only at the level of informants, but as researchers, and in the process of returning the new knowledge.

Finally, I would like to refer to the concept of *Vivencia*. According to Fals Borda (2001),

> Participatory Research was defined as a *vivencia* necessary for the achievement of progress and democracy, a complex of attitudes and values that would give a necessary meaning to our praxis in the field. From this time on, PR [participatory research] had to be seen not only as a research methodology but also as a philosophy of life that would convert its practitioners into 'thinking-feeling persons'. (p. 31, original emphasis)

This *vivencia* is clearly connected with the Gramscian idea that the researcher – the organic intellectual in his terminology – not only has to know how people think, but he or she has to feel with people. In fact, Fals Borda (2001) states:

> Another support for *vivencia*, different from praxis, is also necessary because it is not enough to be an activist […] As stated above, participatory action research has not been a question of knowledge. It is also a transformation of individual attitudes and values, personality and culture, an altruistic process. (pp. 31–32, original emphasis)

To summarise, the contribution of participatory research to popular education is focused on the process of creating knowledge as a path to create awareness and to connect education, research and community in such a way as to provide answers to people's hopes and dreams.

5   Popular Education Methodologies

Until now, I have taken an approach to popular education, stressing two different elements: deschooling theories and participatory research. This means that I have focused on popular education as a theory of education more so than a practice. In the following, I would like to say something about methodology and practices of popular education. I will do this in two ways. I will briefly reflect on some methodological approaches, and then I will present two different experiences.

I think that methodologies can have two different approaches. On the one hand, the consideration that every educational act is one of producing knowledge. On the other hand, that education is a relational process, and the methodology must reinforce this relational element.

The first approach – education as an act of producing knowledge – is summarised by Martin (1999):

> Moreover, the utility and efficacy of the 'knowledge from below', that is the hallmark of popular education, is defined primarily in collective rather than individual terms. In this sense, popular education is informed by an egalitarian rather than a meritocratic ethic. (p. 6)

There are two significant ideas here. To begin with, popular education is a "real struggle for democracy" (Martin, 1999, p. 7), and democracy includes knowledge democracy. As well, popular education is an attempt to build a different educational process where people can explore new paths of knowledge by confronting the 'official' one.

In this direction, the Freirean concept of dialogue is essential. Dialogue guarantees communication and establishes education as a cooperative process characterised by social interactions between people. Regarding dialogue – one of Freire's most important contributions to methodology – Kirylo and Boyd (2017) state that it is

> An encounter between human beings, and in order for it to be authentic and transformative, the presence of love, humility, hope, faith in humanity, and critical thinking are all necessary aspects to a dialogical relationship. (p. 62)

Dialogue also means multiple voices and multiple directions. As Park (2001) states:

> Dialogue occupies a central position as an inquiry in pursuing the three objectives of participatory research, and the knowledge associated with them, by making it possible for participants to create a social space in which they can share experiences and information, create common meanings and forge concerted actions together. (p. 81)

Finally, dialogue enables people to create "open and trusting relationships between two or more people … One important aspect of dialogue is its ability to build social and emotionally caring relationships between people" (Dale & Hyslop-Margison, 2012, p. 4).

In the end, every process of research is arguably a communicative space where people are sharing knowledge, experiences and relationships. For that, the second approach to methodology – to reinforce social relationships – is important. And this is because "more than a technical means to an end, it is an expression of the human condition that impels people to come together" (Park, 2001, p. 81).

Clover, Follen and Hall (2010) consider that popular education starts from people's intellectual, emotional and physical environment. From this point of departure, the authors organise a program addressed to environmental adult education with a strong emphasis on group relationships. They differentiate five steps: (1) the creation of a plan to define the aim of the program by using tools to motivate, and bring to light fear, or lack of self-esteem, etc. (2) the knowledge of the context where the program will take place. This listening phase (Freire, 1970) includes the selection of venues and the timetable of activities. (3) the knowledge of people holding the group together. This means to know why people attend the course, what are the moments of resistance and the fears that people experience about participating in learning processes, amongst others. (4) the subjects and the processes of learning. Subjects must arise from the desires, interests and curiosity of the people. They must listen to the experience and stories of people involved in them. (5) an evaluation of how people learn, how this learning is useful to them, how the program can be improved.

In short, I wish to stress that the methodology of popular education has, as one of its main features, the group as a place for learning, while people remain the primordial resource for learning. In the following, I shall present two experiences. First an historic experience: the 'Misiones Pedagógicas'. After that, a current experience of researching people's lives: the 'Social and Historical Memory Workshop'.

5.1 The 'Misiones Pedagógicas'

Tiana (2021) defined this experience with the following words:

> In Spain, between the years of 1931 to 1936 an original and interesting popular educational experience was developed. Some people, mainly younger people, most of them connected with teaching activities, together with writers and artists, went across Spain bringing books, music, copies of paintings, projectors, films, plays, and puppets to places and villages,

some of them still very isolated. In these places, they organised exhibitions, theatres, teaching keynotes, public sessions of reading, they worked and played with children and their teachers, and lived together with villagers. After some days, they returned to their homes after planting the seeds of education and culture, as well as leaving books and records in the schools. This lasted for a five-year period and in different seasons of the year. (p. 15, author's translation)

There is no better explanation of this process. The same author refers to the methodology of the experience that he names 'recreational school' to stress that it was open to a diversity of cultural events and activities to break the isolation of Spain's hinterland.

This diversity of activities can be summarised as follows: (1) the study of the natural environment through keynotes, exhibitions, etc.; (2) the 'socialisation' of fine arts with exhibitions of copies of great paintings; (3) the organisation of public readings and listening to music – popular and classic – live or on records, (4) the use of the cinema; (5) citizenship education focused on people's rights and the principles of the Republic; (6) activities to encourage people to read, mainly by the organisation of public libraries in small villages; and (7) actions devoted to teacher training (Tiana, 2021).

Participation in the 'Misiones Pedagógicas' involved not only those connected to education. We can mention individuals such as the poet Luis Cernuda, the philosopher Maria Zambrano or the playwright Alejandro Casona, among others. Most of them went into exile when the fascists won the Civil War in 1939 and the Franco dictatorship began.

Finally, it can be stated that the 'Misiones Pedagógicas' presented a triple dimension. First, by defining a specific model of education and practice; second, it was a great effort in terms of cultural action and communication; and third, it carried a strong political implication to reinforce democracy and the Republic.

5.2 *The Social and Historical Memory Workshop*

This workshop started functioning in 2004 to collect people's life histories as a source of knowledge about repression, incomplete education, precarious jobs, poverty, or migration. López (2011) considers that the defining moment was an interview with María, a woman who had lost her father at the very beginning of the Civil War when she was 5 years old. She expressed her nervousness and difficulties in conveying her memories and feelings related to those years.

The workshop has developed three different research activities. The first was focused on collecting histories from people living in the time of the Spanish Civil War, and the early years of the dictatorship. Interviews were collected, analysed and then organised around three main generative themes: repression either in the Civil War or during the dictatorship, education, and work in the post-war period. Dissemination was done in public presentations – in some cases it was the first time that some of the people involved in the workshop talked in public.

The second research activity was related to the last years of the dictatorship and the period known as *La transición,* the process of recuperating democracy between 1975 – the year of the death of the dictator – and 1978, when the democratic constitution was enacted. The generative themes that arose during a dedicated analysis of the interviews were: (a) the processes of migration – a consequence of the previous research, (b) the first massive workers' strikes, (c) the birth of democratic trade unions (even under the dictatorship), (d) the social and political militancy either in clandestine political parties, or in the first neighbourhood associations, and (e) the condition of women.

Dissemination of this research started with a public presentation in a community theatre in the district where the participants lived. Then, it was presented in diverse places: adult education schools, secondary schools, community centres and the university. Audio-visual material was organised to support these public presentations.

At present, the workshop is involved in a third research project related to one of the most important textile factories in the city of Seville. This factory is also significant for the history of the district and the history of the workers' movement in the city. According to López (2011), a variety of achievements have emerged from the research process. One suggests that participants in the workshop were enabled to learn how to carry out research. Another is related to the acquisition of tools for expressing their voice and for being listened to. For instance, their public presentations showed them how to express their own thinking and ideas.

6   Conclusions

Paulo Freire can be considered the key thinker and the most well-known author in popular education. His work is a cardinal point of reference in looking for a notion of education that helps people to understand their reality – physical and symbolic – to organise a better community and a richer personal life. Without his ideas, it is difficult to understand education – and in particular adult education – focused on the collective, starting from people's problems and their desire to learn. Freire's thought provides philosophical and methodological tools to resist the mainstream of an education only addressed to the labour market and concerned with training people to achieve employability – not a real and decent job. To organise practices of resistance to this dehumanising system, it is important to recall that education is a collective and relational event that must be useful for individuals and communities on the road to achieving wellbeing.

What are the contributions of popular education to resisting the mainstream of Lifelong Learning? Firstly, I think that it is related to the introduction of the real world in the school. In recent years, certain critiques have presented the school as an indoctrinated institution. In Spain, for instance, right wing and fascist parties try to prevent the school from introducing "themes such as sexual diversity, gender, ethnic diversity [...] it must be a school which does not present different views of the world and different views of the way to be in it" (Kohan, 2020, p. 189, author's translation). If the school teaches these notions, it is an 'indoctrinated' school. The aim is clearly for the real world to stay out of schools. A transmissive and bookish school that forgets, for instance, the suffering of people during the Spanish Civil War (Rangel, 2021).

The same reasoning applies when the school is defined as a place where people learn useless things. The school must be focused on transmitting knowledge, competences, and skills so that people are made ready to access the labour market. In doing that, however, the desires, the curiosities, the lives of the individuals are subordinated to the competences that they must acquire. These competences then decide what is useful for people and what is not.

There are, though, other models better adapted to organise educational processes. The 'Misiones Pedagógicas' is an example. The major goal of the experience was to 'socialise' knowledge (Gramsci, 1974) to confront people with other realities, building taste and criticism (Williams, 1983). The recreational school wanted to help people to discover other ways of life, beyond the narrow world that they found in isolated villages.

If the 'Misiones Pedagógicas' can be considered a 'top-down' process, the workshop is a popular education experience that starts from the curiosity of people to know more about their lives, and to unveil a part of their own history never yet told. In the end, both experiences, the attempt to imagine a different education far removed from a school that does not serve people, or the efforts to build knowledge in a different way, become an inspiration that facilitates imagining an education beyond the restrictions of Lifelong Learning policies and practices.

References

Apple, M. W. (1986). *Ideología y currículo*. Akal.
Bourdieu, P., & Passeron, J. C. (1977). *La reproducción*. Laia.

Clover, D., Follen, S., & Hall, B. (2010). *La naturaleza de la transformación. Educación ecológica de personas adultas*. Publicaciones de la Cátedra Paulo Freire de la Universidad de Sevilla.

Dale, J., & Hyslop-Margison, E. (2012). *Paulo Freire: Teaching for freedom and transformation. The philosophical influences on the work of Paulo Freire*. Springer.

Demo, P. (1988). *Ciencias sociales y calidad*. Narcea.

Dickens, Ch. (2008). *Hard times*. Collector's Library. (Original work published 1854)

Fals Borda, O. (1980). La ciencia y el pueblo: Nuevas reflexiones. In M. C. Salazar (Ed.), (1990). *La investigación acción participativa. Inicios y desarrollo* (pp. 65–84). Popular.

Fals Borda, O. (1986). *Conocimiento y poder popular*. Punta de Lanza/Siglo XXI.

Fals Borda, O. (1998). Experiencias teórico-prácticas. In O. Fals (Comp.). *Participación popular. Retos del futuro* (pp. 169–236). ICFES.

Fals Borda, O. (2001). Participatory (action) research in social theory: Origins and challenges. In P. Reason & H. Bradbury (Eds.), *Handbook of action research* (pp. 27–37). Sage Publications.

Freire, P. (1970). *Pedagogy of the oppressed*. The Continuum Publishing Company.

Gramsci, A. (1974). *Antología*. Siglo XXI.

Hall, B. L. (2001). I wish this were a poem of practices of participatory research. In P. Reason & H. Bradbury (Eds.), *Handbook of action research* (pp. 171–178). Sage Publications.

Hall, B. L. (2011). Towards a knowledge democracy movement: Contemporary trends in community-university research partnership. *Rizoma Freireano*, *9*, 1–18. http://www.rizoma-freireano.org/articles-0909/towards-a-knowledge-democracy-movement-contemporary-trends-in-community-university-research-partnerships-budd-l-hall

Illich, I. (1971). *Deschooling society*. Harper & Row.

Kane, L. (1999). Learning from popular education in Latin America. In J. Crowther, I. Martin, & M. Shaw (Eds.), *Popular education and social movements in Scotland today* (pp. 54–69). NIACE.

Kirkwood, C., & Lucio-Villegas, E. (2012). Freirean approaches to citizenship: An interview with Colin Kirkwood. In C. Kirkwood (Ed.), *The persons in relation perspective: In counselling, psychotherapy and community adult learning* (pp. 165–173). Sense Publishers.

Kirylo, J. D., & Boyd, D. (2017). *Paulo Freire. His faith, spirituality, and theology*. Sense Publishers.

Kohan, W. (2020). *Paulo Freire más que nunca. Una biografía filosófica*. CLACSO.

Lewin, K. (1946). Action research and minority problems. *Journal of Social Issues*, *2*(4), 34–46.

López Luna, J. M. (2011). L'oubli est plein de mémoire. Récupération de la mémoire historique et éducation populaire. In J. González Monteagudo (Ed.), *Les histoires de vie en Espagne. Entre formation, identité et mémoire* (pp. 253–288). L'Harmattan.

Martin, I. (1999). Introductory essay: Popular education and social movements in Scotland today. In J. Crowther, I. Martin, & M. Shaw (Eds.), *Popular education and social movements in Scotland today* (pp. 1–25). NIACE.

Osorio, J. (2020). La educación popular Latinoamericana: Trayectoria, debates y vigencia. In *Various authors intelectuales y pensamiento social y ambiental en América Latina* (pp. 333–348). RIL editores.

Park, P. (2001). Knowledge and participatory research. In P. Reason & H. Bradbury (Eds.), *Handbook of action research* (pp. 81–90). Sage Publications.

Rengel, C. (2021, February 6). Por qué la Guerra Civil y el Franquismo son aún un tabú en las aulas españolas. *HuffPost*. https://www.huffingtonpost.es/entry/educacion-memoria-historica-guerra-civil-franquismo_es_601bfddfc5b67cdd1a75f005?ncid=other_email_063gt2jcad4&utm_campaign=share_email

Reimer, E. (1976). *La escuela ha muerto*. Seix Barral.

Stavenhagen, R. (1971). Cómo descolonizar las ciencias sociales. In M. C. Salazar (Ed.), *La investigación acción participativa. Inicios y desarrollo* (pp. 37–63). Popular.

Swantz, M. L., Ndedya, E., & Masaiganah, M. S. (2001). Participatory action research in Southern Tanzania, with special reference to women. In P. Reason & H. Bradbury (Eds.), *Handbook of action research* (pp. 386–395). Sage.

Tiana, A. (2021). *Las misiones pedagógicas. Educación popular en la Segunda República*. Catarata.

Tort, A. (2001). Ivan Illich: La desescolarización o la educación sin escuela. In J. Trilla (Ed.), *El legado pedagógico del siglo XX para la escuela del siglo XXI* (pp. 271–296). Graó.

Turay, T. M. (2005). Popular education. In L. M. English (Ed.), *International encyclopedia of adult education* (pp. 480–484). Palgrave-Macmillam.

Williams, R. (1983). *Keywords: A vocabulary of culture and society*. Fontana.

CHAPTER 3

Lifelong Education in Diverse Communities

Reading Ettore Gelpi and Leonardo Zanier on Complex Environments 'in Transition'

Davide Zoletto

Abstract

The chapter starts by focusing on some of the emerging characteristics within socio-culturally diverse environments, particularly highlighting the overall complexity that researchers and educators have to deal with within such contexts. It then proceeds to present some of the key educational concepts in Ettore Gelpi's analysis of diverse urban environments and of the relations between culture(s) and lifelong education. The paper suggests that Gelpi's idea of culture is close to Williams' seminal idea of "culture as a whole way of life" and that, within the Gelpian perspective, living and vital cultural practices play a relevant role in lifelong education in diverse environments.

At the same time, the chapter suggests that, in a Gelpian view, researchers and educators working in diverse communities should change the way they usually consider migration diversity. They should try to not consider migrants as merely beneficiaries of educational interventions, but as an active cultural and educational reference who make a full contribution to lifelong education within complex environments 'in transition'. To conclude, the paper presents Gelpi's great regard for the educational activity of the Italian educator, trade unionist and poet Leonardo Zanier and in particular his work on the issue of migrants' linguistic education.

Keywords

lifelong – education – diverse communities – complex environments – migrant diversity – Ettore Gelpi – Leonardo Zanier

1 Introduction

In one of the closing chapters of his *Lifelong Education and International Relations* Ettore Gelpi highlights a contradiction that sometimes seems to characterise the relationship between the educational demand emerging in social contexts and the institutional offer drawn up by the various educational institutions themselves (Gelpi, 1985, p. 170).

Gelpi hypothesises that one of the consequences of this contradiction between supply and demand is twofold. On the one hand, educational institutions and educators could find themselves in a situation where they are looking for a public (with its presumed characteristics and 'needs') that in fact, may not even exist in the social educational context. On the other hand, the real public – which includes children, young people, and adults – could end up not seeing their own educational requirements satisfied because the institutional offer of education sometimes "confines them in a traditional and/or technological and/or cultural illiteracy; it is not sensitive to their demand to acquire the means to express themselves in the workplace, in social life, in the family. It sometimes conveys messages (which are) often manipulative, sometimes outmoded, and often not very creative" (Gelpi, 1985, p. 170).

The risk of such a contradiction existing between the 'reproduction' of educational institutions *and* societies 'in transition' which express new demands, new expectations and new needs, is becoming progressively more relevant today in educational contexts that are more and more complex and diverse in their different aspects. One example of this complexity can be seen in the educational contexts within today's urban areas. In fact, in the introduction to a monographic issue of the *International Journal of Lifelong Education*, entirely dedicated to emerging educational issues in contexts of urban diversity, Ruud van der Veen and Danny Wildemeersch pointed out that cities are characterised by many forms of diversity. On the one hand, there is the diversity linked to the consequences of migration processes and to the different ways in which the various components of the migrant and post-migrant population locate themselves within different neighbourhoods. On the other hand, there are other kinds of diversity which can be connected to the socioeconomic differences emerging in the different urban areas or even in the same neighbourhood. Furthermore, there are other differences which naturally emerge in urban contexts related to the age of the population, gender, and lifestyles that can characterise different individuals and groups (van der Veen & Wildemeersch, 2012, pp. 5–6). In each of these fields many transformations have long been underway. These transformations are linked to 'global flows' (Appadurai, 1996; Carney, 2009), as well as to technological changes (Floridi, 2014), but also to the different ways in which changes are localised within different contexts (Hannerz, 1992). This in turn increases processes of individualisation and the deepening of differences within and between different social and geographical contexts.

Van der Veen and Wildemeersch themselves have outlined from a pedagogical perspective at least three fields in which various 'tensions' emerge. The first tension is between institutional places for education and new more open educational spaces. The second tension is between real and virtual environments while the third tension is between social cohesion and social laboratories where new forms of community can emerge (van der Veen & Wildemeersch, 2012, p. 6).

While these three tensions can be seen as something that could lead to new and positive developments, at the same time the intersection of differences (Semi, 2012) can also bring an intersection of vulnerabilities. This is also part of a more general situation in which marginal areas emerge (Save the Children, 2018, pp. 114–132). This is the case, for instance, of some neighbourhoods with a high migrant or post migrant component classifiable as socio-culturally highly complex environments. Of course, in these situations there are many other issues to be taken into consideration. For example, the local job market, housing conditions, family structure and education (at the international level, see, for example, van Zanten, 2001; Butler & Hamnet, 2007; Oberti, 2008; with regard to the Italian situation, see the recent analyses offered by Pacchi & Ranci, 2017, and by Reports such as those of Caritas Italiana, 2018, pp. 131–184 and Save the Children, 2018).

2   Educational Contexts 'in Transition'

Understanding this complexity helps to clarify how current educational contexts, especially urban contexts, continue to be 'in transition', as Gelpi suggested. It is in this perspective that this chapter will try to read, within current educational contexts, some elements emerging from the work of Gelpi (1933–2002) and Leonardo Zanier (1935–2017). Gelpi was a known expert on lifelong learning and an educator himself, while Zanier was a trade unionist and an educator, as well as a poet. Both were active in the field of lifelong education and education of adults, both with a specific emphasis on the issue of migrants, as well as on issues around creativity and cultural and linguistic diversity. Gelpi and Zanier shared great respect for each other and a friendship which grew in the context of the activities of ECAP (Ente Confederale Addestramento Professionale), an organisation for adult education and vocational training founded by the Italian trade union CGIL (Confederazione Generale Italiana del Lavoro) in Switzerland in the seventies (Riccardi, 2014, pp. 103–110). ECAP started working with Italian migrants in Switzerland from the beginning of that period. Their educational programmes were intended to help Italian 'Gastarbeiter' to achieve the middle school exam they lacked and did this within the "150 ore" (150 hours), an Italian programme born in the seventies to promote workers' educational access (Barcella & Furneri, 2020, pp. 83–84). ECAP programmes in Switzerland in the seventies also included vocational courses, language courses, conferences and other cultural activities, as an essential contribution to the integration of Italian migrants (and of their children) in the Swiss schools, labour market and society (Barcella, 2014, pp. 107–121; Zanier, 1977a). In 1974 Zanier himself succeeded in setting up the first CGIL vocational education centre in Germany, where Italian 'Gastarbeiter' in the same years had to deal with difficulties similar to those they were experiencing in Switzerland (Barcella & Furneri, 2020, p. 86).

In the case of Gelpi, we do not want to retrace his complete work as it is vast and spans many different fields (Fiorucci, 2014, p. 9), and there are numerous studies which deal with this, from the more 'classical' ones such as those of Ireland (1978) and Griffin (2001, 2003), to the more recent research by Lima (2016), Riccardi (2014, 2021) and Puglielli (2019). Lima, Riccardi and Puglielli's research highlights specific aspects of Gelpi's work that are relevant today, especially in research fields such as those of lifelong, intercultural and adult education. The aim of this paper is something more specific and focuses on a particular issue that highlights how Gelpian perspectives can provide insights for educators and researchers working within socio-culturally complex environments with a high migrant or post-migrant component.

3 Contexts in Which New Cultural Values Emerge

In his work Gelpi focuses on the emerging characteristics within urban environments, highlighting particularly the issues of diversity, uncertainty and complexity. In fact, he emphasises that "new cultural values" emerge in these contexts and he underlines that among the demands on those living in urban environments there is a call for training and self-education so as to master "the foreseeable and often uncertain future" (Gelpi, 1985, p. 83; see also Gelpi, 1982).

Gelpi is well known for his "dialectical" approach to educational thought (Griffin, 2001, p. 274), thus he is aware that we cannot decide once and for all whether one or another educational approach could work or not or is positive or not. He suggests that we always have to see how each approach works within a context. He does not hesitate to ask, following Paulo Freire's suggestions, when and how lifelong education can be a tool of emancipation and when instead, there is the risk that it perpetuates unequal relationships that already exist within the context (Gelpi, 1985, p. 7)?

When considering urban areas, Gelpi argues that lifelong education can play a relevant role in urban areas for at least two reasons. First, he observes that in urban areas there is a "waste of human creative resources, intellectual and physical", and there is a great disregard for these resources which should be taken into account in education (Gelpi, 1985, p. 83). On the other hand, he emphasises our "limited knowledge" of the "needs, demands" and cultural practices of those who live in the city, the "city-dwellers" (Gelpi, 1985, p. 85).

This is why Gelpi underlines the importance of doing research on the relationships between culture and education in urban areas (Gelpi, 1985, p. 85). This is something that emerges from research in the field of cultural studies in urban environments (García Canclini, 1990), and it is very similar also to Michel de Certeau's work. De Certeau was also very attentive to daily cultural practices (de Certeau, 1980) and to the relationship between these and educational issues, even in multicultural environments (de Certeau, 1994).

Once again, we can pinpoint here one of Freire's lessons on the importance of learning to learn from those we wish to teach. Without this learning from below, we cannot teach anything. This is central for Gelpi's work.

4 Culture in Its Broader Significance

The concept of 'culture' used by Gelpi, therefore, is crucial. He argues that it is necessary to explore culture in urban environments by applying the notion "in its wider significance" (Gelpi, 1985, p. 87). That is, "not as a static end-product, but more as an innovative and creative process" (Gelpi, 1985, p. 87). This is very much in line with Raymond Williams' well-known definition that 'culture' is "a whole way of life", that is, "a way to interpret our everyday experiences" (Williams, 1958, p. 21). Williams developed this concept thanks to his experience as a teacher in courses of *adult education* in the England of the 'fifties (Williams, 1976, p. 13; see also the essays collected in McIlroy & Westwood, 1993). He states that it was a question of studying the "actual language", that is "the words and sequences of words that particular men and women have used in trying to give meaning to their experience" (Williams, 1958, pp. 21–22).

Gelpi, similarly, underlines that the focus on the role of 'culture' should not lead to an "academisation" of our idea of culture itself. But it is rather thanks to the introduction of a lived culture within education that "we can bring life into the educational experience" (Gelpi, 1985, p. 88). For Gelpi, if an educational project is to be a tool for promoting self-reliance in the learners, a "life culture" needs to be introduced in that project. Gelpi sees it as a "pre-condition" (Gelpi, 1985, p. 88) for an education that aims at being relevant for real people.

For both Williams and Gelpi, building on this broad idea of culture seems to have a strong impact on the way in which we choose specific cultural practices that we introduce in education. For example, Williams refers to adult education courses in the late 'forties where adults attended courses in a huge range of cultural practices (Williams, 1989, p. 154). In this broad sense, Gelpi speaks about both folk cultures and mass cultures. Following his dialectical approach, he is aware that they can both contribute "to promoting democratisation and development processes", but in other cases they can also lead "to the strengthening and reproduction of the existing social system" However, he also stresses that when cultural practices "promote self-reliance rather than dependence in the social, economic and educational fields" they permit individuals to "have a greater participation and control in all areas of life" (Gelpi, 1985, p. 87).

5 Cultural Services and Migrant Communities in Diverse Urban Areas

As already mentioned, Gelpi's perspective is based on a dialectic awareness that building on cultural practices emerging within urban environments does not in itself guarantee an education promoting inclusion, equity and social mobility for all individuals and groups. Gelpi uses the availability of cultural services to migrant communities as an example. He points out that "the city can sometimes limit itself to providing migrant workers only some of its cultural and educational services", while in other cases the city can "put all public facilities at their disposal and can thus become centres for cultural creation and inter-communication with the native population of the various districts of the city itself" (Gelpi, 1985, p. 87).

Gelpi points out that this is not just a question of accessibility. In his view, we also have to ask ourselves what role migrants can actually play within cultural services in diverse communities. He states that we have to change the idea of "education for migrants", which our plans and interventions are sometimes still based on, writing that "education for migrant workers is but one dimension of an issue that extends beyond literacy training and educational assistance both for workers and for their families" (Gelpi, 1985, p. 97). For he makes it clear that educational interventions with migrants should not be interventions that maintain or strengthen already existing relationships of dependence. They should rather be a part of a broader effort to work towards a "new world order of education" in which "migrant workers would not only be the beneficiaries, but to which they would also make a full contribution" (Gelpi, 1985, p. 97).

In many respects there is a real shift in perspective here: for Gelpi we should clearly not consider migrants as merely 'defective' people, that is, people who only have needs, or are at most potentially employable. Gelpi asks us to consider them as "an active cultural and educational reference" (Gelpi, 1990, p. 137), as people who have personal and collective histories, with knowledge, skills, and cultures from which to build a common project together (see also Riccardi, 2014, pp. 8–9).

6   Reading (and Building on) the Plural Character of Urban Cultures

Gelpi points out that in order to explore this diversity, we have to change the way we usually consider migration diversity. In a chapter of *Lifelong Education and International Relations* with the meaningful title "Migration and creativity" Gelpi notes that research and studies concerning migrants reflect the perspective of institutions and the governments of the society of immigration and do not reflect (or only partially reflect) the perspectives and stories of the migrant workers themselves (Gelpi, 1985, p 97).

This is a perspective shared by other authors researching in the same years that Gelpi was writing, for instance by Abdelmalek Sayad, a well-known scholar in the field of migration. Sayad, a few years earlier in his essay of 1981, significantly entitled "*Le phénomène migratoire, un relation de domination*" (later collected in a volume of his essays *The double absence* of 1999), noted that we almost always "tend to refer to the issues related to migrants and migration from the perspective of the so-called immigration sciences" (Sayad, 1999, p. 164). This is because "it is easier to establish a science of immigration and immigrants (i.e. a science based on the perspective of the society of destination) rather than to start from a science of emigration and emigrants (that is, a science which reflects the perspective of the society from which the migrants originate)" (Sayad, 1999, p. 164).

Gelpi's line of thinking is similar to that of Sayad, however, in the Gelpian perspective this attention to the migrants' point of view and their cultural practices takes on educational and pedagogical relevance. Understanding migrants' perspectives is fundamental in order to answer the questions and expectations of migrant workers, while avoiding two opposing risks. The first risk is to reduce our response to migrants simply to educational training interventions related only to economic factors and questions of employability. The second risk is that of falling into forms of "sentimentalism, pity and paternalism" (Gelpi, 1985, p. 97). These two risks may have opposing effects, but they both reflect, as both Sayad and Gelpi stated, the same often stereotyped answer our society employs.

Moreover, Gelpi writes that "the culture of the city also includes the culture of migrant workers who fight for better living conditions, not only for themselves, but also for those who still live in their home countries" (Gelpi, 1985, p. 88). Gelpi is clearly aware that the diversity of urban cultures can also be seen in what subsequent research would later define as a transnational or translocal perspective (Vertovec, 2009), especially (but not only) as a result of the networks that migrant and post-migrant components of the population have with their countries of origin, as well as with migrants of other countries or places.

Gelpi emphasises how important it is to deepen the study of the cultures and educational traditions of migrants so as to "develop more fruitful intercultural relations" for all those involved – both migrant and native populations (Gelpi, 1985, p. 97). He is neither naive nor unrealistic as he knows that 'intercultural' research, too, can run the risk of becoming "an instrument to maintain forms of dependency" (Gelpi, 1985, p. 99). On the other hand, when and if the relations between migrants and non-migrants are equal relations, then "education and culture will no longer be products only to be given ... to immigrants", and migrants themselves will be able to "take part in political life, in cultural life creation, in production, in communication" (Gelpi, 1985, p. 100; see also Gelpi, 2000, pp. 41–42).

7   Zanier and the Creativity of Migrant Cultural Practices

As we have seen, within the Gelpian perspective cultural practices which should enter lifelong education should be those living and vital practices that are part of a person's everyday experience. He notes that if education is built on culture as "the expression and the creative manifestation of each of us at home, at work, in leisure time, in social life", then this type of education would help "to locate a person in relation to his environment" (Gelpi, 1985, p. 111). Such creative cultural and educational experiences would be fully capable of being, he argued "the action of all, and by all" (Gelpi, 1985, p. 174). This is one of the clearest definitions that we can find in Gelpi's work on lifelong education. An example Gelpi refers to is Leonardo Zanier's work.

Gelpi declares that despite the diverse fields of his activities – which range from vocational training, trade unions, and the cooperative movement, on the one hand, and his poetry and literature, on the other, the main aim of Zanier's educational action was "to make everyone in individual and collective terms, master of his work and his choices, and, above all, capable of creation and production" (Gelpi, 1985, p. 174).

This is a question that emerges, for instance, in the way in which Zanier deals with issues of adult education and vocational training (Barcella, 2014, pp. 93–121), especially in connection with diverse migrant communities, languages and education. The field of diversity in languages, was one of the fields that Gelpi highlighted as typical of the 'in transition' contexts in which migrant workers live (Gelpi, 1985, pp. 111, 114). On these questions Zanier organised a conference in 1975 in Muttenz (Switzerland), entitled *La lingua degli emigrati* (The language of emigrants)' (ECAP-CGIL, 1977). Gelpi was also involved and in the proceedings of this conference he affirms that the linguistic education of the migrant workers is "one of the challenges for lifelong education" (Gelpi, 1977, p. 31). For Gelpi it is more than just a matter of learning the host country language, but rather promoting "the practice and learning of the mother tongue", as well as the "participation" of migrants in the different spheres of life: "in cultural life, in the workplace, in housing communities, in community life, in trade unions, etc." (Gelpi, 1977, p. 39).

This awareness can be seen both in Zanier's works and in his work with ECAP-CGIL in issues related to the linguistic training of migrant Italian workers in Switzerland. Zanier underlines that there are different factors, both social and organisational, that are connected both to "strengthening the mother tongue" and to the "acquisition of the second language" (Zanier, 1977a, p. 9). He also pinpoints how, starting from language issues, we have to rethink the 'integration' of migrants (in this case Italian migrants in Switzerland) because this should not be seen as "acculturation", but as a form of "participation" and "creation of a critical attitude in order to understand and deal with the social reality" in which migrants and also the native population live (Zanier, 1977a, p. 14). Zanier never abandoned this approach towards the factors involved in the social integration of migrants, not when he returned to Italy to work in the CGIL central offices in Rome, nor when he went back to Switzerland after the mid 'eighties. Significantly, as both the socio-historical context and migration flows changed, bringing more and more non-European migrants to Italy, Zanier's attention turned increasingly to the difficulties of these new groups of migrants in the Italian context.

Not surprisingly, in his poems mainly written in Friulian, the language of the migrants coming from his region in the Italian Northeast, Zanier (1981, p. 118) explains that when as a young man he first started writing poems, he started to think and write about "emigration". During this period, he tried to understand and describe the collective and individual reasons that bring people to move (see Zanier, 1998). However, year after year he went on to broaden his perspective, and the issue of migration then became an opportunity to think about "every other acculturation process" (Zanier, 1981, p. 118; see also 1979). Thinking (and writing poems) about migration thus helped him to better understand certain aspects of the social reality in which he lived (Zanier, 1981, p. 119). This awareness emerges clearly in Zanier's cultural (and poetical) production both in the 'eighties and 'nineties. As Barcella and Furneri state: "after the mid-'eighties, [Zanier] integrated the issue of foreign immigration into his trade union and cultural work and, on the wave of the conflicts that – around immigration itself – were starting to spread within Italian factories and in Italian society, the question as well of the Italians' real or alleged xenophobia, which, in the view of many observers, was a striking contradiction for a people who had emigrated for so long" (Barcella & Furneri, 2020, p. 105).

In conclusion, both Gelpi and Zanier tried to promote the creation of a "critical attitude towards social reality" (Zanier, 1977a, p. 14) and this attitude may be seen basically as one of the results of lifelong education in the Gelpian perspective. In relation to the diverse communities of the time in which they wrote, Gelpi and Zanier tried to suggest the relevance of building on the histories, expectations and resources (including the linguistic resources) of all sections of the population, migrants included. In a Gelpian view, this effort can perhaps lead to a better understanding of social reality in its broader sense, in a perspective embracing the whole, diverse community where both migrants and non migrants live together.

Referring back to Van der Veen and Wildemeersch's findings on the tensions presented by urban life (van der Veen & Wildemeersch, 2012, p. 6), this Gelpian perspective seems highly relevant today for those working as educators or researchers within environments which are characterised by complexity and diversity, as well as by the ambivalence of being 'in transition'. The tensions highlighted by van der Veen and Wildemeersch call for new attention to respond to the gap between that which is offered by institutions and the educational demands emerging today in increasingly diverse communities. How then is it possible to respond to Gelpi's and Zanier's invitation to build on the resources of whole communities, in the current context in which "practices of non-formal and informal education became incorporated in education institutions" (van der Veen & Wildemeersch, 2012, p. 7)? And how should we recontextualise today, when "technological innovations make it possible to be simultaneously connected with multiple and distant here and nows" (p. 9), the attention that from the 'eighties on both Gelpi and Zanier were giving to transnational factors of migration? Steps in these directions – in the Italian context – can be seen, for instance, in the ways in which CPIA (Centri Provinciali per l'Istruzione degli Adulti, which are local public institutions for adult education, belonging to the Italian Ministry of Education) are trying to "translate" newly arrived migrants' informal and non-formal learning experiences and competencies, in order to build on these competencies and experiences within CPIA's educational programmes (see Floreancig et al., 2018).

Gelpi would have said that lifelong education is not a magic wand. However, if we learn to stay within uncertainty and we try to read complexity emerging within environments 'in transition', we can activate the resources that we find within diverse communities, which are not reduced to migrants, but are seen in a relationship with the whole community itself. In this way lifelong education can help to empower people living in those communities, concurring in enabling them to deal with the challenges that they find in their everyday life. Valuing their own experiences and practices, histories, and origins.

Acknowledgement

The author would like to thank Mityana Vaccaro, who gave fundamental help in preparing the final English version of this chapter.

References

Appadurai, A. (1996). *Modernity at large: Cultural dimensions of globalization*. University of Minnesota Press.

Barcella, P. (2014). *Migranti in classe. Gli italiani in Svizzera tra scuola e formazione professionale*. Ombre Corte.

Barcella, P., & Furneri, V. (2020). *Una vita migrante. Leonardo Zanier, sindacalista e poeta*. Carocci.

Butler, T., & Hamnett, C. (2007). The geography of education: Introduction. *Urban Studies*, *44*(7), 1161–1174. https://doi.org/10.1080/00420980701329174

Caritas Italiana. (2018). *Povertà in attesa*. Rapporto 2018 su povertà e politiche di contrasto in Italia. Maggioli.

Carney, S. (2009). Negotiating policy in an age of globalization: Exploring educational "policyscapes" in Denmark, Nepal, and China. *Comparative Education Review*, *53*(1), 63–88. https://doi.org/10.1086/593152

de Certeau, M. (1980). *L'invention du quotidien: Vol. 1. Arts de faire*. Gallimard.

de Certeau, M. (1994). *La prise de parole et autres écrites politiques*. Éditions du Seuil.

ECAP-CGIL. (1977). *La lingua degli emigrati*, Guaraldi Editore.

Fiorucci, M. (2014). Prefazione. In V. Riccardi, *L'educazione per tutti e per tutta la vita. Il contributo pedagogico di Ettore Gelpi*, (pp. 9–10). ETS.

Floreancig, R., Fusco, F., Virgilio, F., Zanon, F., & Zoletto, D. (Eds.). (2018). *Tecnologie, lingua, cittadinanza. Percorsi di inclusione dei migranti nei CPIA*. FrancoAngeli.

Floridi, L. (2014). *The fourth revolution: How the infosphere is reshaping human reality*. Oxford University Press.

García Canclini, N. (1990). *Culturas híbridas. Estrategias para entrar y salir de la modernidad*. Consejo Nacional para la Cultura y las Artes.

Gelpi, E. (1977). Una sfida all'educazione permanente. In ECAP-CGIL & L. Zanier (Eds.), *La lingua degli emigrati* (pp. 31–42). Guaraldi Editore.

Gelpi, E. (1982). Politiche e attività di educazione permanente in ambiente urbano. Una problematica sulla base di alcune esperienze. In R. Pasini & M. Reguzzoni (a cura di), *La città a scuola. Prospettive di educazione permanente nelle grandi aree urbane* (pp. 46–63). FrancoAngeli.

Gelpi, E. (1985). *Lifelong education and international relations*. Routledge.

Gelpi, E. (1990). Community, education and migrant workers, myths and realities. In C. Poster & A. Kruger (Eds.), *Community education in the western world*, (pp. 137–141). Routledge.

Gelpi, E. (2000). *Educazione degli adulti. Inclusione ed esclusione*. Guerini e Associati.

Griffin, C. (2001). Ettore Gelpi. In P. Jarvis (Ed.), *Twentieth century thinkers in adult and continuing education* (2nd ed., pp. 274–289). Kogan Page.

Griffin, C. (2003). Ettore Gelpi: An appreciation. *International Journal of Lifelong Education*, 22(2), 109–110. https://doi.org/10.1080/0260137032000078605

Hannerz, U. (1992). *Cultural complexity, studies in the social organization of meaning*. Columbia University Press.

Ireland, T. D. (1978). *Gelpi's view of lifelong education* [Manchester Monographs 14]. Department of Adult and Higher Education, University of Manchester.

Lima, L. C. (2016). Revisitação gelpiana da educação permanente: Aambiguidades e erosão política de um conceito. *Investigar em Educação*, 5, 53–71. http://pages.ie.uminho.pt/inved/index.php/ie/article/view/111

McIlroy, J., & Westwood, S. (Eds.). (1993). *Border country: Raymond Williams in adult education*. National Institute of Adult Continuing Education.

Oberti, M. (2008). Ségrégation scolaire et urbane. In A. Van Zanten (Ed.), *Dictionnaire de l'éducation* (pp. 619–621). Presses Universitaires de France.

Pacchi, C., & Ranci, C. (a cura di). (2017). *White flight a Milano. La segregazione sociale et etnica nelle scuole dell'obbligo*. Franco Angeli.

Puglielli, E. (2019). Educazione degli adulti e globalizzazione: La critica pedagogica di Ettore Gelpi. *Pedagogia Oggi*, 17(2), 114–125. https://doi.org/10.7346/PO-022019-07

Riccardi, V. (2014). *L'educazione per tutti e per tutta la vita. Il contributo pedagogico di Ettore Gelpi*. ETS.

Riccardi, V. (2021). Migration, pluralism and "Earth's consciousness": Some reflections starting from Ettore Gelpi's thought. *Journal of Adult and Continuing Education*, 27(1), 10–24. https://doi.org/10.1177/1477971418804264

Save the Children. (2018). *Atlante dell'infanzia a rischio. Le periferie dei bambini*. Save the Children Italia/Treccani.

Sayad, A. (1999). *La double absence*. Éditions du Seuil.

Semi, G. (2012). Differenze, intersezionalità e sintesi mancate: Classi, individui e città. In A. Cancellieri & G. Scandurra (a cura di), *Tracce urbane. Alla ricerca della città*, (pp. 127–135). FrancoAngeli.

Van der Veen, R., & Wildemeersch, D. (2012). Diverse cities: Learning to live together. *International Journal of Lifelong Education, 31*(1), 5–12. https://doi.org/10.1080/02601370.2012.636570

Van Zanten, A. (2001). *L'école de la périphérie. Scolarité et ségrégation en banlieue*. Presses Universitaires de France.

Vertovec, S. (2009). *Transnationalism*. Routledge.

Williams, R. (1958). *Culture and society*. Chatto & Windus.

Williams, R. (1976). *Keywords. A vocabulary of culture and society*. Fontana Press.

Williams, R. (1989). *The politics of modernism: Against the new conformism*. Verso.

Zanier, L. (1977a). Introduzione. In ECAP-CGIL & L. Zanier (Eds.), *La lingua degli emigrati* (pp. 7–14). Guaraldi Editore.

Zanier, L. (1977b). Emigrazione in Svizzera e ruolo dell'ECAP. In ECAP-CGIL & L. Zanier (Eds.), *La lingua degli emigrati* (pp. 17–29). Guaraldi Editore.

Zanier, L. (1979). *Che Diaz ... Us al meriti. Storias e storiutads tradizion e 'migrazion dets e inventets eretics, santus e santons*. Centro Editoriale Friulano.

Zanier, L. (1981). *Sboradura e sanc (Poesie 1977–1980)*. Guaraldi.

Zanier, L. (1998). *Libers ... di scugnî lâ/Liberi ... di dover partire*. Ediesse.

CHAPTER 4

Is Active Citizenship a Forgotten Idea in Europe?
Educational Interventions in Five European Countries

Monika Noworolnik-Mastalska

Abstract

The European Commission is turning its focus again on to the idea of active citizenship, supporting educational projects for civic education. This chapter describes three different educational practices designed and implemented in Germany, Poland, Hungary, Denmark, and Spain during an educational project funded by the EU. Although all of these innovative practices focus on the learning of civic competencies by disadvantaged learners through new relational and participatory teaching methods, they were implemented in different cultural, social, political, and national contexts. I identify four complex challenges: finding and involving participants in the project; nationalist politics, policies of austerity, and dominant LLL discourses; the unequal position of citizenship education in policy and practice in adult education and learning in the five countries; the global context of active citizenship and learning. I argue that a different approach should be promoted by the European Commission.

Keywords

EU projects – adult education and learning – LLL discourse – active citizenship – globalization

1   Introduction

Some recent changes, like the reappearance or growth of nationalistic politics, xenophobia, and reactions to migration from beyond Europe constitute a serious challenge to any democratic project in Europe (Wildemeersch & Fejes, 2018). In this context, the idea of citizenship and the learning of civic competencies has become crucial in European educational programs. However, policymakers seem to see learning as the sole remedy for general social and political problems that are usually very complex, such as the social inclusion of migrant populations and ethnic minorities, conflict reduction, poverty, social exclusion and a need for intercultural mediation. Biesta writes about "a growing tendency in contemporary politics to reformulate policy issues into learning problems" (2011, p. 3). Of course, while education remains a necessary element in any political reform, a different role for education than that which is usually understood by the European Commission in its educational projects seems to be required. An existing threat of violent radicalisation in migrant or citizen populations, for example, or issues of fundamental rights, intercultural understanding and the idea of active citizenship cannot be confronted in European countries without learning democratic values and reflective competencies. Field and Schemmann (2017) note that the understanding of citizenship in European policy documents about education has recently shifted in this direction, but it refers only to children and youth. European documents on lifelong learning policy are still created on the utilitarian or strategic understanding of the active citizenship idea (Field & Schemmann, 2017, pp. 170–171). There is thus a need for more attention to these issues than is usually paid by post-national bodies, as well as changes in the basic understanding of learning active citizenship.

Another problem is that the idea of citizenship is often assumed to be already missing or forgotten in everyday life, in the social practices of local communities, and at work, so that adult learners must be supported to re-learn citizenship through education. Biesta writes directly about a problematic understanding of citizenship education, which is based on "a process of making young people 'ready' for democracy" (2011, p. 11), in other words a situation of "not-yet-being a citizen" (2011, p. 13). Citizenship is seen there as a learning outcome in educational programs, and learners' subjectivity, personal experiences or knowledge and competences from practical life in communities, at work, or in the family is ignored and devalued (Wildemeersch, 2017). Particularly, they may be perceived as people who are not "full-citizens" (Fejes et al., 2020).

Implementing participatory approaches to learning citizenship and civic education, however, faces serious challenges because of the main framework for learning promoted by the European Commission. Merrill notes that "despite increasing commonalities due to the Europeanisation and globalisation of European countries, different cultural, social, political and historical contexts can still be identified" (Merrill, 2003, p. 30). Currently, researchers emphasise not only regional differences in similar European projects on active citizenship for youth (Kersh et al., 2021), but they also point out contradictions that appear during the implementation of European policy in adult education projects locally (Bilon et al., 2016). The European approach evidently lacks a critical global perspective on learning citizenship that recognises the complexity and diversity of learning contexts.

I argue here that the European Commission's current approach to citizenship education demands serious reflection. In this chapter, therefore, I wish to focus on defining and problematising some of the challenges and contexts that are relevant for the process of learning citizenship and civic competencies in Europe, as observed in educational projects funded by the European Commission.

2 Learning for Citizenship in European Projects

One of the main pitfalls in European projects about adult education and active citizenship is that citizenship pedagogy is still seen as the teaching of an individual competency instead of as a lifelong learning process, in which adult learners can learn from life experiences and in communities.

Nicoll and Salling Olesen write about "a new competence regime" at European level (2013, p. 103) and Panitsides states that educational interventions have been increasingly informed by neoliberal regimes since the 1990s (2015, p. 207). This is directly defined as LLL discourse, in which knowledge is private capital (or a commodity), needed primarily on the employment market, while learning is a social phenomenon, situated in a culture necessary for solidarity and participation with others in a community, and for creating social relationships there, but also for taking responsibility for others and their development.

Further, the idea of civic education as well as "the concept of citizenship is being challenged and contested in response to the transformations brought about by postmodernism and globalisation" (Merrill, 2003, p. 22). Santos (2005) claims even more radically that only a counter-hegemonic perspective on globalisation can help restore the moral, political, and legal aspects of the idea of citizenship. However, in Martins' words, "such a renewal requires a global reconstruction of public education and development models" (2010, p. 162).

Finally, the idea of citizenship and education links with the learning of civic values and democratic practices in the everyday course of life and through everyday life experiences, and it has its source in the practice of a community's life, in participation in, and building relationships with others (Johnston, 2003; Kurantowicz, 2007; Lucio-Villegas & Fragoso, 2016). Active citizenship is linked to participation and learning with others, sharing collectively responsibility in everyday practice, or in joint activity (Finger et al., 2000; Vandenabeele et al., 2011).

Thus, citizenship cannot be understood only as a status, but rather as an everyday learning practice, and it cannot be narrowed down to the mere concession of rights or voting. Obviously, it refers to a wholly different understanding of democratic participation, based on critical thinking and on learning a reflective competence with others, as well as taking responsibility for others in a community. I argue that the current European approach to learning citizenship should be rethought in view of the challenges that appeared in the course of the project that will be discussed in the following pages.

3   Educational Interventions and Learning Democracy in a European Project

The European Learning Environment Formats (ELEF) project was aimed at designing, implementing, upscaling and evaluating three educational interventions carried out in the years 2017 and 2018 in five different countries (Germany, Denmark, Spain, Hungary, and Poland). The main objective of all three interventions is to increase the democratic participation of disadvantaged youth in European society by creating innovative learning formats. The three Democratic Learning Environments (DLE) formats: "Investigating Democratic Action" (IDA), "Democratic Camp" (DC) and "Street Education" (SE) explore different types of learning: formal, non-formal and informal. As a complex set of practical teaching and learning interventions, they were designed and implemented to foster social inclusion and/or prevent radicalisation of disadvantage youth in European countries.

3.1   *Access to the Project Data*
As an external evaluator of the ELEF project, I had access to all first-hand documents, meeting-notes, photos, workshops, or reports. In addition, I prepared a workshop with the project team, during which they shared their reflections on, and experiences with, the implementation of the interventions in each of the countries. I describe the three interventions below, focusing on the differences in that were observed in the implementation in different national, cultural and local institutional contexts.

3.2   *Investigating Democratic Action (IDA)*
The first learning format in the project, the "Investigating Democratic Action (IDA)" workshop develops professional competencies of teachers, teacher students or students who work with young people. The IDA format offers teacher training that focuses on creating a democratic learning environment for disadvantaged groups or individual young people in schools. IDA is based on learning through reflection on teaching practice as a core idea in professional

training, which is understood to be vital for creating a democratic culture in schools. The program develops civic competencies, providing teaching and learning tools (the 5 × E method: Educate, Explain, Empower, Evaluate, and Express) in Germany, Hungary and Poland, or alternatively teaching and learning methods for citizenship education, based on research or enquiry-based learning in Spain (in the form of a Youth Parliament), or in the form of seminars and meetings for teachers in vocational training in Denmark. IDA was based on collaboration with local authorities, schools, training centres and universities in different regions of a single country.

3.3 *Democratic Camp (DC)*
The Democratic camp is the second of the democratic educational practices, and it was implemented by three countries in the project, Germany, Poland, and Hungary. The main difference between the partners was the target group chosen. There were three different target groups of disadvantaged young people:
1. Polish youth between 17 and 18 years old with high potential in the shape of good grades, significant activity in their local communities, recognition as class leaders, or active in organisations like the Scouts, yet disadvantaged on account of their socially or economically underprivileged backgrounds;
2. German youth (15 to 18 years old) and younger school pupils (9 to 12 years old), with high potential and motivated to participate in workshops, with the aim of improving already existing school political education;
3. diversified groups of participants in Hungary (both Hungarians and non-Hungarians), disadvantaged because of their different cultural background as immigrants or refugees.

The intervention links the abstract concepts of democratic values with practical activities based on the personal experience of participants, through participation in drama projects, community projects and learning through political participation. The DC learning format was based on collaboration with local authorities and/or experts, journalists, activists, and artists who supported the political or social engagement of young people.

3.4 *Street Education Practice (SE)*
The last educational intervention in the project was Street Education. The main format for the practice is based on the idea of direct interaction with people on the streets in each of the countries. The practice addresses disadvantaged students from secondary or vocational schools and pupils and/or individual

groups of adults who have different socio-cultural backgrounds. However, the learning format was implemented in different ways in the project. Street Education took the form of a city game in Hungary (the Dystopian City Game) and was employed at open events during public festivals or directly "on the streets" in Germany. Alternatively, the format was deployed as a relational method of learning and teaching (the Forum Theatre) by educational institutions or in courses which had direct contact with young adult learners in the project (e.g., in VET schools in Denmark and in Poland). Street Education was also developed by civil society organisations in Spain and Hungary and by a street worker organisation in Germany. This practice depended on collaboration with civil society organisations, youth centres and street workers' organisations.

All of the above-mentioned interventions aimed to improve the quality of citizenship education. They constitute an alternative method of teaching, creating not only the possibility to learn civic competencies in new ways, but also to improve existing educational practices in institutions with positive effects on local culture at schools. However, they were implemented in different forms in the partnership countries, not only because of the different institutional backgrounds of institutions involved in the project team, but also because of existing cultural differences, different political contexts, and the respective level of development of citizenship education in formal educational curricula in each of the countries.

4 The Main Challenges of the Project

In this section I identify four main challenges encountered during implementation of educational interventions in the five European countries involved: Germany, Spain, Poland, Denmark, and Hungary.

4.1 *Challenge 1: Reaching Participants in the Project*

Common for all partners in the project was the challenge to reach the target group for the educational interventions. During the *Street Education* learning intervention, the project partners had difficulties contacting adult learners. This was mainly because the project call from the European Commission focused on specific 'target groups' of participants as well as on a traditional approach to educating and learning civic competencies. Thus, the project organisers were expected to approach disadvantaged individuals instead of focusing directly on the local communities and the everyday life contexts in which those adult learners live and act. Ultimately, collaboration with NGOs and youth centres or with street workers was the most useful way for the project activities to reach participants.

In the *Democratic Camp* intervention, particularly two partners in the project (Germany and Hungary) met with difficulties recruiting disadvantaged groups of participants. In Hungary a number of participants from local refugee camps were involved, though only for a short time, because the camps were closed by the government in the next year of the project. The German project team decided to recruit participants to the project using previous collaborations between Bremen University and local schools in the second year of the project.

Some challenges appeared also with *Investigating Democratic Action* (*IDA*) because the democratic learning format did not meet teacher-trainees' educational expectations and needs. In Spain, most of the teacher-trainees requested training in skills, specific contents and methods of the subjects they were to teach: ICT, English, and so on. Similarly, in Poland the trainees expected to participate in something more 'modern' or 'useful', so that they could transfer new knowledge into skills needed directly on the labour market or acquire additional ECTS points. In turn, Hungarian teacher trainees did not know how to give feedback when asked to do so during *IDA* workshops. Moreover, in Denmark and Germany an additional problem affecting the engagement of participants was connected to the time they needed to spend on the course, in the meetings and seminars, and during regular and structured time at work in schools, as well as to the complexity of the topics taught during the *IDA* teacher training.

The problem of participation in political education for active citizenship may, in fact, not be what it seems. Nicoll et al. (2013) claim that the problem in current civic education is perhaps not really a problem with the idea of citizenship but a lack of "identification and exploration of the different forms of citizenship that students already engage in" (p. 828). This is all the more true in that the recent history of Poland, for example, is rich in mass protests, in which young adults also participate (in protests against the government abortion ban, or protests of because of the ongoing constitutional crisis).[1] Similarly, the Danish team also met with difficulties in engaging youth in active participation. The Hungarian team reported also that there were local protests by teachers against the direction of new political reforms implemented by Hungary's national government, including the centralisation of education. Finally, the participation of different countries in the project also revealed a number of important cultural differences in education practices and existing models of education, in which a very diverse distribution of participatory or more traditional methods was found. These cultural differences cannot be simply ignored in such projects, because their existence can clearly create too big a gap between innovative experiences and more dated practices in the diverse contexts in which they are rolled out.

4.2 Challenge 2: European Citizenship Education and National Political Contexts

The second challenge concerns the implementation of the project in countries in which the idea of citizenship in education can be 'loaded' or just difficult in practice, because of the context of recent reforms in citizenship education, on account of new legal/constitutional reforms, or as a result of reforms aimed at the centralisation of the educational system itself.

In Hungary, the current government nationalised and centralised local state schools in 2013 and in 2017, even though teachers were against the reforms. The implementation of educational programmes in the project revealed the national government's basic lack of respect for teachers' autonomy as well as for democratic values like tolerance and freedom in schools.

In Spain, Citizenship Education was eliminated as a compulsory subject in the school curriculum after the reform in 2013, when it became an optional subject called Social and Civic values, according to the Organic Law for the Improvement of Educational Quality (LOMCE). The attempt to introduce this programme for MA students of Secondary Education at Seville University revealed a need to allocate more economic and human resources to increase social and community education interventions (including street education), since this sector has been neglected and has suffered a sharp reduction due to austerity policies implemented in recent years.

In Poland, the context of recent controversial constitutional reforms creates a problematic background for forcing the implementation of citizenship courses in the educational curriculum, mainly because of an overall social aversion to 'democratic topics' in the country caused by the politics of the Polish conservative government.

By contrast, in Denmark, the most recent national reforms emphasise precisely the need to extend citizenship education to the VET school profile, which constitutes strong support for new practices in learning citizenship. The new Danish Law on Vocational Education from 2017 introduces the education of social and civic competencies into the curriculum. However, they still link the idea of learning citizenship with schools, and they narrow it down to the voting skills needed during elections. These are also needed, of course, but in a broader context of understanding the learning of democracy, they are clearly not sufficient.

These contexts clearly show the necessity of introducing and implementing citizenship interventions, though in practice local contexts and diverse political cultures in Europe can render their successful initiation very difficult

4.3 Challenge 3: Different Levels of Development of Formal Citizenship Education in European Countries

All five partners in the project implemented the practice of Investigating Democratic Action (IDA). However, the process of implementation was very different, and ultimately the planned introduction of IDA practice within the bounds of the project was possible only in two countries (Spain and Germany). In Germany, IDA practice was a newly established teacher training programme at LIS (a teacher training institute) in the Federal State of Bremen, and a model for teacher training at universities or at schools in this region of Germany (the IDA toolkit). However, teacher-training curricula were already well developed in Germany before any IDA interventions were introduced. In Spain, the course was implemented at Seville University, and has created a Spanish model of IDA, focusing on collaboration in networks in the Andalusia region to implement IDA practice in the educational curriculum as an obligatory module.

In Denmark, recent changes in educational policy in the country have aided the introduction of new educational practices in secondary schools. The project introduced a new and complex model of learning active citizenship in the Aarhus region of South Jutland. The proposed model of learning affected school practices on multiple levels, including personal and group levels, didactic and administrative practices, collaboration with NGOs, and other schools. In Hungary, the new IDA practice was only tested at university level, but collaboration has also been initiated between a university and an NGO. In Poland, IDA practice has also been tested at the university, and the institutional impact can be seen in the implementation of the IDA program, planned for five classes and with a manual (checklist) of good practices for future sessions for Democracy Coaches. Therefore, the impact of the practice on formal educational programs was uneven between partnership countries.

Overall, the different levels of development of formal citizenship education in each country depended on:
– diverse levels of advancement of citizenship education in particular countries from before the project
– differences in educational policy and local educational practices, and different levels of collaboration in everyday practice between HEI and stakeholders such as NGOs, local authorities, etc.
– different notions of participation, and diverse local educational practices based on the idea of citizenship

4.4 Challenge 4: Active Citizenship and Learning in the Context of Globalisation

The processes of globalisation have created another context for learning citizenship. The project faced challenges related to the definition of topics felt to be relevant by young adults participating in educational programmes, particularly those outside education institutions. This problem appeared particularly in the work of the Danish team when they tried to involve young participants/learners in new forms of learning in the Street Education format of citizenship education. They ultimately focused more on social interactions because of the importance of interaction for young people faced with problems of loneliness and lack of social skills. Acquiring social skills is central for citizenship programmes because of the need to participate with others in social networks and local communities, and the importance of sharing social responsibility. Learning active citizenship requires social learning based on social interactions and participation with others in the everyday practices of a local community or small groups. A perspective for citizenship learning that focuses also on the role of social skills of young learners is important for the development of learning processes that are reflective, participatory and committed to social life rather than being narrowly individualistic in their approach.

5 Conclusion

The European Commission focuses currently on the idea of learning active citizenship through educational projects. However, the EC approach to educational projects for citizenship education in Europe is in need of critical reflection. On the one hand, the European Commission seems to be aware already of the problem of education for citizenship, because they fund projects that are focused on the development of civic competencies through educational interventions. On the other hand, they apply an outdated understanding of the idea of LLL, based largely on individual learning and the 'competence regime', while active citizenship as well as learning democracy is supposed to be learned during social and relational learning and directly in everyday life contexts. It is already clear, however, that it must be based on the real-life experiences of learners, fostering their reflection on political, economic, or global contexts during the process of learning, as well as on ongoing societal processes, which shape the dynamic of learning overall. Therefore, the challenges detailed above require deeper reflection about the different local, national, cultural as well as political factors moving learning processes. Ultimately, these projects apply a top-down perspective for the learning of civic competencies. Some of the challenges described here can be understood as problems arising from citizenship education driven by neoliberal LLL discourse and national austerity programmes. The formats for democratic learning described here clearly call for a radically diverse educational policy and significantly more critical approaches to learning processes, processes that focus not only on the idea of citizenship and learning in Europe, but on diverse, local contexts of learning which include the politics of learning, the biographies of learners, and learning based on the local social bonds of communities.

Overall, the project focuses on participatory methods in teaching citizenship education which aim to be closer to the everyday life experiences of learners. In addition, learning spaces that empower and provide a psychological support for disadvantaged groups of young adults and youth in Europe are centrally important. However, the project has shown that there are significant difficulties in reaching participants for such projects. The answer must be, that the perspectives of the learners themselves, their needs, their life experiences and their local practices as citizens in communities must be taken up.

Concluding, I would like to come back to my main question, formulated already in the title: is the idea of local citizenship really being slowly forgotten? Is it really not needed in practice, given that it seems to be vanishing from national educational policies as well as from schools in some European countries? Is it really irrelevant to the needs and expectations of young people, who seem to show no special interest in this type of education? Or rather, does active citizenship need a new perspective, based on a model of collective, social, relational and cultural learning of civic competencies that is not yet largely recognised by governments and educational institutions, even though the idea is still present in the everyday life practices of adult learners, who participate with others in real, local, social and cultural practices, collecting complex experiences throughout life in the global world? How can citizenship education in practice become more relevant to learning, based on critical, social and cultural learning, fostering key social and reflective competencies of learners, or supporting their learning of active citizenship, and responding better to local contexts and local needs in European countries? What would a new type and form of education, focused on learning, including learning spaces outside educational institution, look like? And what about the potential of learning civic competencies inside local communities in family, work, neighbourhoods, and friendship groups? How can they be included directly into the process of learning democracy and citizenship, alongside critical perspectives of learning and education in the global context of life, learning identities and the everyday struggle with the challenges of the idea of active citizenship?

Acknowledgement

I would like to express my thanks to all members of the international team in the ELEF project for sharing all the information, challenges and experiences connected with this project.

Note

1   See particularly Chapter 10 in this volume.

References

Biesta, G. (2011). *Learning democracy in school and society: Education, lifelong learning and the politics of citizenship*. Sense.

Bilon, A., Kurantowicz, E., & Noworolnik-Mastalska, M. (2016). Community development: (un)fulfilled hopes for social equality in Poland. In M. Shaw & M. Mayo (Eds.), *Class, inequality and community development* (pp. 137–152). Policy Press.

Fejes, A., Dahlstedt, M., Olson, M., & Sandberg, F. (2020). *Adult education and the formation of citizens: A critical interrogation* [Kindle edition]. Routledge.

Field, J., & Schemmann, M. (2017). International organisations and the construction of the learning active citizen: An analysis of adult learning policy documents from a Durkheimian perspective. *International Journal of Lifelong Education, 36*(1–2), 164–179. https://doi.org/10.1080/02601370.2017.1287920

Finger, M., Jansen, T., & Wildemeersch, D. (2000). Reconciling the irreconcilable? Adult and continuing education between personal development, corporate concerns and public responsibility. In D. Wildemeersch, M. Finger, & T. Jansen (Eds.), *Adult education and social responsibility: Reconciling the irreconcilable?* (pp. 1–25). Peter Lang.

Johnston, R. (2003). Adult learning and citizenship: Clearing the ground. In P. Coare & R. Johnston (Eds.), *Adult learning, citizenship and community voices* (pp. 3–21). NIACE.

Kersh, N., Toiviainen, H., Pitkänen, P., & Zarifis, G. K. (2021). *Young adults and active citizenship: Towards social inclusion through adult education*. Springer.

Kurantowicz, E. (2007). Badania krytyczne w lokalnych społecznościach. In E. Kurantowicz & M. Nowak-Dziemianowicz (Eds.), *Narracja-krytyka-zmiana: Praktyki badawcze we współczesnej pedagogice* (pp. 446–458). Wydawnictwo Naukowe Dolnośląskiej Szkoły Wyższej Edukacji TWP.

Lucio-Villegas, E., & Fragoso, A. (2016). A tramp shining. The popular (community) educator in the age of lifelong learning. In R. Evans, E. Kurantowicz, & E. Lucio-Villegas

(Eds.), *Researching and transforming adult learning and communities: The local/global context* (pp. 27–38). Sense Publishers.

Martins, P. H. (2010). Citizenship. In K. Hart, J. L. Laville, & A. D. Cattani (Eds.), *The human economy* (pp. 157–165). Polity Press.

Merrill, B. (2003). Adult education and citizenship: A European perspective. In P. Coare & R. Johnston (Eds.), *Adult learning, citizenship, and community voices* (pp. 22–40). NIACE.

Nicoll, K., Fejes, A., Olson, M., Dahlstedt, M., & Biesta, G. (2013). Opening discourses of citizenship education: A theorization with Foucault. *Journal of Education Policy*, 28(6), 828–846. https://doi.org/10.1080/02680939.2013.823519

Nicoll, K., & Salling Olesen, H. (2013). Editorial: What's new in a new competence regime? *European Journal for Research on the Education and Learning of Adults*, 4(2), 103–109.

Panitsides, E. A. (2015). Towards 'utilitarian' adult education perspectives? A critical review of the European Union's adult education policy. In M. Milana & T. Nesbit (Eds.), *Global perspectives on adult education and learning policy* (pp. 207–217). Palgrave Macmillan.

Santos, B. S. (2005). Beyond neoliberal governance: The World Social Forum as subaltern cosmopolitan politics and legality. In B. S. Santos & C. A. Rodríguez-Garavito (Eds.), *Law and globalization from below: Towards a cosmopolitan legality* (pp. 29–63). Cambridge University Press. https://doi.org/10.1017/CBO9780511494093.002

Vandenabeele, J., Reyskens, P., & Wildemeersch, D. (2011). Diverse views on citizenship, community and participation: Exploring the role of adult education research and practice. *European Journal for Research on the Education and Learning of Adults*, 2(2), 193–208.

Wildemeersch, D. (2017). Opening spaces of conversation: Citizen education for newcomers as a democratic practice. *International Journal of Lifelong Education*, 36(1–2), 112–127. https://doi.org/10.1080/02601370.2016.1254435

Wildemeersch, D., & Fejes, A. (2018). Editorial: Citizenship and the crisis of democracy: What role can adult education play in matters of public concern? *European Journal for Research on the Education and Learning of Adults*, 9(2), 133–137.

PART 2

Knowledge Democracy, New Pedagogies, Creative Inclusion

∴

CHAPTER 5

Co-Constructing Knowledge and Communities

Community-University Research Partnerships and Participatory Research Training

Walter Lepore, Yashvi Sharma, Budd L. Hall and Rajesh Tandon

Abstract

Since 2012, the UNESCO Chair in Community Based Research and Social Responsibility in Higher Education has been engaged in major global research projects designed to provide us with a state-of-the-art of what has been happening in the field of community-based participatory research. This chapter reports on the findings of two surveys used in these studies, which provide a global overview of how higher education institutions and civil society organizations contribute to engaged research processes and knowledge democracy. The chapter ends with thoughts on the implications for the role of community-based knowledge creation.

Keywords

community-based participatory research – community-university research partnerships – community-university engagement – higher education institutions – civil society organizations – knowledge democracy

1 Introduction

The idea of re-making community life has never been felt more deeply or more universally than during these pandemic years. The sense of community, the belief in community as a fundamental source of transformation and change has been continuously under attack as untethered capitalism has broken the idea of the social good in favour of a world of solitary consumers. Well educated individuals have been needed to operate the machines of capital accumulation. Both schooling and adult education have been shaped by the vision of a flexible, mobile, well-trained workforce able to raise productivity and profitability within business structures owned and controlled by a diminishing number of people. The visions of Mahatma Gandhi-ji, Richard H. Tawney, Julius Nyerere, Paulo Freire, Orlando Fals Borda, Moema Viezzer, Martha Farrell, Shirley Walters, and Darlene Clover, among many others, of an adult education centred upon social justice and collective community capacity-building have been pushed aside by neoliberal educational theorists.

The COVID-19 pandemic has exacerbated many of the underlying layers of pre-existing structural inequality and injustice that have become more prominent over these past few years. The gap between the rich and the poor in both global and national terms has grown shockingly (Bucher, 2021; Stiglitz, 2020). Women who have historically been victims of domestic violence have felt this violence dramatically when trapped in homes because of COVID-19 lockdowns (Evans et al., 2020; Usher et al., 2020). Banks are still pouring billions into the fossil fuel industries in the face of scientific evidence that our planet is at risk (Clifford, 2021). Genocides both of a physical and cultural nature of the Indigenous Peoples around the world have continued as the locomotive of Euro-centric knowledge continues down the tracks of *epistemicide* (de Sousa Santos, 2014).

As the editors of this book argue, however, resistance to an instrumentalised vision of adult education and learning abounds. In the last number of years, we have witnessed a slow but steady change in the approach to, and practice of, knowledge production. This is reflected in the concept of 'engaged research' that can be seen in the intersection of various strands of scholarship and practice that have one overlapping characteristic: a democratisation of knowledge and its production (see Etmanski et al., 2014; Hall & Tandon, 2020b). Knowledge democracy refers to an interrelationship of phenomena that intentionally link values of democracy and action to the process of producing and using knowledge. Firstly, knowledge democracy acknowledges the importance of the existence of multiple epistemologies or ways of knowing (such as organic, spiritual, and land-based systems), a diversity of conceptual frameworks arising from social movements, and the knowledge of marginalised or excluded social groups. Secondly, it affirms that knowledge is both created and represented in multiple forms (including text, image, numbers, story, music, drama, poetry, ceremony, meditation and more). Finally, it understands knowledge as a powerful tool for taking action that leads to a fairer and healthier world and underscores the importance of making knowledge products available to all through the dissemination of open access resources (Hall, 2016; Lepore et al., 2021).

The reframing of relationships between society, science, and innovation to ensure wider and more active participation of citizens in research and innovation processes implies institutional arrangements that differ from a purely extractive logic and a traditional approach to research and knowledge creation (Hall & Tandon, 2020a; Owen et al., 2012). Academia cannot hope to contribute to the re-making of community relying solely on the knowledge creation practices of the past. Academics speaking to other academics over Zoom or in journal articles will not have a significant impact on community life. Curating the knowledge located amongst those experiencing homelessness, exclusion, racism and generational poverty, and applying that knowledge to build capacity within communities to take action for their own change is an important alternative strategy. Community-based participatory research (CBPR) is that field of theory and practice, which privileges the experiential knowledge of community members and offers ways for academics and community practitioners to co-construct action-oriented knowledge.

The UNESCO Chair in Community-Based Research and Social Responsibility in Higher Education works at the heart of this thinking about knowledge creation for social change. This UNESCO Chair is a unique formal partnership between the University of Victoria (Canada) and the Society for Participatory Research in Asia (PRIA), an NGO based in New Delhi, India (UNESCO Chair CBR-SR, 2021). The focal point of the work in the Chair is the building of research capacity in the field of CBPR in the global South and what we call the excluded North, that is, diverse 'subaltern' communities, such as homeless, immigrants, urban poor, and differently abled groups. Since its inception in 2012, the Chair has been engaged in major global research projects designed to provide a state-of-the-art picture of what has been happening in the field of CBPR. The first study looked at structures and national policies in place to support community-university research partnerships (CURPs) (Hall, Tandon & Tremblay, 2015a, 2015b). The second global project looked at how and where people were learning how to do participatory research (Tandon, Hall, Lepore & Singh, 2016a, 2016b).

This chapter reports on the findings of two surveys used in these studies, which provide a global overview of how Higher Education Institutions (HEIs) and Civil Society Organisations (CSOs) contribute to engaged research processes and knowledge democracy through the creation of CURPs and the development of capacities for participatory research within and outside the academia. We finish with thoughts on the implications for the role of community-based knowledge creation in the face of the major challenges we face in our homes, our families, our communities, and the world.

2   Community-University Research Partnerships

In the face of global crises – like the COVID-19 pandemic– and the challenges posed by socio-ecological and political uncertainties, researchers, policymakers and governments are called upon to think and respond beyond the implications of health and wellbeing (UNESCO, 2015). The uneven impact of global crises on local communities emphasises the role of HEIs' social responsibility to find solutions that are beneficial to everyone in society (see Hall & Tandon, 2021). HEIs are called to engage with communities in the long term to understand their needs and assets, and to support the creation of alternative knowledge that draws on local, community-based and multiple epistemological resolutions.

Community-university engagement networks and research partnerships are able to mobilise the knowledge, skills and assets of both universities and communities (Spilker et al., 2016; Watson et al., 2011). Such institutional arrangements can use rigorous research, community leadership, and university expertise to democratically find solutions to contemporary challenges (Popp et al., 2013). The evidence provided by Hall et al. (2015a) shows that democratic knowledge partnerships, where community action is united with academic knowledge, have the potential for social transformation in ways that the narrow application of university scientific knowledge solutions cannot achieve. We thus embrace an instrumental view of research partnerships which is based on the assumption that ownership and mutual accountability can enhance partnership outcomes, and expand disciplinary knowledge by exposing alternative epistemologies, ontologies and ethics (Fransman et al., 2021).

3   What Is a Community-University Research Partnership?

A Community-University Research Partnership (CURP) is a formal partnership between the university and the organised community (e.g., NGOs, social purpose organisations, social enterprises, etc.), which reflects the interests of both partners to address pressing issues facing communities (Hall et al., 2015a, 2015b).

CURP facilitates and nurtures the engagement between HEIs, community groups and CSOs in responding to a wide range of community issues. It often involves capacity-building, knowledge-building, citizen-centric development and policy advocacy, based on an iterative process of learning, reflection and action, whereby the process and results are useful to both community members and university partners in creating positive social and institutional change (Etmanski et al., 2014).

A CURP, largely but not exclusively, involves participatory approaches to knowledge creation as it actively engages community members in the research creation process, ranging from community participation to community initiation, control, and ownership of research (Munck et al., 2014). A CURP thus represents a mutually beneficial exchange in which the community contributes to the in-depth understanding of the community norms, their pressing issues, assets and needs, and the best method for meeting those needs and making use of their community assets. Universities, on the other hand, bring research resources, frameworks, theoretical knowledge, and expertise to the partnership for creating and implementing interventions in the community (Hall et al., 2018; Tandon, 2007)

4   Global Survey on Community University Research Partnerships

As part of the project 'Strengthening Community University Research Partnerships', the UNESCO Chair conducted a survey to gain an overview of trends and patterns around the world on CURP structures and policies. The survey was administered globally between January and March 2014 in over 50 countries and four languages and received 336 responses covering each region of the world. The survey findings were triangulated with 12 country case studies (see Hall et al., 2015a). The findings of the survey revealed:
- Over 95% of all respondents believe that the co-creation of knowledge is a primary goal in their CURPs.
- However, less than 15% of CURP originate in the community. These partnerships are still very much top-down, initiated by HEIs.
- Active participation in decision-making and distribution of funds in research projects is predominately controlled by HEIs.
- Overwhelmingly respondents agree that trust and mutual respect are essential to the creation of CURPs, but also point to sustained funding support for planning and partnership development over time.
- The primary source of financial support for HEIs to operate CURPs are through government research councils. Only in 15% of the cases, HEIs will provide funding for local community partnership initiatives.

5   Principles of CURP

The survey findings also showed that almost 80% of institutions that participated in this global survey have developed some form of structure to support CURP within the last 10 years. This number is indicative of the increasing commitment of HEIs around the world to redefine the use of community knowledge and its social responsibility to civil society. Sporadic institutional efforts or individual demonstrations of CURP are, however, of limited value if not supported by suitable institutional structures having validation and authority within the context of the partner organisations. The following principles are central to the work of institutional support structures for CURPs (Hall et al., 2015a, 2015b).

5.1 Engagement: Working with Rather Than on People

This principle refers to a form of meaningful collaboration that offers an equal chance to all participants to co-share responsibilities in the research process. Knowledge creation to address community issues is increasingly becoming a process of engagement between researchers and other actors who have traditionally been outside of the knowledge production system (Tremblay et al., 2017). Stakeholders' engagement is key to providing results that would have never been developed by either of the implicated parties individually. Thinking about higher education more specifically, engagement means mutual exchange of knowledge between universities and communities in an attempt to produce outcomes that are of benefit to the larger society (Hall et al., 2015b). Such engagement is possible through the teaching and research function of the university, as much as it is through its service function.

5.2 Cooperation and Participation: A Participatory Worldview

A worldview based on participation and cooperation rather than separation and competition should be encouraged and enabled for CURP partners to participate in the decision-making and other aspects of the research process according to their skill and interest. Global, national, and local actors need to be involved early in the process as co-developers of ideas and institutional arrangements that help knowledge-driven innovations to flourish. Promoting the creation, acquisition, validation, and use of knowledge as a collective societal endeavour allows such knowledge to be used for developing basic language and communication skills, solving problems, and developing higher-order skills (UNESCO, 2015).

5.3 Equality in the Research Process

Each person involved in the research process is respected and heard. The partnership is based on mutual respect by valuing diverse perspectives, epistemologies, and ideologies. Tolerance of uncertainty, ambiguity and diversity of knowledge and values is important to harness and integrate social, environmental, and economic considerations at the local and regional level (Everingham, 2012). Building long-term trust among partners facilitates systemic practice, integrative ways of working, and learning across and within diverse social groups (Allan, 2012; Everingham, 2012).

5.4 Co-Production of New Research Knowledge

All participants equally own the research process as well as the research outputs. Participants work together on a research issue and defy discriminatory practices that give privilege to one over the other. CURPs thus deviate from the normal outreach/extension functions toward an approach that is participative, mutually beneficial and committed to the creation and sharing of knowledge. This also involves changing the perception of civic engagement as a philanthropic activity to one of reciprocity, by recognising the value and diversity of knowledge both in the university and the community (Tremblay et al., 2017).

5.5 Social Change: Research Has Social Justice Outcomes

Research is aimed at creating and promoting positive social justice outcomes that reduce inequalities and improve the lives of those involved in the knowledge production process. CURPs can be seen as local catalysers that give visibility to and strengthen local action, support funding opportunities, and aim to better connect academic work to community needs. Empirical evidence shows that the required interaction and communication between implicated actors to make social learning possible can be organised through the institutionalisation of stakeholder engagement in collaborative processes and the creation of partnerships between stakeholders, policy makers, researchers and scientists (Sandstrom, 2010).

6 Global Survey on Teaching and Learning Community-Based Participatory Research

A second global survey was conducted by the UNESCO Chair between November 2014 and May 2015, as part of the project titled 'Building the next generation of community-based researchers: A global partnership' (aka the Next Gen project). The questionnaire was designed in collaboration with a variety of partners in order to capture a broad understanding of concepts, materials, approaches and practices of training and teaching CBPR. The survey was administered in four languages, and it was responded by 413 individuals from 60 countries, covering each region of the world. The Next Gen project also involved 21 cases studies in 15 countries, and four thematic literature reviews (see Tandon et al., 2016a). Key findings of the survey can be summarised as follows:
- Over 90% of the respondents have had previous experience in CBPR. However, most of them have had a brief formal learning experience in this approach to research, and 16% never received any formal CBPR training.

- The predominant ways of acquiring CBPR capabilities are autodidactic, self-directed learning (56.9%) and on-the-job training (47.7%). Among the formal opportunities, the training offered is mainly dominated by workshops (1 to 10 days duration) and university courses (10 to 13 weeks), and to a lesser extent by medium-term training programs (3 to 6 months).
- Over 60% of the respondents consider that the most effective CBPR training is participating in community actions –i.e., any collective action taken with a community to address or engage with a particular issue. Similarly, almost half (47.9%) valued performing creative activities (e.g., music, theatre, storytelling) as very or extremely useful for building capacities in CBPR.
- The most common learning materials offered to students are traditional and grey literatures; however, many students rated those resources as slightly or not at all useful to learn CBPR. Experiential learning activities are still not commonly used in university courses to teach CBPR.
- The survey underscores a strong interest in the provision of training for participatory research: 9 out of 10 respondents manifested their interest in building capacities and receiving more training in CBPR.

The survey findings make evident that there is a high interest in CBPR training around the world, demanding diversified teaching modalities in a variety of settings. The results also show that diverse skills are needed for the new generation of community-based researchers to contribute to engaged research processes and knowledge democracy. These include, for instance, group facilitation skills – in particular, consensus decision-making, conflict resolution, delegation of tasks, and cross-cultural communication-, as well as continuous reflection on ethics, fairness, equity and power issues within participatory research and training initiatives (see also Fransman et al., 2021).

7 Improving Teaching and Training in CBPR

The last part of the Next Gen survey included a set of open-ended questions for the respondents to provide recommendations that can help improve teaching and training in CBPR in both HEIs and CSOs. We grouped those recommendations under five main themes:

1. *Knowledge systematisation and dissemination.* Better documentation and open data help in demonstrating the value and impact (both global and local) associated with CBPR work; for example, how quantative data could be validated and substantiated through mechanisms of CBPR in a variety of settings. Some specific recommendations include the creation

of national and regional hubs where practitioners and researchers could exchange ideas, more avenues for publishing CBPR knowledge products, and regular dissemination events to generate recognition of the importance of CBPR amongst the more 'traditional' sectors in the university and the professional communities.

2. *Leadership and mentorship.* Finding committed people willing to participate and expand CBPR projects to others is critical to build on the passion of the youth and young researchers. Some recommendations in this regard include the employment of good mentors at the undergraduate and graduate levels and experts in the community, who have experience doing quality CBPR and a critical pedagogical approach, and the appointment of innovative decision-makers to drive community-university engagement (CUE) processes and CBPR at the university and community levels.

3. *Funding and incentives.* The lack of support for citizen-focused initiatives and institutional resources is a major obstacle for providing CBPR training. Strengthening the relationships between the community and HEIs is a key condition to do CBPR, but it requires a significant investment to build institutional capacity for CUE. More financial support for community practitioners, dissemination events outside of the northern hemisphere, and university awards and recognition to CUE practices are needed to support the work that CBPR practitioners are doing on the ground. A major recommendation in this area is the institutionalisation of CBPR training within the academic institutions by implementing policies supportive of faculty and students who engage in collaborative projects; for instance, internships and scholarships for students, the use of the institution's facilities for providing training to community members, and the adoption of community engagement as one of the major criteria for the personal promotions of academics and tenure decisions.

4. *Teaching and training.* Encouraging the 'early immersion' of students in participatory methodologies since their first years at the university and mainstreaming the CBPR approach into research methods courses helps exposing as many students as possible to participatory research tools, their principles and benefits as part of their degree programs. This would also help extending university engagement beyond individual thesis research and short-term projects to long term engagement with recognised accountability pathways. Embedding CBPR within the curricula at all levels of HEIs would require, among other actions, not only changes in existing teaching programs but also: co-developing research projects with community partners and students; providing students the

opportunity to work alongside faculty members from the beginning of the project so they can understand and appreciate the time, effort and thinking that happens behind the scenes; and building a fluid learning environment so the community members are invited into the classroom, while students and faculty members go into the community as a platform for mutual learning.

5. *Community-university engagement and partnerships.* Different recommendations were suggested to enhance long-lasting relationships between HEIs and CSOs: for instance, creating community-based advisory communities for long-term projects; providing funding that is specifically directed towards meaningful community-based partnerships (i.e., sustainable projects with longer term impacts and mutual benefits); rewarding scholars who engage in community-based projects and produce community-based knowledge; advocating with funders to provide resources and reward to non-profit organisations that pursue research connections with universities; and supporting institutional framework for CUE and CBPR at higher organisational decision-making levels.

8   Discussion

On the one hand, the first global survey unfolds the impact of policies and practices at the national, regional, and institutional level on how to integrate CURPs into HEIs' mandates. The survey findings also support the idea that for CURPs to flourish, governments and HEIs must support the concepts and philosophies of Community-University Engagement (CUE) and Community Based Participatory Research (CBPR).

Based on the evidence generated through this survey and case studies, the following inferences can be drawn:

– After realising the need to engage HEIs in active community engagement, many governments have issued guidelines and allocated funds to institutionalise CURP structures in universities. For example, the UK government has created the National Co-ordinating Centre for Public Engagement (NCCPE), a structure to encourage public engagement in higher education. Similarly, the University Grants Commission in India has also allocated significant funds for fostering social responsibility and community engagement in HEIs through programs like Unnat Bharat Abhiyan (UBA) and compulsory community engagement courses (University Grants Commission, 2020). Through national policies and frameworks like these, HEIs tend to

show greater commitment and readiness, and are likely to allocate funds to promote community engagement in HEIs.
- Historically, civil society has not so far adequately engaged with institutions and structures of higher education. The disconnection between the world of academia and the world of practice has been historical in most societies, and more so in the Global South. The knowledge contributions of civil society and social movements are rarely acknowledged by academia, which furthers the chasm (Brown, 2001; GUNI, 2008; Tandon, 2007). This situation needs to change if CURPs are to be mainstreamed as community calls for accountability of HEIs. Engagement in research could be increased in both frequency and volume with positive results, if civil society is willing to partner with academia and able to identify through its direct practice issues that require urgent attention and further investigation by academia.
- Finally, global networks have been valuable to streamline the agenda of mainstreaming CURPs. These networks bring together the capacities of academics, practitioners, and policymakers, and can make a vast difference to the quality of partnerships and engagements in the co-production of knowledge. Living Knowledge Networks (Europe), Community Based Research Canada, PASCAL International Observatory, Talloires Network of Engaged Universities, AsiaEngage, NCPPE, and Participatory Research in Asia (PRIA) are some examples that have been sources of inspiration and sites of innovation in strengthening CURPs across the world. However, such networks and institutions do not widely exist. There is a crucial need to strengthen these networks to further streamline CURP structures within and outside academia.

On the other hand, the Next Gen global study on training and teaching CBRP clearly revealed a major concern of several respondents, namely, the huge disconnect between the knowledge HEIs produce – and are expected to produce (e.g., journal articles and books) – and the research and knowledge produced and needed in the community. As such, the available teaching and training in CBPR tends to be siloed, marginalised and without the quality of resources often directed towards other teaching and training opportunities. The second survey also made evident a strong interest in learning about methods of CBPR, while there is a critical shortage of formal learning opportunities in this field. Often, researchers go through the entire research degree with no exposure to the methods, ethics, and potential of CBPR. Evidence from the Next Gen project suggests that the main challenges for knowledge workers within and outside the academia are to meet the increasing demand for effective modular training in CBPR, add to existing opportunities, generate contextually important learning materials, and develop praxis-based learning, while taking into account regional differences (learning cultures, infrastructures, languages) and the range of local learners and training needs.

Overall, the Next Gen study shows that more training is needed not only on participatory research methodologies and theories, but also on knowledge mobilisation and dissemination, consultation and community engagement, research ethics and equity in interdisciplinary partnerships. Such skills will help the future generation of community-based researchers to actually work in, and with, the communities building relationships based on mutual respect and accountability. Research methods can always be developed and learned, but a way of being that makes community partners feel valued and builds their confidence, so that they can fully participate, is a skill that takes time to master. As a participant expressed, "what many researchers need is not only an open mind but also an open heart, sit down and listen with empathy".

9 Conclusion

As we write this chapter, humanity in its entirety is still grappling with the serious impacts of the continuing COVID-19 pandemic that has laid bare serious fault-lines not just in the access to health, but also livelihoods and social protection. All forms of inequalities hitherto hidden within countries and across the globe have become visible and have been exacerbated. As calls for 'build back better' are being heard, it is important not to lose sight of 'build back equal', too.

On what basis, which worldviews and what knowledge domains would leaders of the world plan to 'build back equal'? The value of contextually relevant knowledge produced in partnerships between universities and local communities becomes critical in this effort. The relevance of authentic, mutually respectful, and sustainable CURPs, and engaged scholarship becomes all the more urgent in the 'reconstruction' of local and global communities. The findings of the studies described in this chapter offer guidance towards building and nurturing the movement towards knowledge democracy across regions and countries.

As the studies have shown, several types of investments will be required urgently if such CURPs and collaborative training initiatives are to become effective institutional arrangements. First, national policymaking bodies have to provide public policy and resource support towards CURPs and CUE. Second, philanthropists and funders of higher education and research need to create special vehicles that incentivise research collaborations between universities and civil society organisations, including funding windows for active engagement by communities and civil societies. Third, civil society and social movements need to be 'brought in' to these conversations in modes, methods and idioms that are the mainstay of the world of practice (not just through academic articles like this). Fourth, the diversity of perspectives, knowledge cultures, research methods and ways of being and knowing would have to be respected by all parties to such partnerships as the essence of CURPs and CUE is harvesting diversity with mutual respect.

The creation and/or support of administrative structures in higher education institutions which facilitate community access to the social infrastructure of universities can contribute to community capacities for recovery and rejuvenation. But perhaps of even more importance is the support for new architectures of knowledge. It is time to put community at the heart of the knowledge curation process.

References

Allan, C. (2012). Rethinking the 'project': Bridging the polarized discourses in IWRM. *Journal of Environmental Policy & Planning, 14*(3), 231–241. https://doi.org/10.1080/1523908X.2012.702012

Brown, D. (Ed.). (2001). *Practice research engagement for civil society in a globalizing world.* Hauser Center for Nonprofit Organisations and CIVICUS: World Alliance for Citizen Participation.

Bucher, G. (2021, January 25). COVID-19 has shown us the true extent of global inequality. In 2021, let's commit to ending it. *World Economic Forum.* https://www.weforum.org/agenda/2021/01/covid19-inequality-virus-report-oxfam/

Clifford, C. (2021, April 22). These are the world's largest banks that are increasing and decreasing their fossil fuel financing. *CNBC.* https://www.cnbc.com/2021/04/22/which-banks-are-increasing-decreasing-fossil-fuel-financing-.html

de Sousa Santos, B. (2014). *Epistemologies of the South: Justice against epistemicide.* Routledge.

Etmanski, C., Hall, B., & Dawson, T. (Eds.). (2014). *Learning and teaching community-based research: Linking pedagogy to practice.* University of Toronto Press.

Evans, M. L., Lindauer, M., & Farrell, M. E. (2020). A pandemic within a pandemic – intimate partner violence during Covid-19. *The New England Journal of Medicine, 383,* 2302–2304. https://doi.org/10.1056/NEJMp2024046

Everingham, J.-A. (2012). Towards social sustainability of mining: The contribution of new directions in impact assessment and local governance. *Greener Management International, 57,* 91–103.

Fransman, J., Hall, B. L., Hayman, R., Narayanan, P., Newman, K., & Tandon, R. (2021). Beyond partnerships: Embracing complexity to understand and improve research collaboration for global development. *Canadian Journal of Development Studies*, *42*(3), 326–346.

Global University Network for Innovation (GUNI). (2008). *Higher education in the world 3 higher education: New challenges and emerging roles for human and social development*.

Hall, B. L. (2016). Towards a knowledge democracy movement. In R. Evans, E. Kurantowicz, & E. Lucio-Villegas (Eds.), *Researching and transforming adult learning and communities* (pp. 15–26). Sense.

Hall, B. L., Lepore, W., & Bhatt, N. (2018). The community-based university. In C. D. Wang, M. Sirat, & D. A. Razak (Eds.), *Higher education in Malaysia: A critical review of the past and present for the future* (pp. 164–177). Penerbit University Sains Malaysia.

Hall, B. L., & Tandon, R. (2017). Decolonization of knowledge, epistemicide, participatory research and higher education. *Research for All*, *1*(1), 6–19. https://doi.org/10.18546/RFA.01.1.02

Hall, B. L., & Tandon, R. (2020a, November 28). Community-university engagement in a time of COVID-19. *University World News*. https://www.universityworldnews.com/post.php?story=20201128094605500

Hall, B. L., & Tandon, R. (2020b). Editorial: Knowledge democracy for a transforming world. *Gateways: International Journal of Community Research and Engagement*, 13(1). Article ID 7225. http://dx.doi.org/10.5130/ijcre.v13i1.7225

Hall, B. L., & Tandon, R. (Eds.). (2021). *Socially responsible higher education: International perspectives on knowledge democracy*. Brill Sense.

Hall, B. L., Tandon, R., & Tremblay, C. (Eds.). (2015a). *Strengthening community university research partnerships: Global perspectives*. University of Victoria; PRIA. https://unescochair-cbrsr.org/unesco/pdf/UNESCO%20Book%20Web_with%20BookCovers_Aug202015_FINAL.pdf

Hall, B. L., Tandon, R., & Tremblay, C. (2015b). *Institutionalizing community university research partnerships: A user's manual*. PRIA/University of Victoria. https://unescochair-cbrsr.org/unesco/pdf/CURP_Guidelines.pdf

Lepore, W., Hall, B., & Tandon, R. (2021). Knowledge for change consortium: A decolonising approach to international collaboration in capacity-building in community-based participatory research. *Canadian Journal of Development Studies*, *42*(3), 347–370. https://doi.org/10.1080/02255189.2020.1838887

Munck, R., McIlrath, L., Hall, B., & Tandon, R. (Eds). (2014). *Higher education and community-based research: Creating a global vision*. Palgrave Macmillan.

Owen, R., Macnaghten, P., & Stilgoe, J. (2012). Responsible research and innovation: From science in society to science for society, with society. *Science and Public Policy*, *39*(6), 751–760. https://doi.org/10.1093/scipol/scs093

Popp, J., MacKean, G., Casebeer, A., Milward, H. B., & Lindstrom, R. (2013). *Inter-organisational networks: A critical review of literature to inform practice*. Alberta Centre for Child, Family and Community Research.

Sandstrom, A. (2010). Institutional and substantial uncertainty: Explaining the lack of adaptability in fish stocking policy. *Marine Policy*, *34*(6), 1357–1365.

Spilker, R., Nagel, R., Robinson, J., Brown, L., & Tremblay, C. (2016). *Creating citizen communities? Innovation and impacts in community-university engagement networks*. University of Victoria. https://www.academia.edu/22059900/Creating_Citizen_Communities_Innovation_and_Impacts_in_Community_University_Engagement_Networks

Stiglitz, J. (2020). Conquering the great divide. *Finance & Development*, (September), 17–19. https://www.imf.org/external/pubs/ft/fandd/2020/09/pdf/fd0920.pdf

Tandon, R. (2007). *Civil engagement in higher education and its role in human & social development*. Society for Participatory Research in Asia (PRIA). https://www.pria.org/knowledge_resource/Civil_Engagement_in_Higher.pdf

Tandon, R., Hall, B. L., Lepore, W., & Singh, W. (Eds.). (2016a). *Knowledge and engagement: Building capacity for the next generation of community based researchers*. PRIA. http://hdl.handle.net/1828/7989

Tandon, R., Hall, B. L., Lepore, W., & Singh, W. (Eds.). (2016b). *Training the next generation of community-based researchers: A Guide for trainers*. PRIA/University of Victoria.

Tremblay, C., Singh, W., & Lepore, W. (2017). Mutual learning and empowering support: Networks and balance between local and global demands. In X. C. Grau, F. Escrigas, J. Goddard, B. L. Hall, E. Hazelkorn, & R. Tandon (Eds.), *Higher education in the world 6. Towards a socially responsible university: Balancing the global with the local* (pp. 391–401). Global University Network for Innovation. http://www.guninetwork.org/report/higher-education-world-6

UNESCO. (2015). *Rethinking education: Towards a global common good?* https://unevoc.unesco.org/e-forum/RethinkingEducation.pdf

UNESCO Chair in Community-Based Research and Social Responsibility in Higher Education (UNESCO Chair CBR-SR). (2021, October 25). *About UNESCO chair*. https://www.unescochair-cbrsr.org/about-unesco-chair/

University Grants Commission. (2020). *Fostering social responsibility & community engagement in higher educational institutions in India. National curriculum framework and guidelines*. https://www.ugc.ac.in/e-book/UNNAT%20BHARAT%20ABHIYAN.pdf

Usher, K., Bhullar, N., Durkin, J., Gyamfi, N., & Jackson, D. (2020). Family violence and COVID-19: Increased vulnerability and reduced options for support. *International Journal of Mental Health Nursing*, *29*(4), 549–552. https://doi.org/10.1111/inm.12735

Watson, D., Hollister, R., Stroud, S. E., & Babcock, E. (2011). *The engaged university: International perspective on civic engagement*. Routledge.

CHAPTER 6

Women's and Gender Museums

Feminist Pedagogies for Illumination, Imagination, Provocation, and Collaboration

Darlene E. Clover

Abstract

This chapter focusses on Women's and Gender museums which can be found in 96 countries across the globe. Some of these institutions are virtual, others come in the form of travelling exhibitions whilst others have their own physical spaces with both permanent and temporary exhibitions. What I illustrate in this chapter is how these institutions operate as spaces of feminist adult education, working to (re)historicise (herstory), (re)represent, (re)imagine and (re)educate the past and the present with future intention. Although each institution is distinct with its own cultural and political challenges and opportunities, women's and gender museums share an epistemological mandate to disrupt the problematic gendered representations and narratives that proliferate in most of the world's museums and art galleries, as well as across society. Through exhibitions, conferences, seminars, arts-based workshops, talks, university courses, adult literacy classes, podcasts, and collaborations with scholars and women's organisations, women's and gender museums work to programme a new feminist consciousness and a basis for action for change by bringing women's histories and contributions out of the shadows. The pedagogical contributions women's and gender museums are making to the struggle for socio-gender justice and change makes them valuable resources for feminist adult educators around the world.

Keywords

women's and gender museums – feminist adult education – representation – herstorying – gender justice – socio-gender change

1   **Introduction**

> History is made out of common dreams, groundswells, turning points, watersheds – it's a landscape more complicated than commensurate. (Solnit, 2004, p. 57)

A central pedagogical role of public museums is to programme historical consciousness with contemporary epistemic intention. History matters because what we learn about the past has an impact on our present structures of thought, meaning and identity as well as our future actions and anticipations. Museums perform and mobilise historic-contemporary consciousness through their practices of representation, artworks, images, objects, artefacts, displays, dioramas, labels and curatorial statements that are carefully choreographed to visualise and story particular understandings of the past as it 'was' and the present as it 'is' (e.g., Sanford et al, 2020). This raises for Hall (2013) the question of whether representations reflect a truth about the world that exists out there or if representations produce meaning by representing it?

As a feminist adult educator researching museums for over two decades, and the current Co-President of a women's heritage site organisation, the answer is both. Museums do represent the world based on the physical objects, artefacts, and factual historical information they have to hand. But representation is neither simple nor transparent because there are always elements of invention, (re)interpretation and judgement. What is collected and represented – visualised, storied and imagined – takes place within existing socio-cultural epistemic constructs of what and who matters or counts. Museum representations are therefore never neutral nor objective, yet these institutions project such a powerful façade of impartiality that "museumgoers and non-visitors alike see the museum as the most trustworthy source of historical knowledge" (Gosselin & Livingston, 2016, p. 11).

Yet museums are masters of a sleight of hand pedagogy that actively shapes gendered 'epistemic injustice' (Bergsdóttir, 2016; Fricker, 2007; Sanford et al., 2020) by teaching visitors "to see what they [are being] taught to see and to remain blind to what they [are being] taught to ignore" (Cramer & Witcomb, 2018, p. 2). What we are consistently being taught to see is a world where men perform intentionally and actively as knowers, adventurers, inventors, artists, discoverers, athletes and more (Sanford et al., 2020). With equal consistency, to borrow from Criado Perez (2019), they "provide little space for women's role in the evolution of humanity [...] When it comes to the lives of [this] half of humanity, there is often nothing but silence" (p. XI). Even when women are represented, they are frequently relegated to underdeveloped, passive, domestic roles or shadowed behind a stereotype of idealised femininity that is riddled with issues of class, race, ability, and sexuality (Bergsdóttir, 2016; Sanford et al., 2020). Representations as powerful pedagogical mechanisms colour masculinities and femininities that seep into our consciousness with highly negative epistemic (knowledge/knowing) and social (identity and agency) consequences that range from the merely irritating to life threatening (Clover et al., 2016; Criado Perez, 2019).

While the majority of the world's museums continue to manufacture and mobilise gender injustice, my aim in this chapter is to introduce the critical and creative museum spaces that both story and allow us to see with what Bloom (1999) calls "other eyes" (p. 1). Established in 96 countries across the globe, Women's and Gender Museums act as intentional feminist adult education forces to (re)historicise (herstory), (re)represent, (re)story, and (re)imagine to (re)educate. Although each institution is distinct and all have challenges, they share in common an epistemological directive to upend narrow gendered representations by programming a new feminist historical consciousness. Drawing on the past and the present for the future through exhibitions, conferences, podcasts, collaborations, and a variety of other pedagogical devices, women's and gender museums illuminate, imagine, challenge, provoke women's and gender diverse lives out of the shadows to open up new possibilities of thought and action. As I outline some of the feminist pedagogical contributions women's and gender museums are making to the struggle for socio-gender justice and change in this chapter, I introduce what they offer as resources for adult educators.

2   Women's and Gender Museums: A Brief Introduction

> Women's equality remains an unfinished business ... in every single country of the world. (United Nations, 2019, p. 1)

Like feminist adult education, women's and gender museums (hereafter simply 'women's museums') are a result of the legacies of struggle by women's and feminist movements for social, political, cultural, aesthetic and particularly, epistemic justice, what Fricker (2007) calls the right to be a 'knower'. Epistemic injustice is particularly insidious because it is a distinctive kind of injustice where a wrong is done to an individual or an entire group such as women in their capacities as holders, speakers and "givers of knowledge" (p. 7). Epistemic injustice is constructed and mobilised visually through the representational power of images and narratively through the stories we tell that bolster the exploits and knowledges of a particular group such as men whilst discrediting those of others such as women and the gender diverse. Women as a group have had their capacities as knowers persistently discounted or belittled in private and the public spheres and the result is a weakened ability to function "fully as subjects of social understanding ... and participate unequally in the practices through which social meanings are generated" (p. 2). Until women can recover and share their own herstories and represent themselves as they are and wish to be portrayed, they will remain subject to manipulations and idealisations that fall well short of their interests (e.g., Criado Perez, 2019; Sanford et al., 2020).

Women's museums operate as what Wolff (1990) calls 'feminine sentences', negotiating "the complexity of the category of 'women', the constructions of the feminine [and] the constrictions and silences of women in patriarchal society [through] processes whereby women intervene ... and articulate their own experiences" (p. 10). These institutions are also responses to Wolff's (1998) queries of firstly, where the spaces are that allow for different feminist representations of history, culture or society and, secondly, what these spaces look like when they are "no longer mediated by the point of view of men?" (p. 509). Wolff calls these 'wild zones' because they offer possibilities of acting "outside the dominant culture and language of men" (p. 510). We must be mindful, however, that as we live in a patriarchal world, the women who create and enter these institutions have been socialised within this dominant ideology, meaning there will be constraints, complexities and compromises.

The first Women's Museum was founded in Bonn, Germany in 1981 in direct response to the concerns by women's movements about the representation and knowledge gaps that existed in museums across Germany and worldwide (Gonzalez, 2021). There are currently 96 women's and gender museums attending to, as the Zambian Women's History Museum website notes, the "dearth of documented knowledge and information in mainstream historical narratives of ... women and from [a] woman's perspective. These are histories that have been excised out of the mainstream socio-economic and cultural historical narrative" (n.d., para. 2).

According to Krasny (2013) there is no one definition of either women's or gender museums because "each is distinctly marked by its location, context, and history" (p. 12). She therefore describes them as a type of "living forum in which contemporary stories are made and a platform for reflection" (p. 12). At a gathering in 2008 in Merano, Italy, a global group of women's and gender museum founders, curators and educators characterised these institutions in the *Resolution of the 1st International Congress of Women's Museums* as reflecting the

> political, cultural, artistic, economic, and social roles and situations of women in the past and the present. They preserve and deepen women's

cultures, challenge prejudices and contribute to the respect of women and human rights. They are a mirror of society and also a means toward changing of the world. (Schönweger & Clover, 2020, p. 253)

Many women's museums are completely volunteer-run with little funding and no physical space of their own. These institutions operate as virtual spaces, hosting exhibitions or podcasts online. Others come in the form of large-scale travelling multi-media exhibitions researched and designed in collaboration with universities or women's organisations and curated in diverse public spaces. The Stockholm Museum of Women's History website describes the potential of their nomadic existence like this:

> Rather than having a fixed location, we appear in different shapes all over the city with tours, exhibitions, talks and other activities, to be present in our everyday lives where the history of women has taken place, working to make it part of common knowledge. (n.p.)

Online presences and mobilities mean accessibility to wider and more diverse audiences. Lack of funding allows for greater freedom of choice in subject matter although it calls for a great deal more energy, commitment, and relationship-building to keep the institution afloat. There are, however, many women's and gender museums with diverse physical spaces. The Musée de la Femme in Quebec, Canada is a converted family home; KØN Gender Museum Denmark has its own large municipal building complete with café; the Women's Museum in Merano, Italy is housed in the attic of a disused convent. These institutions enjoy financial support from local or national governments and sometimes, corporate donors. Physical space enables a blending of permanent collections, temporary and pop-up galleries, virtual exhibitions as well as income from cafés or bookshops. One's own space means the ability to host and facilitate a variety of public education activities at any time. However, as women's organisations know all too well, funding can come with strings attached in terms of content and direction.

If any generalisation can be made about women's museums it is that gender, as a powerfully influential social construction, is central to the diverse issues they tackle through their socio-educational activities. Yet a scan of museums around the world shows the vast majority maintain the word 'women'. As unstable as the category of 'women' is, it is still a category these institutions believe they need to continue to employ. For the Museo de Mujeres in Buenos Aires, "'women' fuels our struggle. Keeping 'women' is essential to maintain coherence with our objectives as a museum because it is a tool for understanding that half of the population has been exposed to specific gendered oppressions over 10.000 years" (Gonzalez, 2021, p. 10). They are motivated by and respond to deep and persistent inequalities and oppressions related to women's historical erasure, femicide (sexualised and domestic violence, rape as a weapon of war), female body control (reproduction, fashion) and constricting visualisations and social constructions of 'womanhood' and 'motherhood'. The primary audience of women's museums is women and girls; their mission to inspire through new knowledge about women's lives and encourage some form of activism (e.g., Akkent & Kovar, 2019; Gonzalez, 2021).

Gender museums tend to see their pedagogical role as educating both men and women equally and focus much less on normative male-female binaries. In 2016 the Women's Museum in Denmark renamed itself the KØN Gender Museum. Their first mandate had been to concentrate on the obscured history of Danish women, but they shifted to respond to contemporary sexual orientation changes because, as trans-feminist Scott-Dixon (2006) argues,

> gender is never just gender. It is a slippery thing that rubs up against other social signifiers in indecent ways. Individual gender expression is embedded in systems and structures of power [...] Just as the critical examination of whiteness within structures of racial inequality enables us to see how the norm is a constructed and to ask questions about both normative and trans genders and observing how they intersect with other social relations facilitate a rich critical analysis of the gender system as a whole. (p. 19)

This broader take up of gender is an important continuum in feminist thinking and practice based in a belief that all violence and oppression have the same roots: dominant patriarchal masculinities (Scott-Dixon, 2006). I have found, however, that a lack of name change does not prevent women's museums from operating in this broader gendered context. While the permanent collection in the Musée de la Femme showcases 400-years of women's history in Quebec, its temporary galleries exhibit contemporary stories of LGBTQI2+ communities. Yet it is a concern when a museum retitles itself in order, as noted by one Asian museum founder, "to appease men and make the museum more palatable to them" or when the institution is forced to do so by funders for similar reasons. We must also remember that the extent to which a women's museum can focus on diverse gender identities depends upon context. In countries where homosexuality is illegal, it is dangerous for a museum to overtly represent diverse gender identities, although as I discuss below these institutions can be extremely courageous in their subject matter despite the consequences. Adding to this, some countries experience a much higher degree of women's inequality and inequity than others and therefore, as a women's museum founder in the Middle East reminded me, "we just have to continue fighting to get women seen and heard. We are still so far behind". While avoiding essentialism of 'womenkind', maintaining a politics as if women exist is fair "since the world behaves as if they unambiguously do" (Wolff, 1990, p. 9).

A further complexity is that most museums were founded by outspoken feminist activists, are managed by self-defined feminists and institutional websites use the term feminism copiously. The vision, mission, essence, and work of these institutions is grounded in feminism as a critical vision and positioning for the reconstruction of consciousness. Yet no institution calls itself a 'Feminist Museum'. When I queried this, women's museum members in Asia and Europe reminded me that: (a) "no society is ready for that yet"; (b) "the term feminism has been so totally vilified that it would make the word the focus of discussion, rather than the content of the museum"; and (c) "believe me, just maintaining the term 'women' causes trouble enough!"

3 Changing the Imagination of Change

Unlike other museums that tend to focus on collection and perseveration, women's museums see education and learning as their central mandate. For Gonzalez (2021) these institutions

> play an active, critical educational key role in society as places of friction, debate and the empowerment of women and girls. They are places where power relations, dominant culture and patriarchies are questioned, where women are (re)imagined and processes of community participation are initiated. The objective is to contribute to knowledge that can bring about change at micro (personal) and macro (socio-cultural) levels. (p. 28)

Women's museums educate by showing (visualisations and images) as well as telling (narratives, dialogue). Their activities encourage women to represent themselves, to come together to tell their own stories and become more responsible hearers and viewers (e.g., Fricker, 2007). In feminist adult education, we refer to this as adding new knowledge to existing knowledge, giving voice, and activating 'deep listening' to form new understandings of how "women have been shaped but not determined by history and how [they] can bring new possibilities into an old world" (Butterwick & Selman, 2003, p. 18). The Zambian Women's History Museum speaks to this as "salvaging women's histories ... to facilitate 'deep learning', which allows understanding on a visceral and intellectual level that can provide new ways of living … and contribute to enriching the dynamics of ever evolving cultural systems" (n.d., para. 2).

The central pedagogical device of women's and gender museums is their exhibitions. For Jackson (2015)

> to make an exhibition is to create a structure through which we can look at the world, look through to the other side of conventions and experience and develop alternative models of being in the world […] Curating exhibitions is part of creating cultural, aesthetic and historical transformation.

Exhibitions can be thoughtful and caring, challenging and deeply critical depending upon the need and purpose. Many are multi-media, combining art, narratives, poetry, objects, artefacts, and other media in ways that disclose unseen worlds or allow us to see the familiar 'strangely'. Exhibitions can be factual, but they can also display 'imaginary worlds' to which I will return, against which visitors can measure their lived reality. Their subject matters are as diverse as the communities they serve. Alongside or in collaboration with exhibitions, women's and gender museums facilitate arts-based workshops, host conferences and offer ongoing discussion fora such as monthly study groups that bring together intergenerational groups to discuss topics relevant to their lives. They also undertake collaborative research and creative projects and intervene into the public sphere and policy. Positioning themselves as community resources, many publish or make available resources such as books.

In the next section, I highlight a global selection of feminist adult education strategies and initiatives. While there is much to choose from and they are also important, I have chosen examples of how they are raising historical consciousness, tackling dark histories, and collaboratively intervening into the public sphere.

4 Remaking Historical Consciousness: Illumination and the Imagination

Although there is no single definition of historical consciousness, feminist museologists Gosselin and Livingstone (2016) refer to it as creating a collective memory of the world upon which to build the present and the future. In a world where the majority of herstories have been disappeared, overshadowed, belittled or misrepresented, women's museums decolonise and re-historicise through practices of illumination, making their lives and experiences visible for the first time or clearer "in order for newness of thought to enter"

(Priyadharshini, 2012, p. 548) and imagination, creatively envisaging into being another world so it can become "thinkable and actionable" (Manicom & Walters, 2012, p. XI).

A ubiquitous practice of historical consciousness-making is to design and curate exhibitions that portray the lives of local or national trailblazing women who have broken through traditional barriers. Exhibitions showcase prominent political leaders or artists for example, but also lesser-known women who have "transcended borders of time and space" (Museum Frauenkultur Regional-International, n.d., para. 3). An example of this comes from the Women's History Museum in Zambia. Their exhibition, *Leading Ladies,* is a series of podcasts, short animations that feature women from the 17th to the 19th century who held significant positions of leadership or played otherwise significant social roles. Part of the series focusses on women who have excelled in male-orientated occupations such as "The General" (military) and "The Innovator" (science). Other prominent women profiled were activists in the public sphere, including "The Feminist" and "The Peacemaker". The aims are to provide role models, sources of inspiration and representations of the possible. Portraying feminist activisms, something that is central to women's museums, is vital, a member of the women's museum in Egypt reminded me, because "women's historical struggles form the basis to engage in ongoing struggles". In addition, while critical and deconstructive practices are vital to exposing the logic of patriarchal systems of representation, celebratory aesthetic approaches such as these have important capacities to engage new ways of seeing and knowing. But let me return to another important element of the work of Zambian Women's Museum which is the use of the creative device of animation. Sometimes referred to as 'artefiction' it is a blurring of the lines between the 'fictional' and the 'factual'. While the art practice is powerful and effective, artefiction is also frequently a necessity. As noted above, women's lives have been so 'uncollected' and 'under-storied' that both images and facts can be short on the ground. Faced with this absence, women's museums are forced to use other means to imagine into being a more full and complete account. How they tell women's stories is active exercise of imagination towards a reality of perspective-making. On the problematic side, this can place women's museums in the battle of what Vendramin (2012) calls "true and false" (p. 89). However, what is critical is not whether something is true or false but "what counts as 'truth' and how this is used to enable women "to see another way round" (p. 89).

Building on this, women's histories are multifaceted, and women's museums are expert at showcasing dichotomies for pedagogical purposes. To do this, they frequently take a very small, somewhat unassuming object and create a provocative social narrative to stimulate discussion, debate, and reflection. An excellent example is the Swedish Museum of Women's History's exhibition entitled *War of the Corsets*. This exhibition tells the story of how in the late 1800s the corset became the focus of intense debate in Sweden. As the curatorial statement on the website notes, "A small garment turned into a major political issue. The corset became an ideological battlefield, triggering debates about power, gender, identity, and class. The exhibition is about the shapes and limits of femininity. About the past, present and future". Through the channels of the corset, literally and figuratively, we are invited into a world of nuances and major differences in the lives of men and women that range from movement and breathing to the very act of voting. As we are reminded how "the corset's role was to enhance the female form, to clearly show that the wearer was a woman and nothing else" (2021, para. 2) and how critics labelled them as in fact dangerous to women's health with no place in a modern society, we are also introduced to stories by women who had more complex relationships with these pieces of cloth. For example, many defended them "as decent, healthy, and modern rather than harmful and outdated" (para. 4). Among other things, these types of exhibitions visualise the forces of society that 'victimise' women without simply positioning them as victims. Further, to encourage deeper discussion and reflection, women's museums organise pedagogical activities around exhibitions like this that focus on how fashion has controlled women's lives historically and today, issues of complicity whereby women conspire against their own best interests in support of patriarchy or the dichotomy of 'choice' as a process of control and manipulation as well as an exercise of power.

5   Looking into the Darkness: Other Ways of Telling and Showing

Exposing dark histories and wading into divisive topics are key pedagogical strategies of many women's and gender museums. With courage and tenacity, these institutions raise fingers of defiance to oppression, exploitation and silencing even when they know there will be consequences.

Both the Women's Active Museum on War and Peace (WAM) in Tokyo, Japan and The War and Women's Human Rights Museum (WWHRM) in Korea bring to light from different perspectives and means, the 'dark histories' of Japan's military sexual slavery which had never been included "as part of the 'official history' in museums until courageous survivors testified and documentary evidence was unearthed in the 1990s" (Watanabe, 2015, p. 236). With "few material objects of sexual violence" to draw upon, WAM used testimonies as the significant element of their exhibition (p. 236). The museum created a series of panels of testimonies from both women survivors and former soldiers to bring to life the entirety of an era. While the exhibition dramatically narrates an historical 'truth' from the standpoint of those who experienced it, the museum accompanies this with pedagogical opportunities to explore the persistence of sexual enslavement and trafficking in women's and children's lives today. In this same context, the women's museum in Korea uses the power of sensory and embodied learning. A dark basement has been created in a replica of the military brothels, what are known as 'comfort stations', where thousands of women "were abducted, tricked and coerced into forced labour" (WWHRM, n.d., para. 1). This approach enables visitors to experience in a small way the isolation, fear and helplessness of the prison cells. A balance women's museums carefully maintain, similar to the challenge of victimisation and victims I outlined above, is to illustrate as fully as possible these violent histories without simply reproducing the violence (e.g., Akkent & Kovar, 2019).

Of course, it is not just 'histories' that are dark. We live, as Solnit (2004) reminds us in 'dark times' and we need an imagination adequate to responding to the dangers. An excellent example is a travelling exhibition entitled *Cultures of Headscarves* that was curated by the Women's Museum in Bonn. *Cultures of Headscarves* educates a feminist intercultural understanding of women within the challenging context of contemporary sexist xenophobia. There are in fact fierce debates as governments in countries such as France and Canada legislate against allowing women wearing 'religious' head wear to work in the public sector. *Cultures of Headscarves* uses something small, in this case the pieces of cloth that women have worn on their heads for centuries for aesthetic, convenience or religious purposes to tackle this enormously troubling issue. The exhibition illustrates a multiplicity of 'truths' from how headwear has fuelled male sexual fantasies and been used to control and repress women, to its use for shelter from the weather for health reasons, and the sense of identity or freedom it has given women. The absurdities of dress codes are illustrated creatively in cartoon form. Specifically, an image depicts an incident in France in 2016 where "male police officers forced a woman to take off her burkini, a full body swimsuit, while on the beach. Women going topless on the beach is seen as an act of freedom while covering is an act of oppression" (Franger & Clover, 2020, p. 297). As the exhibition moves around Europe educators design public activities around topics of resistance, xenophobia and racism, choice, women's bodies and control and religious intolerance. While showing in Belgium, the exhibition received a bomb threat.

Building on the above, the Iranian Women's Movement Museum (IRWMM) is an example of how seriously the work of these institutions "is taken by officials in society because of the impact they can have on changing women's consciousness" (Schönweger & Clover, 2020, p. 261). The museum is a virtual site initiated by Mansoureh Shojaee, an Iranian feminist activist. The aim was "to provide a peaceful strategy for voicing our demands for the equal treatment of women" (Shojaee, 2013, p. 221). The museum has a permanent section of images "devoted to the history of women's movements, and introduces the effect of those struggles, their success and failures" (p. 222). The museum also curated an exhibition of the handicrafts of women "imprisoned for the past ten years in Evin Prison" to shed light on the "harsh criminal penalties women experience as a result of women's rights activities" (p. 224). The museum was shut down for 'security reasons' and Shojaee was forced to flee her country and is now a political refugee in Europe (Schönweger & Clover, 2020, p. 261).

6   Collaborations and Public Interventions: New Memories and Experiences

Women's and gender museums, as noted above, engage in a variety of collaborations and feminist public interventions which often lead to new projects. In 2018 the German Fürth Museum of Women's Cultures Regional-International curated an exhibition entitled *How feminine is the city? Fürth and its sister cities*. Using images, portraits, narratives, installations, and the work of national and international artists, the exhibition inspired visitors to think about what a city could look like if it was for all, rather than for some. Refracted through a female perspective the exhibition sparked not only a great deal of dialogue about the invisibility and forgotten lives of women on the urban landscape but resulted in broad gender community mapping that exposed "the hidden curriculum of gendered norms, values and practices that are transmitted through urban street names, monuments and so forth" (Schönweger & Clover, 2020, p. 259). The aim of the map was to lock women into the historical memory of the city.

The Merano Women's Museum organised a major conference based on a temporary exhibition they had curated of the history of women and psychiatry in fascist Italy. The museum then worked with women's organisations and the Gender Studies department at the university to facilitate workshops around the exhibition that explored everything from the gendered politics of mental health to food insecurity (Schönweger & Clover, 2021). In the spaces created, women are able to make sense of their own social or cultural experiences, "to recover memory of their collective, material and immaterial heritage" (Gonzalez, 2021).

Violence against women is a profound problem worldwide but in Argentina the Museo de la Mujer has created many initiatives and joined others to fight for women's right to a life free of violence. Since 2008, this museum has been addressing this issue by working with performance artists to design specific theatre activities in connection with their exhibitions and displays with the pedagogical mission "to communicate, to impact, to transform" (Gonzalez, 2021, p. 74). The projects are aimed specifically at the most vulnerable women in terms of their socio-economic contexts, "who rarely have the opportunity to go to the theatre or to a museum, and who have few opportunities for dialogue, to be heard and to reflect with others on their experiences" (p. 74). This museum-theatre collaboration is a space of community building, dialogue and critical self and social reflection but it inspired the creation of the yearly National Festival of Theatre Against Gender Violence.

7 Changing the Imagination of Change: Final Thoughts for Adult Educators

> I do not deny that the effects of the past are still with us. But I refuse to strengthen them ... to confer upon them an irremovability the equivalent of destiny [...] Anticipation is imperative. (Cixous, 1976, p. 416)

Women's and gender museums exist worldwide to educate new feminist historical consciousness. Regardless of form, the cultural politics of these institutions is located in the heart of the complex order which (re)produced epistemic and social injustices that (re)produce sexual divisions in societies around the world. Using a variety of strategies and devices, they take up the complexities of women's and gender diverse lives, practising their cultural politics in ways that are once subversive and intentional, critical and celebratory, mobilising and deconstructive. I conclude this chapter with some further thoughts on why these institutions are invaluable resources for adult educators.

To begin, these institutions are accessible. They are located in communities across the globe, responding to local community and national needs through a plethora of education activities and collaborative projects that are free and open to the public. They are equally accessible through their travelling and online presences. The alternative herstories of these institutions matter because they will have impact on how women and the gender diverse live in the present and imagine and create the future. Women's museums are sources of an historical feminist imaginary, the practice of performing and presenting the world differently by visualising the absent presences of social and epistemic injustices and connecting these to the present to change the future. To borrow from feminist adult educator Butterwick (2016), these institutions look back to move forward.

Women's museums are places that celebrate women and the gender diverse, drawing attention to lives, achievements and activisms for change to inspire and motivate. They also wield the powers of imagination and representation such as animation, theatre, artefacts and artefiction as pedagogies of epistemic responsibility, the responsibility to present, to see and to know the world differently. Women's and gender museums are embroiled in the most difficult issues of our time, tackling everything from xenophobia and religious intolerance to issues of choice and complicity. Through illumination, imagination, provocation, and collaboration, through exhibitions, conferences, workshops, theatre and more, women's and gender museums provide adult educators with platforms to explore, discuss and contemplate everything from feminism to food insecurity, fascism to fashion in ways that can change the imagination of change.

References

Akkent, M., & Kovar, S. (Eds.). (2019). *Feminist pedagogy: Museums, memory sites and practices of remembrance*. Istanbul Kadin Muzesi.

Bergsdóttir, A. (2016). Museums and feminist matters: Considerations of a feminist museology. *Nordic Journal of Feminist and Gender Research, 24*, 126–139. https://doi.org/10.1080/08038740.2016.1182945

Bloom, L. (Ed.). (1999). *With other eyes: Looking at race and gender in visual culture*. University of Minnesota Press.

Butterwick, S. (2016). Feminist adult education: Looking back, moving forward. In D. E. Clover, S. Butterwick, & L. Collins (Eds.), *Women, adult education and leadership in Canada* (pp. 3–14). Thompson Educational Publishing.

Butterwick, S., & Selman, J. (2003). Deep listening in a feminist popular theatre project: Upsetting the position of audience in participatory education. *Adult Education Quarterly, 54*(1), 7–22. https://doi.org/10.1177/0741713603257094

Cixous, H. (1976). The laugh of the Medusa. *Signs, 1*(4), 875–893.

Clover, D. E., Butterwick, S., & Collins, L. (Eds.). (2016). *Women, adult education and leadership in Canada*. Thompson Educational Publishing.

Cramer, L., & Witcomb, A. (2018). Hidden from view? An analysis of the integration of women's history and women's voices in Australia's social history exhibitions. *International Journal of Heritage Studies, 25*(2), 128–142. https://doi.org/10.1080/13527258.2018.1475409

Criado Perez, C. (2019). *Invisible women: Data bias in a world designed by men*. Abrams Press.

Franger, G., & Clover, D. E. (2020). Cultures of headscarves: Intercultural feminist education through a challenging exhibition. In K. Sanford, D. E. Clover, N. Taber, & S. Williamson (Eds.), *Feminist critique and the museum: Educating for a critical consciousness* (pp. 284–305). Brill Sense.

Fricker, M. (2007). *Epistemic injustice: Power and the ethics of knowing*. Oxford University Press.

Gonzalez, S. (2021). *El Museo de la Mujer Buenos Aires: Una comunidad de aprendizaje* [Unpublished thesis]. Universidad Cardinal Herrera.

Gosselin, V., & Livingstone, P. (Eds.). (2016). *Museums and the past: Constructing historical consciousness*. UBC Press.

Hall, S. (2013). The work of representation. In S. Hall, J. Evans & S. Nixon (Eds.), *Representation* (2nd ed., pp. 1–59). Sage.

Jackson, G. (2015). And the question is … In P. O'Neill & M. Wilson (Eds.), *Curating research* (pp. 60–78). Open Editions.

KØN Gender Museum Denmark. (n.d.). https://konmuseum.dk

Krasny, E. (2013). Women's museum curatorial politics in feminism, education, history and art. In E. Krasny & Frauenmuseum Meran (Eds.), *Women's: Museum curatorial politics in feminism, education, history, and art* (pp. 11–29). Loecker Verlag.

Manicom, L., & Walters, S. (2012). *Feminist popular education in transnational debates: Building pedagogies of possibility*. Palgrave Macmillan.

Museum Frauenkultur Regional-International. (n.d.). Retrieved February 22, 2022, from https://inklusionvekadinmuz-eleri.wordpress.com/2017/06/12/museum-frauenkultur-regional-international/

Priyadharshini, E. (2012). Thinking with trickster: Sporadic illuminations for educational research. *Cambridge Journal of Education, 42*(4), 547–561, https://doi.org/10.1080/0305764X.2012.733344

Sanford, K., Clover, D. E., Taber, N., & Williamson, S. (Eds.). (2020). *Feminist critique and the museum: Educating for a critical consciousness*. Brill Sense.

Schönweger, A., & Clover, D. E. (2020). The critical advocacies and pedagogies of women's museums. In K. Sanford, D. E. Clover, N. Taber, & S. Williamson (Eds.), *Feminist critique and the museum: Educating for a critical consciousness* (pp. 250–266). Brill Sense.

Scott-Dixon, K. (2006). *Trans/forming feminisms: Trans-feminist voices speak out*. Sumach Press.

Shojaee, M. (2013). The Iranian Women's Museum Initiative. In E. Krasny & Frauenmuseum Meran (Eds.), *Women's: Museum curatorial politics in feminism, education, history, and art* (pp. 220–223). Loecker Verlag.

Solnit, R. (2004). *Hope in the dark: Untold histories, wild possibilities*. Nation Books.

Stockholm Museum of Women's History. (n.d). Retrieved February 22, 2022, from https://www.kvinnohistoriska.se/eng

United Nations (2019). *UN75 2020 and beyond: Shaping our future.* United Nations. https://esaro.unfpa.org/en/news/un75-2020-and-beyond-shaping-our-future-together

Vendramin, V. (2012). Why feminist epistemology matters in education and educational research. *Solsko Polje (School Field Journal ERI Ljubljana), 23*(1–2), 87–96. https://www.pei.si/ISSN/1581_6044/1-2-2012/1581_6044_1-2-2012.pdf

Watanabe, M. (2015). Passing on the history of 'comfort women': The experiences of a women's museum in Japan. *Journal of Peace Education, 12*(3), 236–246. https://doi.org/10.1080/17400201.2015.1092713

Wolff, J. (1990). *Feminine sentences.* Polity Press.

Wolff, J. (1998). Women's knowledge and women's art. In E. Dayton (Ed.), *Art and interpretation: An anthology of readings in aesthetics and the philosophy of art* (pp. 508–517). Broadview Press.

Women's Active Museum on War and Peace. (n.d.). Retrieved February 22, 2022, from https://wam-peace.org/en/

Women's History Museum. (n.d.). Retrieved February 22, 2022, from https://www.whmzambia.org

CHAPTER 7

Living and Learning with Dementia

Implications for Re-Making Community Life

Jocey Quinn

Abstract

People living with dementia have been largely absent in debates on adult learning and positioned on the margins of communities. This chapter presents an alternative vision of people living with dementia: as open to the possibilities of learning, as vital parts of communities and as avant-garde agents of change. Proceeding from the understanding that people with dementia can and do learn, which was generated through earlier research (see Quinn & Blandon, 2020), the chapter focuses on the implications for re-making community life. It generates the following discussions: the extent to which people living with dementia are already active community members; how they free up non-humanistic ontologies and generate visions of more than human and more than social mutuality, which contribute to moves towards decolonisation; and finally, how they help to highlight hopes for the future, not nostalgia for the past, and usher in a more corporeal and creative andragogy.

Keywords

dementia – corporeality – decolonisation – mutuality – creative andragogy – posthuman – non-humanistic ontologies – feminist new materialists

1   Background

Dementia is one of the most significant global social issues of our time and one that is likely to touch everyone in some form or other. Living with a range of dementia symptoms which relate to memory, cognition, spatial awareness, or speech, and which affect individuals to varying degrees and in different ways, has increasingly become a normal part of life as populations live longer. The numbers are sobering. According to the World Health Organisation (2020) around 50 million people currently live with dementia with ten million new cases every year: by 2030 the total is projected to reach 82 million. The pandemic has focused attention on the vulnerability of such people. In the UK, the Office for National Statistics (2020) noted a sharp rise in 'unexplained excess deaths' amongst people with dementia, which Alzheimer's Society research (2020) partly attributed to increased cognitive decline caused by lockdown isolation. Forcibly apart from families and friends, people with dementia have lived and died as discarded members of the community. In planning for a post-pandemic future, communities need to radically revise how they understand and treat people living with dementia, recognising their capacities, slowing their decline, and promoting integration. Adult education has a vital but unacknowledged role to play in this process. Although evidence exists that people with dementia can learn something new unrelated to previous skills or competencies, even at late stages (see Quinn & Blandon, 2017, 2020), they are mostly positioned as outside lifelong learning policy and practice. At best they are offered training to retain existing skills, at worst they are implicitly regarded as waste with huge implications for sustainability. They have moved centre stage in culture, but without a concomitant social response to their needs. Dementia has become a socio-cultural 'sensation', providing substance and frameworks for TV shows, films, and plays. The Oscar winning film *The Father* based on the play by Florian Zeller is just one example. Nevertheless, dementia support remains inadequate. In the UK, for example, adult social care sustains many deep-seated problems: whilst demand for dementia care has gone up, provision has declined (Bottery & Babalola, 2021). Despite numerous research studies and campaigns, support for people living with dementia is minimal and they are perceived as being on the margins of communities. Moreover, the profound ontological and epistemological challenges living with dementia raises have scarcely been addressed.

2   Finding a Place for People with Dementia in Lifelong Learning

Adult education is neglected within education policy with much uncertainty about its validity and meaning. Does it mean being eternally ready for employment even in old age as the recent EU Green paper seems to suggest (European Commission, 2021)? Is it about indulging in leisure activities at all ages, as in media portrayals of hearty baby boomers who are unfeasibly healthy and wealthy? Or is the role of adult education to change communities through radical acts of knowledge transformation? Researchers and theorists cannot agree. Debates include Edwards (2010) recognising that lifelong learning needs rethinking to meet the demands of a posthuman world, whilst Biesta (2014) has critiqued the very concept of lifelong learning as promoting 'learnification' instead of education. With the Black Lives Matter movement and associated seminal literature such as *In the Wake* (Sharpe, 2016), the role of education in both colonisation and decolonisation has come to the fore, placing it at the heart of one of the most important social debates of our time. However, people living with dementia have not featured within any of these debates and visions, including those that focus on social justice. They have been placed outside the realm of the productive, the pleasurable or the democratic.

Despite strong evidence that exercising cognitive functions can help delay the development of dementia, lifelong learning neglects dementia. Even the Adult Education and Lifelong Learning for 21st Century Britain report (Centenary Commission on Adult Education, 2019), stops before any mention of dementia. The literature on dementia pays little attention to learning and education: most reference to learning has been to courses that train people to retain as much functionality as they can to survive (Richeson et al., 2007) or activities aimed to reconnect them with memories of the past (Cheng et al., 2014). Innovative community arts projects such arts4dementia or vamostheatre exist and demonstrate what it is possible to achieve, but the neoliberal discourse of self-management still dominates (Mountain & Craig, 2012). 'Appropriate learning' for people with dementia is commonly couched as containment and the retention of skills, with little sense of the openness to and from something new that constitutes learning. The European Association for the Education of Adults' *Manifesto for Learning in the 21st Century* (2019) does mention dementia and highlights some innovative care homes in Norway and the UK. However, the emphasis here is still functional: a limiting perspective positioning dementia as outside of the innovative realm of learning, cut off from one of the vital agencies of life. Moreover, the possibility that people with dementia have much to teach others does not seem to be entertained in the literature.

3   Research with People Living with Dementia

This chapter builds on research conducted in the UK which included people with advanced dementia, *Beyond Words* (Quinn et al., 2017, 2021). The project was funded by Arts Council England as part of its Research Grants Programme and conducted in collaboration with Plymouth Music Zone, an innovative community music project which focuses on using music to foster inclusion for marginalised groups. The focus of *Beyond Words* was on those the research came to name as 'post-verbal' (rather than using the deficit term 'non-verbal').

They were people who did not use words as their primary means of communication: people living with advanced dementia. stroke, learning difficulties, autism or acquired brain injury. The research combined eighteen months of ethnographic observations of 25 participants and their involvement in music, 44 interviews with families and carers, 30 arts workshops with participants and four focus groups with arts practitioners. The project employed posthuman theory to understand the processes of learning for post-verbal people and the role of music, drawing on feminist new materialists such as Braidotti (2013), Bennett (2010), Barad (2007), and Alaimo (2010). This approach has been coined PhEmaterialism by educational researchers (see Ringrose et al., 2019) and employed in research in early years, schools, or Higher Education, but has had little influence in adult and lifelong learning up to now. Rather than focusing on the inviolate individual who possesses a 'self' that s/he can communicate through words, posthuman theory moves away from the articulate human to focus on acts and bodies (Braidotti, 2013), on materiality (Barad, 2007) and the agency of things (Bennett, 2010). It validates and explores the significance of silence (Mazzei, 2016). In posthumanism the unit of experience is not the individual human, but the "agentic assemblage" (Bennett, 2010) where the human is part of a web of matter all contributing to the combined agency of the assemblage.

The ability to think and articulate meaning in words is repeatedly hallmarked as the distinguishing feature of a human. This trope is repeated endlessly from philosophical texts to popular media. A recent example is the podcast *What makes a human?* where actor and writer Stephen Fry simply responded: "words, words, words". This positions people living with dementia outside the category human. Often, they cannot speak coherently, and they are not in control of their thoughts or body, they put themselves in different 'irrational' relations to the objects around them, they are not sure where they are. Posthuman modes of thinking can provide a more productive way of entering and understanding their worlds. Using them in *Beyond Words* provided a positive and hopeful perspective on people living with dementia and other post-verbal people and revealed their learning potential. This provided the framework for our analysis of fieldwork data and enabled us to enter the world of the participants, rather than trying to fit them into a humanistic mould which would always position them as lacking. In line with previous writing (see Quinn, 2013), we were alert to potential problems in posthumanism, such as its tendency towards utopian thinking, so, rather than seeing possibility as unbounded, we also paid close attention to structural inequalities and how they shape access to learning. The project demonstrated the multiple ways that post-verbal people can create and learn and the benefits of inclusive music practice in releasing their potential.

A key finding of the study was that even at a very late-stage people living with dementia showed a potential to learn, which music facilitated. It also showed that people living with dementia have much to teach about being in the world. For carers and family members these findings gave hope and comfort. There was important recognition that even if the learning moment was transitory, it was worth facilitating. The recognition that people living with dementia are adult learners too has been developed and discussed further (see Quinn and Blandon, 2017, 2020). Taking this understanding as a starting point, the purpose of this chapter is to focus specifically on where people living with dementia stand in relation to discussions on re-making community life.

4   People Living with Dementia as Adult Learners and Teachers: Implications for Remaking Community Life

Extending the discussion on remaking community life and adult learning, so that people living with dementia can take their rightful place, is far more than a matter of inclusion. If the person living with dementia is recognised as a legitimate community member and learner, then many assumptions and practices must change. The nature of the learning community changes and the sense of how it could and should function changes radically too, providing multiple challenges. It is not sufficient to argue that the value of learning in communities and resources to promote it must be supported and extended to people living with dementia; even though both these aspects are vital first steps. There are assumptions about the nature of personhood and the process of learning that need to be unpicked. I will proceed to discuss some of these implications.

5   Already Active Community Members

Amongst people living with dementia there is already a rich history of coming together to lobby for justice for people living with the disease, to share experiences and to influence policy. For example, in the UK the 3 Nations Dementia Working Group which works across England, Wales and Northern Ireland is led by people living with dementia and co-ordinates multiple activities to demonstrate the capabilities of their peers and their contributions to the community. Different members of the group share their computing expertise with visitors to local libraries, work with journalists and film makers to share knowledge about people living with dementia or review research proposals for research councils. They organise and run webinars to support their networking. Another interesting example is the international Reimagining Dementia network, coordinated from the USA, which positions itself as a 'creative coalition for change'. This brings people living with dementia together online with artists, carers, health and social care professionals and researchers to challenge negative discourses and practices regarding dementia. Research has shown the campaigning power of activist groups of people living with dementia in Scotland (Jenkins, 2014) and demonstrated how they can be co-producers of knowledge (Stevenson & Taylor, 2019). So, to suggest that people living with dementia are not already active community members, quite apart from their ongoing personal roles in families and friendships, would be a significant mistake. These examples of activism show people living with dementia remaking communities for themselves and demonstrate how communities cross international borders and are remade by online connections. As I shall discuss, community is about doing rather than place and people living with dementia are already doing the remaking.

6   Non-Humanistic Ontologies: Beyond the Neo-Liberal or Radical

Nevertheless, as discussed above, this active community membership is not acknowledged in discussions about the future of adult learning; whether the focus be neo-liberal or radical people living with dementia are not present. Moreover, neither a neo-liberal nor a radical vision of the learner will do full justice to them. In both discourses and traditions there is a valorisation of voice and identity. In neo-liberal contexts the person is seen in terms of their individuality and agency, their autonomy to make what they can of the world through merit. In a radical tradition there is a focus on 'voice', on coming to consciousness and from that to join with others who are oppressed to work to make positive change. Being able to speak, to articulate, is at the heart of both traditions and whilst there are eloquent advocates for people with dementia, this focus on voice and agency leaves many firmly outside. Both neo-liberal and radical traditions circulate around a version of the human which excludes many people with dementia. This is a version of the human which is a bounded entity who can tell a unified story about themselves and is secure in place and time, even if there are different stories valorising individual triumph or collective unity. In contrast, for many with dementia boundaries are porous, time and space are not always clear, and an articulate voice is not accessible. In a sense they highlight the relational nature of existence and the non-linear, non-rational world in which we all actually live, which neoliberal or radical stories tend to glide over. This posthuman vision of the person. not as autonomous. but as connected across multiple forms of matter provides a productive way forward for adult education more generally as it shows a different way of understanding community and the world.

7   More than Human and More Than Social Mutuality

It therefore follows that to recognise people living with dementia as part of communities we must be able to understand different non-humanistic ways of being. As people living with dementia see the world in non-humanistic ways, they move the emphasis from the individual self to systems of relations: not only amongst humans, but with the more than human world. Seen from this perspective, the community is not just formed of humans but of animals, birds, trees, insects, water, rocks, materials, machines, digital environments and so on, all with a part to play. Yet such a flat ontology, where no one aspect of the world is seen as more important than another, is quite difficult to attain after being acculturated in the West to see (a certain kind of) human as the top of the pinnacle: a human who is white, male, and well educated. Some people with dementia have no problem with disrupting this hierarchy, giving just as much credence and attention to the non-human as the human. This is generally seen as a negative symptom of their disease, but it could also be regarded as a form of freedom, placing them in the posthuman vanguard.

Such a breakdown of hierarchies of knowledge and of persons is fundamentally important in the move to decolonisation mentioned earlier, in which adult education should play a vital role. It is a feature of indigenous ways of knowing, for example: "recognising the ways in which land is alive, agentic, and relating through a plurality of 'voices' so different from our own" (Higgins & Madden, 2020, p. 294). This different perspective on the world opens up new possibilities, not just for people with dementia, but for all community members. It helps change visions from individuality, where education is seen as a personal investment and students as consumers, to sustainability where preserving a multiform community is what matters. Along with decolonisation sustainability must be central to remaking community life. This means that nothing should be carelessly wasted: including the potential of people living with dementia. Neal et al. (2019, p. 82) see community as 'a continuous act of social mutuality'. This mutuality should be extended to the more than human, with community more than a solely social form. Thus, one aspect of remaking community is to marry adult learning with literature and research that furthers this vision. Fertile examples include Bennett's (2010) work on vibrant matter, which sees all forms of matter as humming with shared vitality, or Alaimo's (2012) work on the transcorporeality of the human and the more than human. If community is to be remade it must be extended to all forms of matter and adult educators and researchers need to refresh and stimulate their ideas and practices. Adult education is already transdisciplinary and boundary breaking in its approach, but this can be taken much further combined with new forms of community engagement (see Taylor et al., 2021). Researching with and learning from people living with dementia has acted as a stimulus in this regard: they have been teachers as much as learners.

8   Hopes for the Future, Not Nostalgia for the Past

The heyday of adult education is often seen as in the past, a lost treasure, or a redundant field, depending on your perspective. Similarly, community is perceived as a bounded entity that 'is joined' or has been 'lost' or is 'lacking' (Wills, 2016). Trying to resurrect the past will inevitably result in disappointment. A different vision of community, which not only embraces all those humans placed on the margins, but all those forms of more than human matter which were hardly visible previously, ensures that adult education is future oriented and vital. Tett and Hamilton (2021) stress that there are hopeful signs for this future, highlighting the role of online learning in making connections that are unconfined by time and space; the role of movements like Black Lives Matter in bringing supressed voices to the fore and the significance of new partnerships across education, other professions, and civil society. This future orientation speaks to the inclusion of people living with dementia. One of the issues in working with people living with dementia is how far this should be a process of recouping memory and a past self? Many of the activities and processes in the field of dementia care are characterised by trying to help the person with dementia remember or employing nostalgic environments to give them comfort. In Quinn and Blandon (2020), we argue that to focus mainly on the past does not allow respect for the person living with dementia as they are now and neglects their present and future capabilities. We show how lifelong learning could play a key role in taking a positive and productive approach to living with dementia. Similarly, in thinking about what adult education is and might be, nostalgia can be a trap that is best avoided.

9   Interdependence: Remaking Community as a Material Process

The phrase 'remaking community life' under which these chapters are gathered recognises that this is a material process as well as a conceptual one, it is a doing. This accords with recent sociological debates about community (see Neal et al., 2019). For example, Studdert and Walkerdine (2016a, 2016b) suggest that there has been too much focus on what 'community is' and a lack of attention to 'how it works' (2016a, p. 617). As Neal et al. (2019, p. 72) argue:

This repositioning of community as process and practice, or as Ben Rogaly (2016, p. 660) puts it, community as 'a verb rather than community as a noun' pushes community away from being a geographically or socially bounded category of identity and axis of belonging towards being about a sociality of interdependent necessity.

People living with dementia bring this community interdependence into focus. They highlight what is necessary for themselves now, but also what may be necessary for any of us in the future given that one in six people over 80 develop dementia. What is done for and with them now is also for their networks (who are also potential learners) and for networks to come. The community is not static, it is perpetually being remade and learning plays a key role in this process as does dementia itself. Neal et al. (2019) demonstrate community as a 'doing' by studying how diverse people come together in leisure activities. Adult learning in all its forms is potentially a similar mechanism of community generation across boundaries and people living with dementia can play a significant role. In Quinn and Blandon (2020) for example, we show how children and people living with dementia can create intergenerational bonds by learning together. Adult learning for an interdependent community must be part of a network of services across health, care, arts, and leisure: connected, not acting in isolation. Many innovative practices already exist and are located imaginatively in multiple spaces including care homes, refuges, museums, or football grounds. However, they tend to be fragmented and subject to the whims of funders. In *Beyond Words* for example we found that family members found it impossible to negotiate the chaotic web of care services, let alone to trace what was available in terms of adult learning opportunities. Resourcing, planning, and mapping an interdependent lifelong learning is vital, however optimistic such a vision might be.

There are also pragmatic issues to face. For people living with dementia to take part in this 'doing' there are material needs that must be addressed too. In the UK dementia friendly guidelines have been produced by the Alzheimer's Society for sectors such as the arts and heritage, but not as yet for education; re-enforcing the idea that this is not a sphere where people living with dementia are considered participants. This is an omission that needs redressing: but general principles such as consulting with groups led by people living with dementia when designing provision, providing good information beforehand and good clear signage, quiet spaces to retreat and room for spontaneity in activities, help provide the steps that organisations need to follow to ensure that people living with dementia are not just included in learning, but that the provision is comfortable and safe for them.

10   Corporeal and Creative Andragogy

In terms of andragogy, both as adult education theory and didactics, research with people living with dementia helps to illustrate that bodies are an active part of learning, not just as shells for the mind but fundamentally imbricated in the process. In researching with women students, I argued for what I termed 'the corporeality of learning' (Quinn, 2004) stressing that we must understand learning as an embodied process. The pleasures and pains of the body help to shape what is learnt and how that happens, not just when considering disability issues. but for everyone. Researching with people with dementia highlights and accentuates this. One example might be the habit of roaming of wanting to move and not sit still which is characteristic of some people with dementia. In Quinn and Blandon (2020) this was visualised as a spider web process, a necessary movement that had its own logic and function. Expecting a static learning activity is not productive, instead flexibility and a different use of space must be employed. Seeing the learning environment in terms of multiple forms of relations and movements is a prerequisite for learning for people with dementia but is also key for learning overall. Thinking beyond words is a necessity when it comes to dementia, but it is also a productive quality for learning environments as Lees' work on silence in schools has helped to illustrate (2012). New information and new capacities may be transmitted and expressed through the body and not in words: respecting silence and attending to its meanings can be profound. The *Created out of Mind* programme funded by the Welcome Trust 2016–2018 included scientists, visual artists, musicians, broadcasters, clinicians and carers exploring understanding of dementia via science and the creative arts. Whilst not focusing on learning as such, it highlighted the significance of arts methods to foster engagement as a process of co-creativity (Zeilig et al., 2018). In remaking community, creativity cannot be hived off into discrete boxes, seen as a personal interest or the preserve only of those with special powers but as fundamental andragogic practice.

11   Conclusion

At the beginning of the chapter, I raised a number of questions: the extent to which people living with dementia are already active community members; how they free up non-humanistic ontologies and generate visions of more than human and more than social mutuality, which contribute to moves towards decolonisation; and finally, how they help to highlight hopes for the future, not nostalgia for the past, and usher in a more corporeal and creative andragogy.

The chapter provides positive answers to these questions and hopeful examples of how people living with dementia are remaking communities and understandings of what learning might be. However, this must be put beside the negative trends which intend to close down community rather than open it up. In Europe there are many examples of those wishing to use 'community' for reactionary ends, as a mode of reification and exclusion. Brexit is one illustration of how powerful such moves can be. Shifting focus from 'who belongs?' to 'what do we do together?' will not be easy but is essential. Learning, in formal or informal contexts already plays a key role in shaping culture, whether this is acknowledged or not, but efforts need to be made to support learning that works for mutuality not division. Bad lessons swirl around us, for example in social media, fostering hatred and misinformation: what MacKenzie et al. (2021) call 'dupery by design'. The role of adult learning as a site of resistance is an ever more urgent one, but the terms need to be rewritten to move beyond limited humanistic visions of what humans are and what they can do. As discussed in this chapter, people living with dementia are adult learners too and provide lenses through which community can be remade as more than human but also attentive to vulnerable human needs. It might be considered that given limited resources, focusing on people with dementia is a risky venture. On the contrary, ensuring that people living with dementia are considered and included in adult education is an investment not only in their present but in anyone's future. Moreover, as this chapter has illustrated, thinking through their role in remaking community life opens some key debates and visions.

References

Alaimo, S. (2012). States of suspension: Transcorporeality at sea. *Interdisciplinary Studies in Literature and Environment*, *19*(3), 476–493. https://doi.org/10.1093/isle/iss068

Alzheimer's Society. (2020, June 5). *Thousands of people with dementia dying or deteriorating – Not just from coronavirus as isolation takes its toll.* https://www.alzheimers.org.uk/news/2020-06-05/thousands-people-dementia-dying-or-deteriorating-not-just-coronavirus-isolation

Barad, K. (2007). *Meeting the universe halfway: Quantum physics and the entanglements of matter and meaning.* Duke University Press.

Bennett, J. (2010). *Vibrant matter.* Duke University Press.

Biesta, G. J. J. (2014). *The beautiful risk of education.* Paradigm Publishers.

Bottery, S., & Babalola, G. (2021, May 6). *Social care 360.* https://www.kingsfund.org.uk/publications/social-care-360/access

Braidotti, R. (2013). *The posthuman.* Polity Press.

Centenary Commission on Adult Education. (2019). *'A permanent national necessity …': Adult education and lifelong learning for 21st century Britain.* University of Nottingham. https://doi.org/10.17639/nott.7027

Cheng, S.-T., Chow, P. K., Song, Y.-Q., Yu, E. C. S., Chan, A. C. M., Lee, T. M. C., & Lam, J. H. M. (2014). Mental and physical activities delay cognitive decline in older persons with dementia. *The American Journal of Geriatric Psychiatry, 22*(1), 63–74. https://doi.org/10.1016/j.jagp.2013.01.060

Edwards, R. (2010). The end of lifelong learning: A post-human condition. *Studies in the Education of Adults, 42*(1), 5–17. https://doi.org/10.1080/02660830.2010.11661585

European Association for the Education of Adults. (2019). *Manifesto for adult learning in the 21st century: The power and joy of learning.* https://eaea.org/our-work/influencing-policy/manifesto-for-adult-learning-in-the-21st-century/

European Commission. (2021). *Green paper on ageing: Fostering solidarity and responsibility between generations.* https://op.europa.eu/s/uVIa

Higgins, M., & Madden, B. (2020). Refiguring presences in Kichwa-Lamista Territories: Natural-cultural (re)storying with indigenous place. In C. Taylor & A. Bayley (Eds.), *Posthumanism and higher education: Reimagining pedagogy, practice and research* (pp. 293–313). Palgrave Macmillan.

Jenkins, N. (2014). Dementia and the inter-embodied self. *Social Theory and Health, 12*(2), 125–137. https://doi.org/10.1057/sth.2013.24

Lees, H. (2012). *Silence in schools.* Institute of Education Press.

MacKenzie, A., Rose. S., & Bhatt, I. (Eds.). (2021). *The epistemology of deceit in a post-digital era: Dupery by design.* Springer.

Mazzei, L. A. (2016). Voice without a subject. *Cultural Studies – Cultural Methodologies, 16*(2), 151–161. https://doi.org/10.1177/1532708616636893

Mountain, G. A., & Craig, C. L. (2012). What should be in a self-management programme for people with early dementia? *Ageing & Mental Health, 16*(5), 576–583. https://doi.org/10.1080/13607863.2011.651430

Neal, S, Bennett, K., Cochrane, A., & Mohan, G. (2019). Community *and* conviviality? Informal social life in multicultural places. *Sociology, 53*(1), 69–86. https://doi.org/10.1177/0038038518763518

Office for National Statistics. (2020, July 3). *Deaths involving COVID-19 in the care sector, England and Wales: Deaths occurring up to 12 June 2020 and registered up to 20 June 2020 (provisional).* https://www.ons.gov.uk/peoplepopulationandcommunity/birthsdeathsandmarriages/deaths/articles/deathsinvolvingcovid19inthecaresectorenglandandwales/deathsoccurringupto12june2020andregisteredupto20june2020provisional

Quinn, J. (2004). The corporeality of learning: Women students and the body. In S. Ali, S. Benjamin, & M. Mauthner (Eds.), *The politics of gender and education* (pp. 174–188). Palgrave Macmillan.

Quinn, J. (2013). Theorising learning and nature: Posthuman possibilities and problems. *Gender and Education, 25*(6), 738–754. https://doi.org/10.1080/09540253.2013.831811

Quinn J., & Blandon, C. (2017). The potential for lifelong learning in dementia: A posthumanist exploration. *International Journal of Lifelong Education, 36*(5), 578–594. https://doi.org/10.1080/02601370.2017.1345994

Quinn, J., & Blandon, C. (2020). *Lifelong learning and dementia: A posthumanist perspective.* Palgrave.

Quinn, J., Blandon, C., & Batson, A. (2017). *Beyond words project report.* https://www.plymouth.ac.uk/uploads/production/document/path/9/9063/Beyond_Words-_Final_Report-12-6-2017.pdf

Quinn, J., Blandon, C., & Batson, A. (2021). Living beyond words: Post-human reflections on making music with post-verbal people. *Arts & Health, 13*(1), 73–86. https://doi.org/10.1080/17533015.2019.1652194

Richeson, N. E., Boyne, S., & Brady, E. M. (2007). Education for older adults with early-stage dementia: Health promotion for the mind, body, and spirit. *Educational Gerontology, 33*(9), 723–736. https://doi.org/10.1080/03601270701364438

Ringrose, J., Warfield, K., & Sarabadi, S. (2019). Introducing feminist posthumanisms/new materialisms & educational research: Response-able theory-practice-methodology. In J. Ringrose, K. Warfield, S. Zarabadi (Eds.), *Feminist posthumanisms, new materialisms and education* (pp. 1–15). Routledge.

Rogaly, B. (2016). 'Don't show the play at the football ground, nobody will come': The microsociality of co-produced research in an English provincial city. *The Sociological Review, 64*(4), 657–680. https://doi.org/10.1111/1467-954X.12371

Sharpe, C. (2016). *In the wake: On Blackness and being.* Duke University Press.

Stevenson, M., & Taylor, B. J. (2019). Involving individuals with dementia as co-researchers in analysis of findings from a qualitative study. *Dementia, 18*(2) 701–712. https://doi.org/10.1177/1471301217690904

Studdert, D., & Walkerdine, V. (2016a). Being in community: Re-visioning sociology. *The Sociological Review, 64*(4), 613–621. https://doi.org/10.1111/1467-954X.12429

Studdert, D., & Walkerdine, V. (2016b). *Re-thinking community research: Inter-relationality, communal being and communality.* Palgrave Macmillan.

Taylor, C., Quinn, J., & Franklin-Phipps, A. (2021). Rethinking research 'use'. Reframing impact, engagement and activism with feminist new materialist, posthumanist and postqualitative research. In K. Murris (Ed.), *Navigating the postqualitative, new materialist and critical posthumanist terrain across disciplines* (pp. 169–190). Routledge.

Tett, L., & Hamilton, M. (Eds.). (2021). *Resisting neo-liberalism in education.* Policy Press.

Wills, J. (2016). (Re)locating community in relationships: Questions for public policy. *The Sociological Review, 64*(4), 639–656. https://doi.org/10.1111/1467-954X.12431

World Health Organisation. (2020, September 21). *Dementia*. https://web.archive.org/web/20201228055259/https://www.who.int/news-room/fact-sheets/detail/dementia

Zeilig, H., West, J., & van der Byl Williams, M. (2018). Co-creativity: Possibilities for using the arts with people with a dementia. *Quality in Ageing and Older Adults, 19*(2), 135–145.

PART 3

Social Learning and Activism for Change

CHAPTER 8

Regaining Lost Community Knowledge
The Impact of Individual and Collective Biographical Work

Rozalia Ligus

Abstract

The aim of the *Migrating Biographies* project is to analyse and categorise meanings in the autobiographical narratives of the second, third and fourth generations in Poland of 're-emigrant families' from Bosnia, which reveal dynamic transformations of biographical identity. The chapter presents a synthetic summary of selected (re)interpretations, which illustrate changes that take place generationally and are the dynamic and ongoing processes that remake community through intergenerational identity conceptualisation which is a result of bottom up individual and community biographical work. The theoretical framework of the project is based on the interpretative-constructivist and critical humanist paradigm, where qualitative research strategy is meant to reinforce the inductive generation of empirical material. Data were collected through autobiographical narrative interviews and through oral history. Research participants (25 people) were recruited on the basis of their unique biographical characteristics as members of a 'post-Yugoslavian' family and their specific situation within their family systems, which made them the medium for intergenerational experience of repeated migration, from Galicia to Bosnia (end of 19th century) and from Bosnia back to Poland (in 1946).

Keywords

learning in/with a community – family and symbolic heritage – lost knowledge – individual/group biographical work – mnemonic experience – historical memory

1   Project Background

The post-1989 political transformation in Poland has strongly influenced the current shape of local communities while the formerly named 'Western and Northern Territories' which became part of Poland as a result of the Yalta and Potsdam conferences in 1945 and which were earlier dubbed the 'New' or 'Recovered' lands (Sakson, 2014, pp. 149–150; Strauchold, 2012), have slowly become a more distant historical category. However, the dynamics of localism in the Western and Northern Territories still differ significantly from other regions of the country, in great part due to the accumulation there of profound experiences of war and resettlement. The shaping of post-war Poland has had an enduring impact on the development of local/regional images of localism and/or collective memories, identities and learning processes within communities (Connerton, 2012; Halbwachs, 1992; Kurantowicz, 2007; Kurczewska, 2006; Słowińska, 2017; Sulima, 2001).

After three decades of transformation, involving the Polish western borderlands as well, the question "Where are you from?" still remains relevant, even though it no longer stigmatises, but rather enables the expression of personal identification (Ligus, 2009; Mach, 1998; Niedźwiedzki, 2000, 2003; Strauchold, 2012; Wylegała, 2014). The need to answer it may be one of the manifestations of both post-war individual and collective 'biographical work' and learning processes that occur within the community, performed by both individual residents and local communities as a whole (Kaźmierska, 1999; Kurantowicz, 2007; Schütze, 2012a, 2012b, 2012c). Ideas, values, symbols, collective images, collective beliefs, and opinions, accumulated over a long time, as well as commonly shared experience derived from various ideologies of the modern and postmodern worlds (Kurczewska, 2006) have become sources of 'local ideologies' used in constructing a social or/and cultural programme for the locals to learn in a community and re-shape their understanding of 21st century localism. Another concept of local community development was proposed by Lyn Tett (2010) using the Scottish example, in which she highlighted the importance of cultural continuity and intergenerational communication that is part of everyday collective life. In her work *Community education, learning and development* (2010), Tett described the development of a community as a "relay race", in which people consciously take from their predecessors and look forward to their descendants having a better understanding of both self and society, leading on to a more equitable life for everyone (Tett, 2010, p. 107).

In such dynamically reconstructed local history, scholars often use biographical research to reveal the processes of reconstruction and redefinition of both individual and collective identity. The concept of biographical work was introduced by Anslem Strauss (2012, pp. 515–527) and further elaborated by Fritz Schütze and others. Thus, "The person's orientational relationships to the present, personal history, and future are altered. The alteration of the person's relationship to herself or himself is accomplished by biographical work. This is the work of recalling, rehearsing, interpreting, and redefining, and this involves the communicative work of fellow interactants, especially significant others" (Riemann & Schütze, 1991, p. 339). Proponents of critical humanism also argue that biographical analysis needs to be extended to include and demonstrate the 'instability of the subject' (Plummer, 2019; Stanley, 2016). In their view, identity, belonging or embeddedness should not be presented as a state of being, but rather as a process. The idea of subject instability provides a useful route to recognising the situated, contextual and temporally grounded character of what it is to be a person over a life course, and how people are – and how they feel they become – changed over time (Stanley, 2016). Heather Blenkinshop (2016) argues that 21st-century critical humanism should move from the epistemological stance towards a more ontological approach centred on who 'they' (narrators) are and who 'the researcher' is, and how they are all situated. Moreover, critical humanism argues against the use of binary oppositions – such as public vs. private, insider vs. outsider – instead opting for a continuum of interrelationships with many points of interconnection that depend upon context, situation and who is telling and who is listening to the story. Researchers should thus not rely solely on what has been said or written, but take note of more physical, performative ways in which people tell the story of who they, things, events and other people are (Blenkinshop, 2016, p. 131).

The case of Lower Silesian families, when compared with those from other regions in Poland, is quite special. The inhabitants of Lower Silesia, the region which was both geographically and historically part of the (former) 'Western and Norther Territories', from the moment of their settlement (around 1945) have been (re)constructing their regional identity through novel interpretations of their heritage and the analysis of their own cultural resources, conducted both by individuals and by collective entities (Kuszyk, 2019). One of the focal points or 'centres' of local knowledge is the intergenerational narrative being told on a daily basis in families, as well as within formal and informal local collectives (Tett, 2010). Paul Thompson, who is considered one of the pioneer scholars of intergenerational narratives within families, pointed out the power and meaning of family events and casual information exchanged in a natural and spontaneous way within the space of everyday family life (Thompson, 2007, p. 13). Such information is revealed through life stories told by narrators who not only refer to the events they remember, nor interweave their own experience with the story, but who in their narratives also include stories which have been passed down for generations within their families.

Michał Kaczmarek (2006), who focuses on peasant narratives called this technique mnemonic experience. Regardless of the sources of knowledge revealed by the narrative subject, their narrative, and their past experience – both direct and mediated through oral or written text – is transformed into a mnemonic experience. In practice, this means that knowledge becomes part of memory knowledge, transformed into a narrative or text, into a form of expression in which the narrative subject *knows that* because they *remember that*, without needing to know the source of information or episode they retrieve from their memory (Kaczmarek, 2006, p. 6). Biographical researchers should thus not be surprised that life stories they collect include episodes that their narrators could not have possibly remembered as children, as well as episodes that predated the narrators altogether.

According to Thompson, the act of telling one's life story is necessarily an intergenerational narrative. What other generations receive as a story has been retrieved and selected from the vast repertoires of family recollections and mnemonic experiences of previous generations, and as such, it is meaningful and impactful on the ongoing process of identity construction by the present family members. Individual life stories reveal meanings that have been ascribed within the family to selected events and those that have become an important symbolic heritage passed down the generations. Because of the density and depth of narrative threads, meanings and interpretations involved in family members' life stories, Thompson suggested that researchers should ask two crucial questions: the first question, as in the narrative interview designed by Schütze (2012a), relates to processual structures identifiable in the life story being told, while the second question explores the scope and content of the intergenerational narrative within the narrators' family, as well as individual meanings ascribed to them by the narrative subject (Thompson, 2007, p. 13).

2 Research Motivation and Participants

Migrating Biographies in the Process of Retrieving Lost Community Knowledge – Identity Reconstruction by the Descendants of Re-emigrants from Bosnia in the 21st Century is an ongoing project initiated in 2017 in the city of Bolesławiec and its surrounding area (Poland, Lower Silesia, approx. 60 km from Wroclaw). In 2007, post-Yugoslavian families started to become more vocal in the public space, taking as their point of reference the 19th-century migration of their families from Galicia – part of partitioned Poland under Austrian rule – to Bosnia, and their subsequent (1946) re-settlement into the Western Territories of Poland (Drljača´, 1997; Lis, 2016; Ligus, 2019, 2020; Strauchold, 2016; Strauchold & Nowosielska-Sobel, 2007). In the descendants' narratives both of these pivotal moments are presented as a repeated exodus, experienced by the same members of their families twice over a period of fifty years, which prompts the descendants to start biographical inquiries into their own ambiguous identity (Ligus, 2019) and efforts to regain lost community knowledge (Ligus, 2020).

This research was motivated by the identity decisions of a group of inhabitants of the region of Lower Silesia in Poland, and their 2018 identification as *"We, the Poles from Yugoslavia"*. My encounters with 'post-Yugoslavian' family members were initiated through a conversation with a woman who introduced herself as "a Polish woman from Yugoslavia". Such self-representation offered by Weronika both surprised and intrigued me. I asked whether she had been born in former Yugoslavia and about her present age and she replied that she was 22 and had never visited Yugoslavia. Indeed, she was born a year after the collapse of the Yugoslavian state (1995). Based on this information, I was even more intrigued by her labelling herself as a "Polish woman from Yugoslavia". Following Charles Tilly (2000) and the research findings presented by Blenkinsop (2016, pp. 121–132), I assumed that Weronika's experience was probably firmly rooted in her family history and the intergenerational transmission of mnemonic experience (Kaczmarek, 2006, pp. 3–22). In the generational repertoire of events, there will be stories that the narrators learned, interpreted, and included in their own life stories. It is important to note that the mnemonic experience seems to radically impact the life stories depending on the group, individual interpretation, the context of storytelling and the social context within which it occurs, as well as on the generation.

3   Research Methodology

The theoretical framework of the *Migrating Biographies* project is based on the interpretative-constructivist and critical humanist paradigm, where qualitative research strategy is meant to reinforce the inductive generation of empirical material. Data were collected in autobiographical narrative interviews (Schütze, 2012a, pp. 141–278) since life stories include information on the biographical processes of learning, predicated on the individual, reflexive structuring of experience, knowledge, and skills, along with the biographical formation of bonds and social processes, collective knowledge, and practices.

Research participants were recruited based on their biographical, unique characteristics of being part of a 'post-Yugoslavian' family and their specific situation within their family systems, which made them the medium for intergenerational experience of repeated migration (from Galicia to Bosnia, from Bosnia back to Poland). The *Migrating Biographies* project is based on 25 narrative interviews conducted between March 2017 and November 2018.

The aim of the *Migrating Biographies* project is to analyse meanings included in the autobiographical narratives of the second, third and fourth generation of 're-emigrant families' from Bosnia, which reveal dynamic transformations of biographical identity. The concept of biographical identity developed by Schütz (1976) and Strauss (2005), emphasises the processual and transformative nature of personal identity for every human being that has its own way of being. Biographical identity is constituted through subjective experience gathered in the social space (Schütze, 2012a; Strauss, 2012.) but goes beyond the process of traditional socialisation. It refers to the whole-life process of constructing and interpreting the self-image. It is a continuum, in which the present is formed by the past, but also includes the project of the future (Clandinin & Connelly, 2000). One of the research questions that focused on the motives and inspirations for re-making community life asks about the transformation processes which have influenced both the individual process of identity-constitution within the community and the learning processes in the background.

I present below the analysis of two interviews that I consider to be representative of two successive generations. The narrative offered by Anatol (the interview was conducted on November 15, 2018 in Boleslawiec), seems representative of the oldest living 're-emigrants', who came to the Western Territories as children, traveling with their parents and often also their grandparents. At the time of his arrival in the Western Territories, Anatol was 9 years old. The interview with Anna, a representative of the younger generation, was conducted on March 13, 2018 in Wrocław. At the time of the interview, Anna was 55 years old. She is the daughter of Agata, aged 85, who at the age of 12 resettled to the Boleslawiec area with her parents.

Based on these two carefully selected narratives, we can identify generational patterns of personal identity reconstruction. The analysis of the collected narratives shows how identity and cultural resources (historical, social, cultural, communicative memory) are reconstructed. These resources are different for each generation, but they constitute the basic source of reflection on the continuity of one's own identity against the background of family history and local history.

4   Anatol's Narrative

Anatol (81) is an active member of the Re-emigrant Association. His story begins with a manifesto, which serves as a preamble to the overall interview:

> Extract 1
> Well yes, you have to talk, you have to talk about this, because (.) they don't know anything about it, that there were such and such and such people ... like my grandfather, others too. This was our Galicia, there were many, many are, many were in the Balkans. Because their numbers, seventeen

thousand of them returned here. They returned, because of this land, the so-called 'recovered' land. Following the Potsdam deal we got, instead of the one in the east, we got this. And our people come from there, from that Galicia. In the beginning of this (.) 20th century. (Interview An/81/4, lines 21–27)[1]

The first part of the preamble in Anatol's interview is only seven lines long and presents a non-fictional narrative, which the narrator begins with an emotionally saturated call: "Well, yes, you have to talk, you have to talk about it, because ... they don't know anything about it, that there were such and such and such people [...]" The narrator distances himself from the post-war political division of Europe, which is evidenced by such expressions as "this land, the so-called 'recovered' land we got, instead of the one in the east, we got this". In the preamble, the narrator emphasises the need to share the 19th-century history of migration of Poles living in the Podkarpacie region (then the Galician partition), to preserve their memory and the obligation to provide information about their experiences. It is not only about factual or historical truth, but about specific experiences which the folk literature dubs 'eternal truth' or 'age-old truth', which lasts continuously, which is the truth that was, is and will be relevant in the "past, present and tomorrow" (see Kaczmarek, 2006, pp. 6–12). Just like the 'age-old truth' is the condition of existence of the world being described, Anatol's preamble seems to set the conditions for the existence of memory about Poles in Bosnia (Interview An/81/4, lines 21–27).

Anatol seems to tie his own personal biography with the biography of his ancestors by adding one short expression: "my **grandfather**, others too .... This **was our Galicia**, there were many, many are, many were in **the Balkans**. Because their numbers, seventeen thousand of them **returned** here ... They returned, because of this land, the so-called '**recovered**' land". Combining present tense with past tense in such a short narrative piece, especially the combinations of was/many are/many were, next to the toponyms of Galicia/the Balkans, reflects the narrator's personal situatedness within both the milieu and in history (Czyżewski, 2016; Kaźmierska, 2008; Piotrowski, 2016). It may also be evidence of the narrator's rich mnemonic experience and its frequent use in his narratives.

It is also interesting that the narrator used the rhetorical device of reiterating an expression, with an element of inversion: "returned here ... They returned (PL. "wrócili tu"/"Tu wrócili"). By using the grammatical form of 3rd person plural in "[They] returned ..." he situated himself in an opposition, at a distance from the experience of his parents and grandparents. Even though Anatol participated in the collective 'return' as a nine-year-old child, and we may have expected that he perceived himself as an active subject of the event, he chooses not to identify with it, not identify himself as part of the group of re-emigrants from Bosnia 'returning' to their ideological and not private homeland (Ossowski, 1967, p. 210). For Anatol and his generation, i.e., children born in Bosnia, the arrival in 1946 in the 'Western Territories' was in no way a return. Only their parents and their grandparents thought that they were 'returning' to their homeland, even though no one could have associated the Western Territories with the landscape of the private homeland they remembered, as it was located in the Podkarpacie (Subcarpathia) region, which they had left.

The sentence "they returned, because of this land, the so-called 'recovered' land" expresses doubts and skepticism ("so-called"). In fact, something that was a promise, a dream come true, an expectation, which meant months of organisation and logistical efforts, did not become a source of joy but rather a source of uncertainty for those who returned. Anatol included himself as sharing the experience of his parents and grandparents, but also the collective national experience. The transition we see in Anatol's statement – from 'They' to 'We' ("we got, we noticed, they made us believe"), may testify to the act of 'solidarity' with the experience of disillusionment of the generation older than oneself, who, faithful for years to their symbolic and imagined homeland, 'return' to the land which in no way resembles either the memories/imaginings of the Galician land preserved for three generations, or the familiar Bosnian land. It could also be a sign of resignation, surrender and acceptance, together with the parents, of this 'substitute' land with all material goods that came with it. Distancing oneself from the modernist architecture of the city, along with German inscriptions on the shops (Wrocław, Bolesławiec) increased the feeling of alienation, which could not be overshadowed by appreciation of the advantages of civilisation.

> Extract 2
> Everyone looked at these buildings, at these houses. It was wonderful and so different from what they had left there ... in faraway Kunowa [village], in faraway Bosnia. Everything was completely different here, completely different. They did not believe that it was theirs, that it would be theirs. Because ... because they were afraid that ... it was too good, too great, too serious, too expensive to be given to them. After all, you don't get anything for free. Although they left their farms there and on that basis they could settle here. (Interview An/81/4, lines 123–128)

> Extract 3
> Eeee iii ... what we noticed. They made us believe that everything that was here was Polish and it was ours for good. We looked at it, at it ... The

city was empty, the inscriptions written in Schwabacher … We couldn't read it they were German inscriptions. It was all sooo beautiful. The city was wonderful. Some people saw such a big city as Bolesławiec for the first time. (Interview An/81/4 115–119)

Anatol's distance from the experience of return is, in the context of his natural history (process), fully justified. It was "they" (grandparents, parents, their peers) who returned to their country of origin (Poland), which they had left, but not Anatol. The 'returns' of Anatol (and his peers), which he tells about later in the narrative, have a completely opposite direction and lead from Poland to Bosnia. Whenever Anatol returns it is "back to our Bosnia", his private homeland, to which he feels "emotionally attached" as the place of his birth and his first consciously remembered experiences

Extract 4
In 1962, I came to visit that area [Bosnia – RL] again☺. Of course, it was completely different, a completely different situation … and … Naszyce … But it was there that I first saw electricity, the first time I was taken to the cinema, the first time I went to the cinema. It was all firsts … Just like I saw the sun for the first time there, I saw everything for the first time … and the city. Ayyyyy. So, I remember it fondly, I remember those times fondly, because … because … it somehow stayed in me … it stayed in my memory … (Interview An/81/4, lines 172–177)

In the second part of the preamble (lines 28–72), the narrator, using historical memory, enters the role of a chronicler or a historian. He introduces meta-narrative comments and remarks. The specificity of the chronicle-style fragments is, once again, the narrator's use of mnemonic experience, i.e., his own and others' historical memories, which can be oral or written down, which allows him to use a relatively objective historical memory, which is characteristic of historiography, including chronicles, but also autobiographical prose (Kaczmarek, 2006). Thus, Anatol assumes the role of a chronicler, but also exposes himself as representative of the generation whose duty it is to proclaim the 'age-old truth', that is, to cultivate the memory of the ancestors.

5 Anna's Narrative

At the time of the interview, Anna was 55 years old. She represents a generation younger than Anatol and can be considered to symbolically constitute the generation of his children. Anna acquires knowledge about the place where her ancestors lived in various ways. She collects publications – mostly, these are memoirs, diaries and studies written by the inhabitants of Bolesławiec, Nowogrodziec, Ocice (Ligus, 2020). She collects family documents, photographs, and talks to her mother (she was 83 in 2018 and had come to Lower Silesia as a 12-year-old child). Anna wants to learn more about the birthplaces of three generations of her ancestors who came to Bosnia at the turn of the 20th century from Galicia.

Anna does not explicitly say what prompted her ten years ago to focus on learning about her family history, but in the structure of her narrative there is an accumulation of 'vignettes', images retained in memory, including, in large part, sensory memory (Modrak, 2016), which provide Anna with arguments to support her personal process of gathering "evidence" and "maturing" to begin challenging her identity and imbuing it with knowledge of her family history – which she had perceived as "irretrievably lost" (Interview A/55/1, lines 25–26). Her life story and identity dilemmas start to gain meaning only in connection with the re-invoked memories of her relatives, the local community, regular trips to Bosnia, and collaboration with the Association of Bosnian Reemigrants and their Descendants and Friends.

For Anna, one of the clues that was meaningful in terms of reconstructing knowledge about herself and her family, was the language used by her parents and grandparents. When she was a child, many words seemed strange (*tamo, trajno, majstor, zdrawo*), and it was only in her adult life, when she arrived in Bosnia for the first time, that these previously foreign-sounding words acquired meaning and triggered a stream of associations stored in the recesses of her childhood memory. On her first visit to Bosnia, the intergenerational transmission of Serbian and Croatian – became meaningful. Anna's narrative structure focuses on references to earlier stages of her life, cataloguing the 'evidence' for what she perceives as a lost part of her identity. This way of narrating may indicate that the narrator has already undertaken biographical work. This 'evidence'-seeking is done by looking for witnesses whom Anna considers to be a "living bridge" between the pre-1946 history and the present.

> Extract 5
> So, we knew that Dragan J., because that was the neighbour's name, that he was still alive, was eighty something and that he was a person … we could go to and learn something more from him. (Interview A/55/1, lines 162–166)

It was about impressions, conversations, (self)observations, childhood memories, sounds, smells, chance encounters, including the description of the place where the grandparents' house used to be:

Extract 6
Dragan showed us more or less where my parents' house was. We got to the place where you could expect that there had been a house, because there were fruit trees there, old apple trees were there, grape vines, pear tree just like mum told us. I will tell you frankly that I was moved. (Interview A/55/1, lines 383–387)

Following Anna's narrative, one can trace a 'checklist' in which the basic question the narrator asked is: "What do I have more of in me – Poland or Bosnia?" On the other hand, Anna does not challenge her Polish origin, but on a symbolic level she identifies with the culture contributed by her grandmother from Bosnia and her aunts from Sarajevo. The biographical work, which consists of Anna's (re)constructing and (de)constructing her identity, is a process of applying known and unknown fragments from her family's life to herself and repeatedly trying to check their conformity to the 'pattern' based on biographical, social and collective memory (Kaźmierska, 2008). She tells how she started "recovering from memory" fragments of recollections, including imaginary visions of the space she then had not known personally, but which she associated with the magical world of her aunts from Sarajevo. The language of the passage, repetitions and pauses, testify to a trajectory experience (Schütze, 2012b) that, through continuous biographical work, assuages a sense of guilt.

6 Conclusions – Remaking Community Through Intergenerational Identity

The narratives of Anatol are selected examples of patterns of behaviour adopted by the descendants of families coming from Yugoslavia individually or collectively, depending on the knowledge accumulated within the family. These specific ways of acting and accumulating knowledge about themselves against the background of family experience is akin to gaining scientific knowledge, which also includes documenting family histories – the practice which following 2000 became evident in many places in the Bolesławiec area, where 'hearths' of post-Yugoslavian families still remain (Ligus, 2020).

Below, I present a synthetic summary of selected (re)interpretations, which illustrate, on the one hand, the durability and strength of intergenerational transmission, and on the other hand, the ability to "detach" oneself from generational burdens and to reconstruct one's identity within the perspective of the future. Changes in attitudes take place generationally, from the most nostalgic and rooted in mnemonic experience and historical memory (Assman, 2015), through those of younger generation, who reflectively approach their cultural resources, to those of the youngest, drawing on cultural and communicative memory with an awareness of their origin and orientation towards future.[2]

Generation I "We are people with two hearts" – the oldest generation, aged 80 and older, who came to the Western Territories as children, with their parents and grandparents. In their interviews there is a sense of losing places associated with a happy though "barefoot childhood". In 2011 they set up the *Association of Re-Emigrants from Bosnia, their Descendants and Friends* in Bolesławiec. The questions they keep asking themselves are: Who am I to others? Who were my parents and grandparents? Why do they call us Serbs? – after all, we have always been Poles.

Generation II "What do I have more in me? Poland or Bosnia?" – representatives of the group aged 50 and older, are a rather enthusiastic group focusing on tracking the past with a positive attitude towards any evidence of double identity in themselves. They glorify experiences of their parents and grandparents, but not to the same extent as the generation older than them. They reinforce their research and analysis intuitively with sensory memory, so as not to miss any clues from the past. However, they also face dilemmas and tend to ask the following questions: Who am I for myself? How can I benefit from my cultural resources?

Generation III "I know who I am and who my ancestors were" – representatives of the group aged 30 and older, reconstruct their identities through gathering knowledge of their families' places of origin and combine imagination with strong empathy towards their ancestors' experiences. "I am a strong woman because my grandmother came from Serbia" (Ewa). Ewa's statement is constructed partly on the basis of media coverage documenting the strength of Serbian women during the Balkan war in the 1990s.

Generation IV "I am a Polish woman from Yugoslavia" – people aged 20 and older, – in whom the present and the past stand side by side. On the one hand, they are aware of the past, but their thinking is firmly oriented towards the future. They have adapted stories they have heard many times and the knowledge they have gained from them. They accept diversity of cultural resources and occasionally include and celebrate the tradition in which their origins have been documented in the history of their own lives.

Thus, the continuous process of individual and collective identity formation demonstrates, among others, the strong heterogeneity of the social fabric formed by the local communities of the Lower Silesia region. Individual and collective experience in intergenerational transmission is constantly reinterpreted, providing a rich source of knowledge, often recovered in the process of social dialogue and informal learning.

Notes

1 The excerpts provided in this article include transcription markers, such as italics, fragments in bold which denote parts stressed by the narrator, ☺ for laughter, (.) or (.3.) for pauses and their duration in seconds.
2 Partial results of this study were presented at two international conferences, on May 21, 2021 as "Identity in Flux. Past, Presents and Future of Migrant Communities across Europe", UCD Humanities Institute Dublin, Irish Research Council, Irish Center for National Studies, Ireland and on August 31, 2021 at the Cultural Heritage for Social Responsibility: Bridging Universities and Communities conference (dsw.edu.pl).

References

Assman, J. (2015). *Pamięć kulturowa. Pismo, zapamiętywanie i polityczna tożsamość w cywilizacjach starożytnych*. Wydawnictwo UW.
Blenkinsop, H. (2016). Forgotten memories? Silence, reason, truth and the carnival. In L. Stanley (Ed.), *Documents of life revisited: Narrative and biographical methodology for a 21st century critical humanism* (pp. 121–132). Routledge.
Clandinin, D. J., & Connelly F. M. (2000). *Narrative inquiry: Experience and story in qualitative research*. Jossey-Bass.
Connerton, P. (2012). *Jak społeczeństwa pamiętają* (M. Napiórkowski, Trans.). Wydawnictwo UW.
Czyżewski, M. (2016). Generalne kierunki opracowania, wymiary analityczne. In R. Dopierała & K. Waniek (Eds.), *Biografia i wojna: Metoda biograficzna w badaniu procesów społecznych*. Wybór Tekstów (pp. 73–80). Wydawnictwo UŁ.
Drljača, D. (1997). *Między Bośnią, Bukowiną, Serbią i Polską*. Polskie Towarzystwo Ludoznawcze.
Halbwachs, M. (1992). *On collective memory* (L. A. Coser, Ed. & Trans.). University of Chicago Press.
Kaczmarek, M. (2006). Genologia pamięci: Od wspomnienia prostego do wspomnienia literackiego (z problemów mnemologii Vicenza). *Literatura ludowa, 2*(50), 3–22.
Kaźmierska, K. (1999). *Doświadczenia wojenne Polaków a kształtowanie tożsamości etnicznej: Analiza narracji kresowych*. Wydawnictwo IFiS PAN.
Kaźmierska, K. (2008). *Biografia i pamięć*. NOMOS.
Kurantowicz, E. (2007). *O uczących się społecznościach*. Wydawnictwo Naukowe DSW.
Kurczewska, J. (2006). Robocze ideologie lokalności. Stare i nowe schematy. In J. Kurczewska (Ed.), *Oblicza lokalności. Tradycja i współczesność* (pp. 88–129). Wydawnictwo IFiS PAN.
Kuszyk, K. (2019). *Poniemieckie*. Wydawnictwo Czarne.

Ligus, R. (2009). *Biograficzna tożsamość nauczycieli. Historie z pogranicza*. Wydawnictwo Naukowe DSW.

Ligus, R. (2019). "We are the Poles from former Yugoslavia": Transformation processes shifted in time – the biographical perspective. *Qualitative Sociology Review, 15*(4), 96–111. https://doi.org/10.18778/1733-8077.15.4.05

Ligus, R. (2020). Retrieving lost knowledge: Researcher, 'native researchers' and shifts in participatory action research. *Kultura i Edukacja, 2*, 15–37. https://doi.org/10.15804/kie.2020.02.02

Lis, T. J. (2016). *Z Bośni do Polski*. Bolesławiecki Ośrodek Kultury.

Mach, Z. (1998). *Niechciane miasta*. Universitas.

Modrak, B. (2016). *Pamięć sensoryczna, czyli myśleć ciałem. Doskonalenie zasobów pamięci zmysłowej*. Wydawnictwo Difin.

Niedźwiedzki, D. (2000). *Odzyskiwanie miasta: Władza i tożsamość społeczna*. Universitas.

Niedźwiedzki, D. (2003). *Władza-tożsamość-zmiana społeczna*. Universitas.

Ossowski, S. (1967). *Dzieła: t. 3. Z zagadnień psychologii społecznej*. PWN.

Piotrowski, A. (2016). Wprowadzenie do projektu: Biografia a tożsamość narodowa. In R. Dopierała & K. Waniek (Eds.), *Biografia i wojna: Metoda biograficzna w badaniu procesów społecznych. Wybór tekstów* (pp. 43–52). Wydawnictwo Uniwersytetu Łódzkiego.

Plummer, K. (2019). *Narrative power: The struggle for human value*. Polity Press.

Riemann, G., & Schütze, F. (1991). "Trajectory" as a basic theoretical concept for analyzing suffering and disorderly social processes. In D. R. Maines (Ed.), *Social organization and social process: Essays in honor of Anselm Strauss* (pp. 333–357). De Gruyter.

Sakson, A. (2014). Socjologia pogranicza społeczności postmigracyjnych Ziem Zachodnich i Północnych Polski. Kilka uwag o jej uprawianiu. In M. Zielińska & B. Trzop (Eds.), *Transgraniczność w perspektywie socjologicznej: Pogranicza i centra współczesnej Europy* (pp. 149–156). Lubuskie Towarzystwo Naukowe.

Schütz, A. (1976). Collected papers II. In A. Brodersen (Ed.), *Studies in social theory* (Photomechanical reprint). Martinus Nijhoff.

Schütze, F. (2012a). Analiza biograficzna ugruntowana empirycznie w autobiograficznym wywiadzie narracyjnym. Jak analizować autobiograficzne wywiady narracyjne. In K. Kaźmierska (Ed.), *Metoda biograficzna w socjologii: Antologia tekstów* (pp. 141–278). Nomos.

Schütze, F. (2012b). Trajektorie cierpienia jako przedmiot badań socjologii interpretatywnej. In K. Kaźmierska (Ed.), *Metoda biograficzna w socjologii: Antologia tekstów* (pp. 415–458). Nomos.

Schütze, F. (2012c). Koncepcja świata społecznego w symbolicznym interakcjonizmie oraz organizacja wiedzy w nowoczesnych złożonych społeczeństwach. In K. Kaźmierska (Ed.), *Metoda biograficzna w socjologii. Antologia tekstów* (pp. 489–514). Nomos.

Słowińska, S. (2017). *Sensy oddolnych inicjatyw kulturalnych w interpretacji ich realizatorów*. Oficyna Wydawnicza Uniwersytetu Zielonogórskiego.

Stanley, L. (2016). Introduction: Documents of life and critical humanism in a narrative and biographical frame. In L. Stanley (Ed.), *Documents of life revisited: Narrative and biographical methodology for a 21st Century critical humanism* (pp. 3–16). Routledge.

Strauchold, G., & Nowosielska-Sobel, J. (2007). *Dolnoślązacy?: Kształtowanie tożsamości mieszkańców Dolnego Śląska po II wojnie światowej*. Oficyna Wydawnicza ATUT – Wrocławskie Wydawnictwo Oświatowe.

Strauchold, G. (2012). Jest dobrze, będzie jeszcze lepiej. Nowe granice zachodnie polski w dyskursie publicystyczno-naukowym lat 40. XX wieku. *Rocznik Lubuski, 38*(1), 39–59.

Strauchold, G. (2016). *Wydzierając puszczy ziemię ... Wspomnienia bolesławieckich reemigrantów z Jugosławii*. Muzeum Ceramiki w Bolesławcu.

Strauss, A. (2005). *Mirrors and masks: The search for identity*. Transaction Publishers.

Strauss, A. (2012). Praca biograficzna i jej powiązania (intersections). In K. Kaźmierska (Ed.), *Metoda biograficzna w socjologii. Antologia tekstów* (pp. 517–527). Nomos.

Sulima, R. (2001). *Głosy tradycji*. Wydawnictwo DiG.

Tett, L. (2010). *Community education, learning and development*. Dunedin.

Thompson, P. (2007). Family myth, models, and denials in the shaping of individual life paths. In D. Bertaux & P. Thompson (Eds.), *Between generations: Family models, myths and memories* (pp. 13–38). Transaction Publishers.

Tilly, C. (2000). How do relations store histories? *Annual Review of Sociology, 26*(1), 721–723. https://doi.org/10.1146/annurev.soc.26.1.721

Wylegała, A. (2014). *Przesiedlenia a pamięć. Studium (nie)pamięci społecznej na przykładzie ukraińskiej Galicji i polskich "Ziem Odzyskanych"*. Wydawnictwo Naukowe Uniwersytetu Mikołaja Kopernika.

CHAPTER 9

Social Learning and Building Solidarity

Learning in the Context of a Natural Disaster

Angela Pilch Ortega

Abstract

Drawing on an empirical study conducted in Juchitán de Zaragoza, Mexico, which focused on the impacts of a strong earthquake in this region, this paper explores opportunities for social learning in combination with distribution conflicts, social vulnerability, and solidarity building. The research findings reveal that this natural disaster elicited social learning processes and the development of strategies for dealing with the related extraordinary circumstances. The paper highlights opportunities and risks for such social learning processes and gives a brief insight into the research findings.

Keywords

natural disaster – community learning – social learning – social vulnerability – solidarity building – sociographicity

1   Introduction

The Mexican region of Istmo de Tehuantepec was impacted by a strong earthquake in September of 2017 that destroyed the greater part of the infrastructure, including schools, hospitals, governmental and residential buildings. Moreover, many fatalities occurred. As a result not only of the numerous aftershocks as well as a hurricane that crossed the region just after the earthquake, the regional population was exposed to a high level of social insecurity and existential vulnerability that resulted in a violent struggle for survival, accompanied by bloodshed and killing, with deep impacts on the functioning of the community. Drawing on an empirical study conducted in this region six months after the earthquake, the paper explores the question of the transformative potential that lies in social crises as well as consequences that such crises bring for social relationships and civil society. Research findings show that the natural disaster is being collectively framed as an experience of abandonment by the government, which did not attend to the population's needs and misappropriated international relief deliveries. Even before this event, the region was affected by a high level of social inequality and poverty, a lack of social support mechanisms, few opportunities for education and employment, political corruption, and a brutal conflict between various drug cartels. In light of the natural disaster, social problems became more evident than before, raising the question of how to rebuild social life and society through collective local effort.

On a collective level, Bourdieu (in Overden, 2000) for instance notes the transformative potential of social crises, even if his theory of habitus tends to overemphasise the perpetuation of social structures. He suggests that social crises have the potential to bring doxic beliefs into question because such beliefs then enter our awareness; if expectations and objective possibilities fail to fit, social agents experience a gap in their perception of self-evident truth (see Bourdieu, 1977, p. 169). The research findings reveal that the experiences connected with the earthquake initiated collective reflection processes in relation to social dynamics and collaborative practices in which social problems are addressed. Dimbath and Heinlein (2020) mention in this context that natural disasters may provoke social upheavals that call for a reorganisation of social structures. Communal life and societal arrangements need to be reflected upon and re-structured. The question of how communities deal with a natural disaster and its impacts gives insights into social learning processes in which challenges and problems are addressed.

Against this backdrop the paper highlights the opportunities and risks for such social learning processes within a situation determined by distribution inequality, social vulnerability, and solidarity building. Additionally, the paper offers some theoretical considerations surrounding the question of how to explore the complex interrelationship between social structures and subjects in relation to social learning. In this context the focus lies on the capacity of humans to critically reflect on and to challenge the scope conditions of individual and shared life circumstances and inherent power regimes (see Pilch Ortega, 2018). In particular, the article will address the role of social learning and emancipatory practise for dealing with the impacts of the natural disaster. Furthermore, I will give a brief insight into the research findings and reflections on social and community learning processes under precarious living conditions.

2 Opportunities for Social Learning in the Light of a Natural Disaster – An Empirical Study

The empirical study entitled *¡Alerta sísmica! Biographical perspectives on narrative and mediatized modes of memorization of a natural disaster,* that I refer to in this article focuses on the earthquake which happened in Mexico 2017 and the question of how social actors and communities frame and integrate this natural disaster biographically. Furthermore, the research includes the impacts of the natural disaster on the dynamics of social life and strategies for dealing with the related exceptional circumstances. As was already mentioned, the state of Oaxaca in Mexico, in particular the region of Istmo de Tehuantepec, was affected by a strong earthquake in the year 2017. According to the Mexican government the earthquake caused 98 deaths in this region along with damage to the majority of the infrastructure, mainly in Juchitán de Zaragoza, but also in other settlements in this region. In the course of the field investigation that took place six months after the earthquake, mainly in Juchitán, the signs of damage were still clearly visible (see Figures 9.1–9.4). Families who lost their homes were still living in emergency shelters (see Figure 9.5), and due to the fact that the school building suffered serious damage, teachers were providing their lessons outdoors in temperatures reaching 40 degrees. Neither the town hall nor the main marketplace had been reconstructed six months after the earthquake took place, even though the market women relocated their commercial activity to the central park of the town (see Figure 9.6). We can suppose that the historical buildings will be pulled down due to the extensive damage they suffered – this will change the cityscape in a fundamental way.

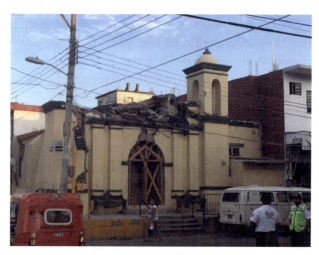

FIGURE 9.1   A church in the centre of Juchitán (© Pilch Ortega, 2017)

FIGURE 9.2   The town hall of the city (© Pilch Ortega, 2017)

FIGURE 9.3   A residential building (© Pilch Ortega, 2017)

The interviewees mainly articulated the precarious social and economic conditions that were accompanied by a high level of social insecurity and vulnerability. Living costs increased due to the natural disaster, the regional economy for the most part broke down and there were few possibilities for employment. The social situation also became more strained due to political corruption in the area and a bloody war between drug cartels. Considering the significant damage and the far-reaching consequences that the earthquake had on the daily life of the population, a return to 'normality' seems to involve

FIGURE 9.4   A residential building (© Pilch Ortega, 2017)

FIGURE 9.5   Emergency shelters (© Pilch Ortega, 2017)

FIGURE 9.6   Temporary marketplace in Juchitán (© Pilch Ortega, 2017)

immense challenges. Against this backdrop, the research interest focuses on social learning processes which seek to address the problems and challenges specifically caused by the natural disaster. The deep impacts on the social structure and infrastructure call for strategies for dealing with this extreme situation in order to rebuild social life.

2.1 Capturing Social Learning and Emancipatory Practice

If we focus on social learning and how it tries to deal with natural disasters among precarious life circumstances, we have to pay specific attention to the complex interplay between social dynamics and subjects. This leads us to the question of how collective learning processes that are related to biography, communities and societies can be theoretically framed. Common theories of the dialectic relationship between structures and subjects (i.e., the critique) overemphasise either the structural or the individual perspective and may overlook the importance of collective modes of learning. In this context "socio-graphicity" (Pilch Ortega, 2018), which has been developed by the author as a draft concept, aims to map such processes of rethinking or rewriting sociality and seeks to highlight the interrelation between biographical and social learning. A central aspect of this concept is the capacity of social agents, groups, and communities to reflect on the social world in which they live. Such collaborative modes of social learning support reflexivity and enable agents to question seemingly naturalised dynamics of social relations and related power regimes. The interactive reflections on shared life circumstances help in understanding some of the 'logic' of the power regimes and may lead to the creation of useful strategies for opposing the perpetuation of power dynamics. In particular, social learning and the formation of social spheres come into focus. These critical reflections are understood as highly reflexive forms of learning that enable people to question dominant discourses which limit and constrain agency.

Bourdieu (1977, 2000) also offers theoretical consideration in relation to social crises and transformation processes. He describes social crises as "periods in which habitus fall out of alignment with the fields in which they operate, creating a situation in which 'belief in the game' (illusio) is temporarily suspended and doxic assumptions are raised to the level of discourse, where they can be contested" (Crossley, 2003, p. 44). With doxa he means an ensemble of assumptions which are postulated tacitly and beyond any query, and which reveal themselves only retrospectively when they are jettisoned in practise. He states in this context that those issues that are consciously being raised are just the "tip of an iceberg" and that social structures are reproduced by the broader and much deeper part, the "unspoken and pre-reflective or 'doxic' assumptions" (Crossley, 2003, p. 46) of societies. He further suggests that in periods of social crises, doxic beliefs can be questioned because they enter our awareness; if expectations of subjects and objective possibilities fail to fit, then the self-evidence of social agents can become broken in a pragmatic way (see Bourdieu, 1977, p. 169). The concept of sociographicity as well as Bourdieu's theoretical considerations in relation to social crises were helpful for understanding and analysing the social modes of learning and how it deals with the effects of this natural disaster.

2.2   Methodological Issues and Challenges

The empirical study I am drawing on in this paper is based on grounded theory methodology and theoretical considerations of biographical research. Part of the development of the theoretical sensitivity (according to grounded theory methodology) was an ethnographic field investigation which was important for identifying basic "logics of the field" (Bourdieu, 1977; Bourdieu & Wacquant 1992). The empirical survey involves narrative-biographical interviews conducted in Spanish half a year after the earthquake took place, together with an analysis of social media and videos related to experiences of the natural disaster. The process of field investigation and data collection was made more challenging by the precarious security situation due to the exceptional circumstances after the natural disaster. Another aspect I had to deal with was the risk of re-traumatisation of the interviewees by conducting narrative biographical interviews. Due to the fact that the interviews were conducted just six months after the earthquake, the risk of re-traumatisation was taken very seriously. The detailed transcriptions of the narrative interviews were translated from Spanish to German. The translation is important as it yields access to the empirical data to a different group of researchers and the scientific community. The translation of empirical data must be done very carefully as translation is always entangled in power regimes. Against this backdrop, the process of translation can be described as a first step of interpretation, as a line-by-line open coding process of data utilising grounded theory methodology (see Pilch Ortega, 2016; see Evans, Chapter 13 for a different approach to the interview transcript and translation of talk).

In accordance with grounded theory methodology, the empirical data was sequentially analysed. The "careful handling" of the data within the analyses process requires a detailed discussion about "how the person quoted has used single words, phrases, and sentences" (Strauss, 2004, p. 170). In this context Strauss argues that it forces researchers "to examine the data microscopically" and "to listen closely to what the interviewees are saying and how they are saying it" (p. 173). The narratives provided by the interviewees give insights into the subjective construction of their social reality and the question of how the individual people experienced the natural disaster and its impacts on their lives and social circumstances. In addition, the interviewees provide their personal and collective strategies for dealing with the state of emergency and related social learning processes. The narrative interviews were empirically linked with videos and other public symbols the interviewees referred to within their narration. The videos had been published on various social media platforms as collective documents in dealing with the impacts of the natural disaster.

2.3   Research Findings: A Brief Summary

In this section I would like to give a brief insight into the research findings of the empirical study. Relating to experiences of natural disasters, the question of how people structure their experiences in terms of temporal, spatial and social issues assumes particular importance. The narratives offer detailed descriptions about how the interviewees experienced the moment of the earthquake. The descriptions of this moment when the earthquake happened show a lot of similarities in terms of the way in which the natural disaster was experienced. A woman of Juchitán describes her experiences in the following way:

> Well, in fact it was a bitter experience, no? Unforgettable I think, for many from us from the Istmo, in particular for Juchitán, the most affected city I guess, we were, it happened shortly before midnight, on this day, 7th of September you know? Unforgettable, we were chatting, right there in the living room, in my home with my husband when everything started to move suddenly, I only panicked, because I experienced that one in 1985 in Mexico City, fortunately I feel each and every old, that's stuck in my mind, […] and immediately I was looking for my daughter Sarah, in her room, Sarah Sarah get up and he [her husband] remained seated over there, well we thought that it will stop but it didn't, it was one of the strongest, of the worst of the worst, in other words it is one thing, do you know what, we were not able to leave the house because it was not possible to open the doors and the things started to fall down on the ground, in the kitchen, all the things, the cooking oil, drinking water, glass, everything fell down on the ground, a mirror fell down on the ground, and then the power went out and you tell yourself I will not move from here, because you couldn't […] and you close your eyes and you say oh my God, and there I stayed in these seconds and I thought I will not be able to see my children again, oh my God […] and everything is crossing your mind at this moment I will not see them again oh my God, I don't know, it's the end. (Interview with Luisa)

The earthquake is described as something which occurred suddenly and immediately interrupted the daily routine. The natural disaster is framed as a collective experience, which can be detected, for example, in the we-perspective of the narration. Moreover, the interviewee introduces her belonging to the region of Istmo as a relevant frame of identification. Details, such as the exact date and the scene of the event are described as well, as they are important temporal and spatial dimensions. The narrations present a world in slow motion where every second and every detail, such as the movement of things falling to the ground, the social interaction in order to find secure exit and the existential threat experienced had been memorized. The fact that it was impossible to open the doors likewise seems relevant for the drama of the narration as it relates to the shock and the panic which occurred.

In addition, the narratives of the interviewees focused on different modes of framing the natural disaster and its impacts on personal and social life. In particular, the interviewees gave insights into individual and collaborative strategies for dealing with this precarious situation along with biographical and social learning processes. The collapse of basic services such as drinking water and electrical power was articulated as well as the arrival of the military and the global press. The people described how they were pushed into to the spotlight of national and global media, with their suffering and their tragedy on display. The narratives reveal an initial coming to terms with the vulnerable and insecure situation the people found themselves in. Various interviewees described collaborative practices of defending their homes from assaults and robberies which started just after the earthquake happened. In some of the urban districts of Juchitán, the neighbourhoods organised day and night watches. One of the interviewees described the situation in the following way:

> Well then in the first days after the earthquake rumours spread that they enter into homes to steal, […] well there were other parts, other districts, where signs were put up, that they will lynch them if they catch them, there in La Zapanda, there was a doll hanged up where it was written those thieves who will be caught stealing, will be hanged it was in la Gustavo, I don't remember very well, where they almost lynched one but they beat one really baldly, well the people organised themselves via districts, via streets, via street blocks, in order to protect their homes, they took turns, some of them were sleeping and then started at 6 am 'til 10 am and they blocked the road, from 5 pm. (Interview with Damian)

The lack of electricity and the high level of insecurity caused by the natural disaster provoked the questioning of everyday social interactions as well. In this context, social relations are re-evaluated and reconfigured. Due to their vulnerable situation, the people affected created and negotiated 'new' social rules and regimes. Social trust became an important social 'currency'. The social practice of self-organisation described can be interpreted as a strategy for regaining control over a random unrestricted space. Taking issues of security to heart also refers to processes of managing the hazards of trajectories of suffering. However, the collaborative strategies for dealing with the situation show different modes of solidarity building, which on the one hand refer to social and community learning processes. On the other hand, distribution conflicts and social vulnerability were omnipresent.

If we focus on the general framing of the earthquake and its impacts on community life, research findings reveal two central 'figures' of sense and meaning (*Sinnfiguren*) which dominate the narratives. The first figure is related to the experience of abandonment by public authorities as the government did not attend to the needs of the people who were exposed to a high level of vulnerability and social insecurity. The second figure refers to community learning processes in which social problems were addressed. The experience of being left to their own devices initiated processes of self-empowerment and collective agency. Sociocultural resources of the people in this region, for instance, became relevant in order to overcome the impacts of the massive physical and social damage.

An old building in Juchitán with a famous mural which was not destroyed by the strong earthquake became an exemplary central symbol of the survival of the people (see Figure 9.7). The mural "la señora anciana" is connected with la sanduga and with música profunda, which symbolises the cultural way of life and its history in this region. The durability of the socio-cultural heritage of the people functions as a central resource for rebuilding social life and helps to create continuity in the face of the extensive damage. A similar perspective is shown in the lyrics of a song which was composed after the earthquake by a young regional rap group with the sentence: "se cayeron las iglesias pero no la fe, se cayó la ciudad pero no mi gente (…) las malas rachas no duran siempre,

FIGURE 9.7   "La señora anciana" (© NVI Noticias, 2018)

mi gente no duerma esta despierta y en pie, cuidando a los suyos a la noche ser" (Juchirap et al., 2017) which can be translated as "the churches collapsed but not our faith, the city is in ruins but not our people (…) the streak of bad luck does not last forever, our people are not sleeping, they are awake and they are on their feet again taking care of their families in the night".

Overcoming the natural disaster and its impacts is also at the centre of some regional art projects. The artist group Collectivo Chiquitraca, for instance, seeks to address the experiences of the earthquake with street art. On various buildings which have been damaged by the earthquake, they created a kind of street art which is linked with sociocultural memory traces. After the natural disaster the artist group was requested to give the tragedy another sort of framing in order to revitalise the soul of the Istmo (see Figure 9.8; see Istmopress, 2018). With the initiative "recuperar la memoria de Juchitán" (Chaca, 2017), another group of artists aims to revitalise the memory of Juchitán as well. They created iconographic images which were placed on buildings in public spaces which had been damaged by the earthquake. The neighbourhood was also invited to participate in this project (see Figure 9.9).

Additionally, various videos which are related to the natural disaster have been explored and analysed. Even if created in an amateur way, they can be seen as documentation of overcoming the experiences of the natural disaster, in which socio-cultural heritage plays an important role. For instance, "El relato del sismo en Juchitán 8.2" (see Figure 9.10) shows an elderly woman sitting at the centre of her home in ruins, narrating how she and her husband experienced the earthquake and its effects. The special feature of this video is the language used; the woman narrates her experiences in her mother tongue of Zapoteco. The elderly woman draws attention to the emergency relief on which the people depend, and narration elicits the involvement of the audience.

FIGURE 9.8   Mural by the artist group "Colectivo Chiquitraca" (© Pilch Ortega, 2018)

FIGURE 9.9   "Señora de las iguanas" by Demian Flores (© Pilch Ortega, 2018)

FIGURE 9.10   "El relato del sismo en Juchitán 8.2" (© Santiago Noriega, 2017)

The final example I would like to give is the video "El Corrido del Terremoto de 7 Septiembre" (see Figure 9.11). The video documentation gives insights into how people experienced the earthquake and its impacts accompanied by traditional music of this region. The song "El Corrido del Terremoto de 8.2 del 7 de Septiembre de 2017" was composed by Victor el Elejido de Oaxaca. El Corrido refers to a genre of music in Mexico which arose during the Mexican revolution and was used as a medium of dissemination of the life histories of poor people. The video is dedicated to the victims of the earthquake and shows images of the damage, rescue operations and the suffering of the people affected. The natural disaster is highlighted as a collective tragedy in which the rich and the poor are similarly affected. These visual formats for summing up experiences retrospectively show the complex interrelation of individual and collective memory. The complexity of different overlapping elements of meaning is intertwined with performative levels of social enactment.

FIGURE 9.11   "El Corrido del Terremoto de 7 Septiembre" (© El Tío Memero Vlogs, 2017)

3   Conclusions

The aim of the chapter was to focus on opportunities for social learning in a context characterised by distribution conflicts, social vulnerability, and solidarity building. The paper draws on an empirical study conducted in Juchitán, six months after a strong earthquake affected the region of Istmo in Mexico. The study explores the impacts of a natural disaster on community life and the transformative potential that lies in such a social crisis. Along with the field investigation, various narrative-biographical interviews were conducted in this region. In addition, initiatives of different regional artist groups and video documentaries related to the earthquake have been analysed. We have seen how the research findings reveal two central figures of sense and meaning (*Sinnfiguren*) which dominate the way people structure and frame the experience of the natural disaster and the consequences that such crises have for their social lives. The first figure we saw refers to the experience of abandonment by the government, which failed to attend to the needs of the people who were therefore thrust into a highly vulnerable situation. The second figure of sense is related to empowerment processes and collective agency resulting from having been left to their own devices. In this context, the people's socio-cultural heritage becomes a useful potential resource in order to overcome the conditions of vulnerability in which the people find themselves. The research findings reveal processes of solidarity building as well as waves of social disintegration and an erosion of solidarity. The power of distribution conflicts caused by a violent struggle for survival and accompanied by bloodshed and killing, as well as the insecure situation remain a strongly influencing factor of the social dynamics. However, the collaborative social practises observed show that, in wake of the natural disaster, social rules and power relationships were questioned by the people. These modes of social reflexivity enable people to analyse their circumstances in order to overcome established power regimes and to create new social practises which respond more adequately to their needs.

References

Bourdieu, P. (1977). *Outline of a theory of practice*. Cambridge University Press.

Bourdieu, P., & Wacquant, L. J. D. (1992). *An invitation to reflexive sociology*. University of Chicago Press.

Chaca, R. (2017, December 10). Con murales, artistas buscan recuperar la memoria en Juchitán. *El Universal.* https://oaxaca.eluniversal.com.mx/municipios/10-12-2017/con-murales-artistas-buscan-recuperar-la-memoria-en-juchitan

Crossley, N. (2003). From reproduction to transformation: Social movement fields and the radical habitus. *Theory, Culture & Society, 20*(6), 43–68. https://doi.org/10.1177/0263276403206003

Dimbath, O., & Heinlein, M. (2020). Einleitung: Soziale Gedächtnisse der Katastrophe. In M. Heinlein & O. Dimbath (Eds.), *Katastrophen zwischen sozialem Erinnern und Vergessen. Zur Theorie und Empirie sozialer Katastrophengedächtnisse* (pp. 1–18). Springer.

El Tío Memero Vlogs. (2017). *El Corrido del Terremoto de 7 Septiembre* [Video]. YouTube. Corrido del terremoto del 19 de septiembre de 2017 en México y Morelos – YouTube.

Istmopress. Agencia de Noticias. (2018). *Colectivo Chiquitraca emplea el arte para reconstruir Juchitán tras terremoto de 7S.* http://www.istmopress.com.mx/istmo/colectivo-chiquitraca-emplea-el-arte-para-reconstruir-juchitan-tras-terremoto-de-7s/

Juchirap, Mani Rap, & Aldri Pineda. (2017). *Mi Gente* [Video]. YouTube. https://www.youtube.com/watch?v=tPbwT-bIATg

Ovenden, K. (2000). The politics of protest: An interview with Pierre Bourdieu. *Socialist Review, 242,* http://pubs.socialistreviewindex.org.uk/sr242/ovenden.htm

Pilch Ortega, A. (2016). Learning and local change in social movements in Chiapas, in Mexico. In R. Evans, E. Kurantowicz, & E. Lucio-Villegas (Eds.), *Researching and transforming adult learning and communities: The local/global context* (pp. 177–186). Sense Publishers.

Pilch Ortega, A. (2018). 'Rewriting sociality'. Sociographicity as a concept for comprehending emancipatory practice and social change. *Andragoška spoznanja, Studies in Adult Education and Learning, 20*(1), 77–88.

Santiago Noriega, S. (2017, October 10). *El relato del sismo en Juchitán 8.2* [Video]. YouTube. https://www.youtube.com/watch?v=feeVpeRVdok

Strauss, A. L. (2004). Analysis through microscopic examination. *Sozialer Sinn, 5*(2), 160–176.

CHAPTER 10

The 'Pulsating Activism' of Polish Activists

Oscillation between the Mainstream and the Margins

Anna Bilon-Piórko

Abstract

The aim of this chapter is to analyse social activism as a lifelong activity that undergoes cyclical changes and understandable as an oscillation between the mainstream and margins. Based on activists' narratives collected during a research project focused on social activism, this chapter identifies triggers of oscillation between the mainstream and the margins. Importantly, mainstream and margins are used in a metaphorical sense to capture the patterns of individual biographies. Mainstream denotes the periods when activists are committed to social issues, whereas the margin stands for the periods in which they withdraw from activities, in the sense of being on the margins of social life. This chapter shows the dynamics of these processes and stresses that learning itself is an important factor that changes the course of events in activists' lives. The chapter also stresses that the study of individual meanings and lifetime trajectories is essential to understand better the members of community groups so as to know the individual motivations for social engagement. An important conclusion is that activism in communities and social movements possesses a dynamic of its own and may follow a pulsating rhythm.

Keywords

social activism – activist biographies – oscillation – pulsating rhythm – triggers – social activity – withdrawal

1 Introduction

In this chapter, I analyse individual processes of oscillation between social engagement on the one hand and withdrawal and social passivity on the other. I use "mainstream' and 'margin' in a metaphorical fashion to capture the patterns of individual biographies. My research focuses on social activists, that is on individuals who become involved in activities which are unconventional (as compared to accepted social norms, policies and aesthetics) and designed to achieve social or socially relevant aims (Anderson & Herr, 2007). Frequently, activism situates people within the *acting communities* (e.g. social movements) and within a course of events leading to social change. By exploring the dynamic of social engagement at the level of an individual, we can better understand the variability of activists' engagement that has been identified in research (Einwohner, 2002; Ollis, 2011; Vestergren et al., 2017). Because intense engagement periods sometimes alternate with withdrawal from activity, I refer to this kind involvement as 'pulsating activism',[1] which can be described as a series of *engagement-withdrawal cycles*, that is, an oscillation. I argue that this oscillation exhibits certain features:

1. from the activist perspective, it may be understood as stepping into the mainstream of a given activity and then taking a step back to its margin, which is especially the case for activists whose involvement is a lifelong practice (Ollis, 2011);
2. such an oscillation may be prompted by various reasons, whereby my focus is on the negative consequences (costs) incurred by activists in and because of their pursuits;
3. facing up to the negative consequences of activism necessitates learning processes and/or the activation of coping mechanisms (Hobfoll, 1998).

To capture and explore this oscillation is the main aim of this chapter. Therefore, this chapter seeks answers to the following questions:

1. Which periods are perceived as 'the mainstream and the margin' within the contexts of activism?
2. What are the triggers for oscillation between 'the mainstream and the margin'?

these questions stem from my attempt to understand the pulsating rhythm of activism, as identified in the literature (Ollis, 2011; Vestergren et al., 2017), and its possible implications for adult education and social organisations. Another important source of my research questions is to be found in a gap I noticed in the existing studies on the learning and biographies of Polish activists in international discourse (Mrozowicki & Maciejewska, 2017; Vestergren et al., 2017).

2   Research Material and Methodological Approach

My analysis is based on the data collected in the project *Socio-biographical costs of activism in the narratives of Polish activists*, where ten deliberately chosen activists were interviewed using the in-depth semi-structured (Wengraf,

2001) biographical-narrative interview method (Seale et al., 2004). Interview questions were only partially pre-arranged. They served as opening questions and requested the respondents to recount their biographies from the angle of activism. The sampling criteria were: (1) involvement in activism in various areas of social life and organisations; (2) age (the narrators were aged between 25 and 89 years old); (3) gender. Ultimately, the sample included a member of the non-military Resistance during WW2, members of human and women's rights advocacy organisations, activists of anti-communist movements, cultural leaders, people active in health organisations, social policies and community activists. Since some interviewees were associated with several organisations simultaneously and were 'life-long activists', they could represent the same organisations.

For the purpose of the chapter, two narratives were selected on the basis of *judgmental sampling* (Mohd Ishak & Abu Bakar, 2014) as they very vividly reflected the intermittent, 'pulsating' nature of activism. The case of the oldest activist respondent is presented for its potential to highlight life-long engagement in social activism and its *'pulsating'* character. To provide meaningful contrast, his narrative is juxtaposed with that of a middle-aged female whose activism also exhibits a recognisably pulsating rhythm and has been a long-lasting process, though it concerns a different sphere and has mainly unfolded within a different political system introduced to Poland in 1989. The selected narrators are:

Krzysztof – an eighty-seven-year-old male who lived through WWII, the communist period and the political transition of 1989. Krzysztof's entire biography is a testimony to his exceptional social engagement. As a child, he took part in wartime fights and resistance activities; under communism, he was deeply committed to furthering the cause of Poland abroad (which was actually a very difficult biographical experience for him since, determined to serve his country, he had joined the communist Polish United Workers' Party which still remained his acute identity-related problem at the time of the interview); and the political transition helped him become the leader of an international NGO dedicated to human rights (one of Poland's first after 1989). His motto was always: "there is always something to be done in the world, and no times are less significant". When interviewed, Krzysztof was still actively involved in social life: he tirelessly participated in public protests against Poland's governing party. He died relatively soon after the interview. The interview with Krzysztof was 9.5 hours in length.

Ewa – a forty-year-old female who grew up after the collapse of the USSR. As such, for most of her life, Ewa has had access to greater civil freedoms and could become involved in international activities as a young person. She is a member of an international NGO committed to human rights, anti-discriminatory education and refugee rights. As a result of a major turn in her life (precipitated among other things by the costs of her activism), Ewa is now a representative of an international political organisation in Poland. This does not mean that she has given up her activist pursuits; on the contrary, she is involved in employee rights advocacy, opposes discrimination and hate speech in Poland and disseminates ecological consciousness and 'slow life' practices. My interview with Ewa lasted six hours.

All the interviews were carried out in Polish. Analyses were conducted on working transcripts. Selected passages from the narratives were translated into English, edited (Mondada, 2007) and adjusted to the receptive capacities of English-speaking readers.

My analysis was primarily based on abductive reasoning and thematic analysis (Anfara & Mertz, 2015; Nowell et al., 2017). My assumption was that a theme is an element that connects various experiences and confers meaning on them. Thus, this was about identifying the main meanings in the narratives. Additionally, I also used elements of sequential analysis (Rosenthal, 2004), since the first research question called for exploring the biographies of activists, the ways they formulated their narratives and the sense they made of various stages of their lives. In this case, sequential analysis was thus a "procedure where the temporal structure of both the *narrated* and the *experienced* life history is analysed" (Rosenthal, 2004, p. 54). In analysing the triggers of oscillation (the second research question), special attention was paid to the interview passages which spoke about the costs of activism (negative consequences) incurred by the participants.

3   The Mainstream and the Margin in Activists' Lives

My analysis of the selected narratives assumes that activism formed the essential core of the activists' biographies and identities around which other aspects of their lives were organised. Given this, activism fundamentally affected their feeling of being at the centre or on the margin of social life. Crucially, the participants invested that 'centre/mainstream' with specific meanings of their own; they sometimes referred to major historical events (e.g., the collapse of USSR) and on other occasions to events which were not of general historic importance but of significance to a given social group/organisation with which they were associated. Hence, it is crucial to recognise the individual meanings that the activists attached to what could be the 'mainstream/centre'. In this context, they tended to cite social values (and events) to which their activities were committed, such as freedom, equality, and justice, even though these values were only significant to a limited group of people. Interestingly, the periods of withdrawal from social involvements made the activists feel that they were at the margin of social life even if their work and family lives were robust at the time.

Krzysztof – in Krzysztof's view, social involvement and activism were essential in making his own life meaningful. He explicitly stated:

> I deeply believe that (...) basically nothing else makes sense other than pushing the world forward, I mean acting in one way or another ...

For this reason, Krzysztof felt profoundly responsible for social matters and values, such as Polish culture, freedom and justice, and thought it was his moral obligation to uphold these causes. Social activity made him, as he stressed many times: *proud, happy, sensible of participating in something of utmost importance and magnitude, which kindled the feeling of being fully human*. Krzysztof resorted to such terms when talking about his attempts to fight for the freedom of his country during WW2 (a young teenager at the time, Krzysztof could not directly participate in warfare), his membership in the delegation that worked on the Helsinki Accords signed at the Conference on Security and Co-operation in Europe in 1975, his contribution to cultural events promoting Polish culture in London, his involvement in protests against the current government of Poland, his work for human-rights organisations and other initiatives in which he (had) participated. He also admitted that his constant sense of responsibility had resulted in a number of personal errors, as he had taken part in activities he had not fully endorsed and with which he could not internally come to terms for many years, including at the time of the interview. The passages below outline Krzysztof's journey:

> I joined the party[2] with the idea that *I wanted to do something for the country right then*, and, the way I saw it, the party was the only forum where one could talk in the first place. You had no other forum if you wanted to have your voice heard. I was always a revisionist in the party, always urged to do something in this department, and I always was in some trouble, but for those times, I can't say that I was a hero, because if I'd been one, they'd have kicked me out quickly ...
> [...]
> It was then, and of course, students took part in it,[3] and they spoke out, and I also spoke out, of course; it was *there that I ultimately got my nickname: a second-hand man. I was a second-hand man there*. Recycled. Yes, recycled. At a bonfire, I confessed everything to them, told the whole story with details (...) so that they knew everything about me, and I was a second-had man, *but it was really huge for me, because I won their trust indeed. That's how my Solidarity-related activity started; after that camp, they immediately got me into work*.

The passages above illustrate how the deep-seated sense of responsibility made Krzysztof feel fulfilled only when he took part in social actions even if this entailed a public admission of prior mistakes. Krzysztof continued to (re-)examine his path in an attempt to establish whether or not his initial choice had been right.

As opposed to that, Krzysztof talked about periods of inaction and social passivity, using words such as 'great weakness', 'poor health', 'depression', 'bad time in life' and 'dissipation'. For him, these were the moments of feeling useless, excluded, and desperate. This pattern persisted throughout his lifetime, starting from his distress at being unable to fight the Nazi occupiers during WW2 and ending with his sadness at his incapacity to educate the young about human rights caused by his health problems and, later, old age. Krzysztof underscored that life without social involvement could not be a fulfilled life for him:

> What I can say is that experience, my observations of the world have led me to conclude that, well, what is actually the point of living in this world? of course, there's family, and it makes a lot of sense and is valuable, but it's not enough, not enough …

When he had no opportunity to satisfy this need to live a life geared to achieving socially relevant aims, he suffered mentally, isolated himself and even abused alcohol. This kind of detachment marked the time of being on the margin of society.

Ewa – for Ewa, social involvement is also associated with the sense of responsibility, social sensitivity, standing up for the right cause and the desire to change reality. What matters to her is participation in social life to make the world a friendly place for future generations. Ewa emphasises more frequently than Krzysztof that her social engagement is directly connected with her family and personal satisfaction:

> United Europe matters a great deal to me because *I want my children to live in a secure place*, without wars, etc. I believe that the Union guarantees this as it were, and when it is not around, well, things may take a different course, so this is extremely important to me, and this fuels me up in this work, of course, because I do my very best for my kids, right, to live in safety and I believe that it is good all in all.

Social involvement makes Ewa feel that she can influence things and that her actions help people in countries afflicted by wars, persecutions, hunger, diseases, and the lack of educational opportunities. Ewa's 'mainstream life' – her activism – enters the 'margins' with a view to making the world a fairer place.

Like Krzysztof, Ewa has experienced an important change in her life. This involved shifting from 'high profile' activism (in an international organisation) to 'everyday life activism' (advocacy for employee rights, educational campaigning, or environmental consciousness-raising on a daily basis and at her current workplace, a political institution). Reflecting on this change, Ewa said:

> For example, I never thought that I'd be fighting for human rights more when I quit [the organisation], and now I'm a hell of an activist for employee rights because it suddenly seems that they're all only on paper at my institution, that things are fine only on paper.
>
> What matters a lot to me and my mission is showing that it's not about opposed camps, but that each party involved can use its own resources, and that it's really a triangle of the member states, EU institutions and civil society, and human-rights organisations, that they can achieve something together, that everybody has their role to play but they are all one team really, aren't they? One team which can, well, make one thing or another better in the world.

I believe that these passages demonstrate that Ewa regards social engagement as multidimensional and coming in many forms, and that what matters most in it is the sense of having a mission and pursuing particular aims. Without this, as Ewa stresses, there is no fulfilment in life.

Ewa talked about the periods of withdrawal from social activity in less emotionally charged terms than Krzysztof, although such moments were associated with a sense of helplessness and irrelevance for her as well. Emphatically, as Ewa's entire work life involves social activism and advocacy for various people and communities, her attitude to these pursuits was more task-focused. If she disengaged from a given activity, this rarely implied abandoning social involvement as such and rather tended to entail a shift in activity/its setting or taking up less mentally cumbersome issues. Ewa's 'margin' produced fewer negative consequences for her.

Both Krzysztof and Ewa repeatedly experienced periods of intense activity and withdrawal in their lives. Therefore, in terms of their biographies, this process unfolded as an oscillation composed of two processes/two directions: the periods of increased activity and involvement and the periods of withdrawal and inaction. Following Trimmer et al. (2015), these may be described as "mainstreaming margin" and "margining mainstream" since they were always associated with learning processes and coping with various challenging situations.

4 Triggers of Oscillation between 'the Mainstream and the Margin'

The identification and exploration of the two processes/directions of oscillation between activity on the one hand and withdrawal on the other helped me establish that there were two distinct sets of 'triggers' initiating these two processes/directions. I examined the activists' narratives for these triggers, and my search yielded a complex picture of the phenomenon as predictably no simple cause-effect relationship was discernible in either of the narratives. Rather, the commencement of action was revealed to have been prompted by a combination of various factors, thus a complex cause-effect relationship.

Individual and personality-related triggers include, for example, personality traits, values, future anticipations, visions of the past, sensitivity to social issues, etc. Activists' agency (Emirbayer & Mische, 1998) and motivation for action also play a considerable role. Some kinds of social engagement were triggered by social factors, such as the historical period, political developments, wars, persecutions, etc., or by factors strictly connected to local communities, small social groups and/or support networks. A separate group of factors were education and formal, non-formal and informal learning, which naturally surfaced in the activists' narratives (for example, school encouraged or discouraged activities for social change). In some cases, involvement in activity was prompted by a random event, a coincidental meeting or other contingent circumstances. My analysis of the narratives revealed a certain profile of factors essential to each of the activists.

Krzysztof – as an activist, Krzysztof lived to have opportunities for social engagement in Poland's three distinct historical periods (occupation during WW2, communist rule, and the times after the political transition of 1989). Given this, Krzysztof's social involvements were naturally shaped by exceptional socio-historical factors. Interestingly, Krzysztof felt an urge to be socially active irrespective of the particular socio-political conjuncture. Krzysztof's narrative testifies to his extraordinary sense of responsibility, moral obligation, common decency and respect for human rights and communal values. He had these sentiments instilled in him in his family home (his almost always absent father was a fervent social activist), which he explicitly stated:

> I lived with my grandma. My father was a loner and very active. He was this very active type of man. That's probably why their [Krysztof's parents'] marriage failed. He was not only a journalist, he was an activist. I wasn't close with my father. I only felt this involvement of his (…) And it was formative in a way. It stirred a need to act.

Factors related to education and learning were also consequential for Krzysztof. He went to primary school during WW2; he remembered his school as a setting where patriotism was prominent and came to be one of the major engines of Krzysztof's militancy:

> Even today I still remember all kinds of essays that we wrote. About Kornel Ujejski's poem "Marathon" [...] Our teacher asked us to learn an excerpt from this poem by heart. And, can you imagine, this excerpt is what I still [...] We did not learn just this excerpt; we learned the entire poem. Because it was very patriotic.[4]

Krzysztof also claimed to have learnt from his biography and from his mistakes, which he would correct to bring his activism in alignment with the value system he endorsed. His 'lived life' appears, in fact, to be convergent with his 'told story' (Wengraf, 2001). His narrative contains multiple passages that depict the moments in his life when Krzysztof indulged in profound analysis and re-directed the course of his life. What he regarded as the most pivotal moment was joining the democratic opposition under communism.

> It was '75, the end of Geneva, of the Conference of Security and Co-operation in Europe, that Great Charter of Liberties is adopted, the Helsinki Accords. In Poland, there is an escalation of ..., no, it was 1976. I'm deeply moved by what I heard in Geneva and ... it is ... I consider it the beginning of my dissidence, I mean, the way I put it to myself was that, my God, I want to do the right thing, but I'm serving a completely different God than I'd like to serve. And it starts gnawing me.

Ewa – as a member of another generation, Ewa has had opportunities for involvement in other kinds of social actions and activism related to new social problems. Besides her sensitivity to social issues, individual personality-related triggers pivotal to Ewa's social engagement include her strong sense of agency, curiosity about the world, aspiration to do something good for the world and a sense of self-fulfilment and personal satisfaction. Ewa openly stressed the importance of agency:

> But I was brought up to have this feeling ..., the feeling of agency is very important, I guess, right, the fact that people have self-confidence. And, I believe, that later it translates, for such an activist, into the feeling that I can do things.

As Ewa emphasised, she developed this feeling at home, at school and in her community. What Ewa considers important is that this feeling tends to help someone achieve more than they perhaps previously expected to do. Therefore, engaging in pro-social pursuits, Ewa encourages her collaborators to be socially active persons. She does so because she believes that:

> to be really effective, one can't use any artificial power, or force, some kind of position, can one? All this must be really authentic and really come from … Natural authority, and not something externally reinforced.

Hence the elements that motivate Ewa include interesting *people*, good atmosphere, collaboration and mutual respect, all of which make her believe that what she does is meaningful. Ewa said that she usually became involved in actions for a cause when:

> I *feel that something needs to be done*, because otherwise things will go on the way they are …

In order to align her life as best as possible with these values, Ewa chose a work career associated with organisations committed to advocacy and helping people.

Notably, in neither of the narratives was there a single dominant factor that triggered the activists' need for involvement and the mainstream-directed process of oscillation (towards action). In each of the cases, such responses were fuelled by a certain combination of factors, of which only the major ones are mentioned above. Both narratives also revealed the role of other factors, such as anger, protesting against the status quo, frustration, resentment at injustice and/or shock. Sometimes the respondents' activity was directly fuelled by these feelings, which have been found to be very important in activism (Horowitz, 2017; Vestergren et al., 2017). In fact, they may play a double role because in certain circumstances the same emotions (for example, bred by the perceived inefficacy of action) cause a sudden oscillation in the opposite direction, i.e., towards withdrawal and inaction. To understand this better, the narratives were explored for the dominant factors behind their processes of withdrawal from social involvement.

5 The Triggers of Withdrawal from Activism and Social Engagement

The triggers of withdrawal from activism identified in the narratives fell into a few categories. Among them, the negative consequences of social engagement, referred to as costs, appeared to be most weighty, being frequently mentioned in the narratives and, besides, were presented as the most transformative factor in the activists' biographies. Their occurrence was given as a reason for making changes and/or undertaking deep reflection. This capacious class of factors includes, for example, burnout, helplessness, risk of sustaining a serious injury (e.g., as a result of being beaten), harassment, Internet slurs, unemployment, disruption of the educational path, etc. Essentially, the burden of such costs depends both on the historical period (the costs were different for the oppositionist in communist Poland and for those protesting against the current government) and on the kind of activity (helping the casualties of war generates other costs than street protests or organisation of cultural events). In some cases, the successful completion of a given venture calls for a period of rest and making sense of the recent experiences. This is all the more likely to happen if group-related factors are more salient, for instance when groups and communities are in conflict with one another, if the social movement does not share the same values or when an unfriendly atmosphere prevails. The respondents tended to discontinue their involvement if they considered their group insufficiently focused on pursuing their goals. Activists also withdrew because of changing socio-historical circumstances.

Krzysztof – Krzysztof's narrative indicated that his withdrawals were very difficult experiences for him. Krzysztof never deliberately calculated gains and losses of his engagement and was ready to sacrifice a lot and brave the consequences of his activities. This attitude is well expressed in his account of the period when he joined the anti-communist opposition in Poland:

The periods of withdrawal were triggered by the moments when Krzysztof realised the pointlessness of his actions or his own mistakes. Given this, his learning played an important role in the process. Krzysztof typically indulged in crucial reflection on himself and his life sometime after the events and would change his approach after reflection.

Krzysztof had a seemingly very elemental need to follow his system of values. As a result, he would disengage from organisations, social groups and communities which he believed no longer fitted the previously adopted principles. He explained:

> So I'm against any radicalism and against fundamentalism (…) Wherever this radical sense of entitlement appears, it's no longer to my liking, and I fear that it'll turn against the cause they want to see accomplished, because they put off people by their, by this radicalism of theirs, they simply put off people (…) So it's a matter of reflection, of separating one from the other; at the beginning I couldn't do it, when it started, and I was not good at separating the one from the other. Entitlement and the core

of the issue. Now I can set the two apart; I'm against entitlement but for the core of the issue.

Noticeably, the moments when Krzysztof withdrew from activism were also related to the dynamic of the social groups with which he was affiliated and to the disappointment they occasioned.

Ewa – Ewa typically withdrew from her involvement and activism for reasons related to the kind of activity and the need to protect herself against burnout and helplessness. Her role as a mother may have taught Ewa to identify the moments and types of action that posed a risk to her mental and physical wellbeing. As a result, she avoided such engagement, a strategy well encapsulated in her account:

> I remember the moment I was reading … perhaps I was exceptionally sensitive then, because I had young kids, and we know that when you've got kids, things change in your head in various ways; I was working for [the name of the organisation] then, and I had to read various reports for the job. And I remember that reading one of them I simply concluded that I'd not finish reading it, that I wasn't up to it. It was about abducted children, some really horrific things, and I had two kids of my own, and simply wasn't able to go on. The next step was when some people came along to hold a meeting and I could come as a guest, and they talked about tortures, how political prisoners were tortured there. And I knew I wasn't up to that either. It just wasn't for me, there simply was a certain level of suffering I was able to absorb and still sleep at night without imagining …, simply to keep some kind of …, well not to get burned out emotionally, right?

The strategy adopted by Ewa may have made the moments of withdrawing from action less difficult for her than such periods were for Krzysztof. While Ewa also perceived problems of the organisations with which she was involved, she tended to look for solutions rather than stopping her collaboration.

6   Implications for Adult Education and Work with Communities

I argue that the complexity of social engagement and activism has important implications for adult education and work with communities. This relevance is borne out by the fact that learning and education surfaced in the activists' narratives as significant factors both in becoming engaged in social activity and in withdrawing from it. The oscillation depicted above, in the same manner that was stressed by Lave and Wenger regarding *participation,* is a "part of actors' learning trajectories, developing identities, and forms of membership" (Lave & Wenger, 1991; p. 36). Because individual identities of activists are not reducible to any single group identity and shared values (Horowitz, 2017), the study of individual meanings and trajectories is essential to understand better the members of these groups and their individual motivations for engaging with them. I believe that we can deduce from Krzysztof's and Ewa's narratives that fostering opportunities for individual reflection on communal/collective action and for (biographical) learning from such action may be a fundamental factor in understanding social engagement, social activity and activism. When arranging social activities, community engagement, and social movements it must be borne in mind that activism has a dynamic of its own and may (though does not have to, as qualitative research does not permit such bold generalisations) exhibit a pulsating rhythm. This means that activism may be punctuated by moments of withdrawal from action. Support for learning and self-reflection by fellow activists and their organisations may help initiate re-engagement in social pursuits, which was the case for both Krzysztof and Ewa. Ultimately, however, the role and significance of negative emotions and frustrations must be taken into account and will be worked through with the biographical resources activists acquire in the course of the shifts demanded of them in a pulsating career of social activism.

Notes

1. The metaphor of 'pulsating activism' has been chosen for at least two reasons. First, it refers to the urge to act, which pulsates like the blood in veins. This drive may subside, but it does not disappear as long as an activist is alive. Second, it proposes activism as an embodied practice which builds up and decreases. At the same time, as activists themselves emphasise, the wish to do things and activism do not always depend wholly on their will; nor do the moments when their activity abates or nearly vanishes.
2. The party meant here is the Polish United Workers' Party, which governed in Poland between 1948 and 1989.
3. Krzysztof relates his gradual involvement in the anti-communist opposition in Poland in 1983–1984. This happened during students' summer camps in which Krzysztof took part for various reasons.
4. During the German occupation, a great deal of education was conducted underground as part of the Polish resistance to Nazi Germany.

References

Anderson, G. L., & Herr, K. G. (Eds.). (2007). *Encyclopedia of activism and social justice.* Sage.

Anfara, V. A., & Mertz, N. T. (Eds.). (2015). *Theoretical frameworks in qualitative research* (2nd ed.). Sage.

Einwohner, R. L. (2002). Motivational framing and efficacy maintenance: Animal rights activists' use of four fortifying strategies. *The Sociological Quarterly, 43*(4), 509–526. https://doi.org/10.1111/j.1533-8525.2002.tb00064.x

Emirbayer, M., & Mische, A. (1998). What is agency? *American Journal of Sociology, 103*(4), 962–1023.

Hobfoll, S. E. (1998). *Stress, culture, and community: The psychology and philosophy of stress*. Plenum Press.

Horowitz, J. (2017). Who is this "we" you speak of? Grounding activist identity in social psychology. *Socius: Sociological Research for a Dynamic World, 3*, 1–17. https://doi.org/10.1177/2378023117717819

Lave, J., & Wenger, E. (1991). *Situated learning: Legitimate peripheral participation*. Cambridge University Press.

Mohd Ishak, N., & Abu Bakar, A. Y. (2014). Developing sampling frame for case study: Challenges and conditions. *World Journal of Education, 4*(3). https://doi.org/10.5430/wje.v4n3p29

Mondada, L. (2007). Commentary: Transcript variations and the indexicality of transcribing practices. *Discourse Studies, 9*(6), 809–821. https://doi.org/10.1177/1461445607082581

Mrozowicki, A., & Maciejewska, M. (2017). 'The practice anticipates our reflections' – Radical unions in Poland. *Transfer: European Review of Labour and Research, 23*(1), 67–77. https://doi.org/10.1177/1024258916679320

Nowell, L. S., Norris, J. M., White, D. E., & Moules, N. J. (2017). Thematic analysis: Striving to meet the trustworthiness criteria. *International Journal of Qualitative Methods, 16*(1), 1–13. https://doi.org/10.1177/1609406917733847

Ollis, T. (2011). Learning in social action: The informal and social learning dimensions of circumstantial and lifelong activists. *Australian Journal of Adult Learning, 51*(2), 248–268.

Rosenthal, G. (2004). Biographical research. In C. Seale, G. Gobo, J. F. Gubrium, & D. Silverman (Eds.), *Qualitative research practice* (pp. 48–64). Sage.

Trimmer, K., Black, A., & Riddle, S. (Eds.). (2015). *Mainstreams, margins and the spaces in-between: New possibilities for education research*. Routledge.

Vestergren, S., Drury, J., & Chiriac, E. H. (2017). The biographical consequences of protest and activism: A systematic review and a new typology. *Social Movement Studies, 16*(2), 203–221. https://doi.org/10.1080/14742837.2016.1252665

Wengraf, T. (2001). *Qualitative research interviewing: Biographic narrative and semi-structured methods*. Sage.

CHAPTER 11

Learning (for) Civil Disobedience in Poland
Extinction Rebellion as a New Form of Social Movement

Marta Gontarska, Paweł Rudnicki and Piotr Zańko

Abstract

This chapter looks at the significance of individual and collective counter-hegemonic practices of the Extinction Rebellion (XR) movement in Poland. Founded on the idea of civil disobedience, these practices essentially contest the passive attitude of political decision-makers vis-à-vis threats associated with the global climate crisis. We explore the dimensions of learning (for) civil disobedience and show the relevance of this activity for the civic awareness of XR activists and as a differentiator for the movement as a whole. Our qualitative research is based on narrative interviews with selected XR activists from Warsaw and Wrocław and serves as a critical exploratory study. Importantly, it is also a tool of pedagogical intervention which aims to demonstrate and strengthen the voice of young people concerned about the fate of our planet in the realities of the hegemony of the neoliberal, neoconservative, populist state.

Keywords

civil disobedience – Extinction Rebellion (XR) – climate change – new activism – public pedagogy – Poland

∙ ∙ ∙

> And if solutions within the system are so impossible to find, maybe we should change the system itself. We have not come here to beg world leaders to care. You have ignored us in the past and you will ignore us again. We have run out of excuses and we are running out

of time. We have come here to let you know that change is coming, whether you like it or not. The real power belongs to the people.
> GRETA THUNBERG (Address at the COP24 UN Climate Summit, December 2018)

∴

1   Introduction

New social, cultural, political and technological realities require an appropriate activist response. In today's world, random actions are ineffective and undesirable, hence the activism approach is a response to the existing realities (Piotrowski & Muszel, 2020). Engaging in social activism requires finding an important glocal topic, appropriate forms of social engagement (hybrid: implemented simultaneously in the real world and social media), precise – almost targeted – distribution of postulates, and have potential to reach out to people who are genuinely interested in a given issue. These requirements are dictated by the habits we have developed under neoliberalism. Efficiency, immediacy and some kind of (expected) spectacularity, have been present for several decades in our private biographies, social life, professional life and culture (Johnson, 2011; Sowa, 2015). Whole generations treat the rules of the neoliberal world as dogmas of modernity. However, just as neoliberalism has made acquisitions of social categories – e.g., participation, democracy or learning – turning them into products and services and us into consumers and people competing for everything (Cervinkova & Rudnicki, 2019), now its tools are being reclaimed for new activism (Korolczuk, 2020; Polanska, 2018).

By investigating the activities of activists from the Extinction Rebellion (XR) Poland movement (members of groups from Warsaw and Wrocław), we identified several dimensions related to new forms of social activism that are significantly different from activist practices undertaken in Poland over the past four decades. The differences are not only the result of easily identifiable transformations related to political movements from the Solidarity Trade Union in the 1980s, by the collapse of the communist state in 1989, or the experience of Poland's political transformation till now (Krastev & Holmes, 2020; Ost, 2005).

The actions of XR climate activists, which started in spring 2019, not only showed the message of climate catastrophe demands, but also used a method of civil disobedience that has not appeared as a tool of resistance in Poland for a long time. XR activists make this form of resistance an emblem of their movement. At the same time, in order to use it in a fully conscious and effective way, they treat it as part of the informal education carried out within the movement. The learning of civil disobedience is a distinctive feature of XR Poland which we analyse in the article. We show the relevance of this activity for the civic awareness of XR activists and as a differentiator for the movement as a whole. Furthermore, we embed civil disobedience in a broader political and social context. In 2019–21, we were able to observe, participate in, and research numerous mass protests directed against the ruling far right. The populist policies of the Polish government from 2015 up to 2021 have been consistently directed against the rule of law, civil society, against women, the LGBT+ community, and minorities of all kinds (Ambroziak & Pacewicz, 2020). The radical right-wing turn has been linked to the deliberate destruction of the environment, the pursuit of irrational energy policies (reliance on coal) and the breaking out of Green New Deal policies. All these actions have intersectionalised activist circles. Slogans related to women's rights, minority rights, climate, and workers' rights appeared at mass demonstrations of tens of thousands of people. This combination of themes of protest and resistance was linked to actions marked by civil disobedience. XR Poland activists were always present at these events.

The activities of the glocal movement Extinction Rebellion, whose practices we analyse in this chapter, show both the specificity of this activist group (themes, actions, dimensions of learning) and certain tendencies in the transformation of activists in a Poland moving towards authoritarianism, practically abandoning liberal democracy.

2 Research Methodology

In our research project we explore and interpret the educational potential of activities by Extinction Rebellion (XR), a global movement whose practices we examine in this article using the example of two Poland-based groups: XR Wrocław and XR Warsaw. Technically, our ethnographic research spanned March to May 2020, but we have in fact studied the pursuits of this movement from July 2019 till the end of 2020, collecting a rich body of research materials, such as leaflets, photos and film footage, both posted on social media and made by ourselves during actions staged by XR in Wrocław and in Warsaw.

Our research largely relied on narrative interviews, which we conducted with nine XR activists (5 females and 4 males) whom we identified as particularly committed to developing the movement, which had first made its mark in Poland in spring 2019. All our interlocutors (IL)[1] were university-educated and worked in big cities (Warsaw and Wrocław) in jobs demanding specialist competencies. Eight of them had prior experience of social involvement (NGOs and/or informal groups), with four of them assessing their commitment as 'activist'. For one interlocutor, XR was the first social movement she had ever joined. Because of the coronavirus pandemic restrictions, we conducted interviews with XR activists online (using a variety of tools) between March 12th and April 10th 2020. The total recording time added up to 504 minutes. The approach to the narrative interviews is defined by Susan E. Chase (2005) as sociological with high interest in the communication skills and language practice and contextualisation of the stories in the broader perspective of the XR movement and other social organisations. In addition, the interaction between interlocutors and how discourses influence, take over and change the activists' narratives was of central importance. It was important from a research point of view to conduct narrative interviews with open questions to open up the narratives of activists as broadly as possible and follow their stories. Recognising the specific dynamics and tensions involved in the new context of our research in the wholly online setting, we were aware, too, of how complex the situation of the activists was in the context of the pandemic, where they were inviting the researchers into their houses, and showing themselves in front of the camera for more than an hour with all the interruptions caused by their everyday lives which could not be isolated out of the act of the interview taking place.

All the interviews were transcribed and then coded by means of the Atlas.ti 8 data analysis software, which supports qualitative data analysis. When transcribing the interviews, we made a decision not to transcribe them word for word, not to include intonation, repetitions and pauses in the interlocutors' utterances, as well as the emotional layer of the expression. Transcriptions prepared in such a way are more useful for detailed conversational, linguistic and psychological analyses. In our case, the transcription was intended to present the statements of XR activists in a way that would be understandable to the general audience (see Kvale, 2007, pp. 95–98; see also in this volume Pilch Ortega and Evans on the topic of transcripts and language in interviews).

All the doubts related to interview analysis (coding) were discussed by us as they arose, in seminars which we held weekly online on Skype. In line with our research goals, we conducted an "analysis focusing on meaning" (Kvale, 2007, p. 104). It took place according to the procedure proposed by Kvale, which covers the following research activities: meaning coding, meaning condensation and meaning interpretation (Kvale, 2007, p. 104). Before starting the analysis, we created an initial list of codes (main analytical categories) related to, among others, the structure of the XR movement, its philosophy, strategies and forms of activity. The codes we selected were assigned to a given fragment of the text, which facilitated the subsequent identification of the statement that interests us and its interpretation. Although we assumed that we would code our research material using predefined codes ('list coding'), we also sometimes used the 'open coding' procedure, which involved assigning codes to selected interview fragments 'bottom-up' while working directly with the text. In total, our code book consisted of 117 codes. The Atlas.ti 8 computer application used by us significantly improves the analysis of the research material. It helps, for example, in the quick identification of codes, and enables the definition of relations between the codes and individual statements of the interlocutors. However, we are aware that it is only a tool of analysis. The researcher is always responsible for the analysis process.

Taking advantage of our collective work on the project, we were able to identify points of tension between our individual levels of engagement which ranged from a generally supportive approach of the sympathetic observer to a position of active engagement in the XR movement. The critical role of each researcher in the project was highly motivated by our individual standpoints and enriched the conclusions of the article by merging our perspectives under the one research goal.

In this paper, we examine the significance of individual and collective counter-hegemonic practices of the Extinction Rebellion (XR) movement in Poland. Founded on the idea of civil disobedience, these practices essentially contest the passive attitude of political decision-makers vis-à-vis threats associated with the global climate crisis. We explore the dimensions of learning (for) civil disobedience and the ways in which the XR movement operates in the public sphere (and in social media). Our research project is embedded in engaged critical and emancipatory pedagogies, in which the practices of social, cultural and political opposition are understood as civil, educational and scholarly responsibilities. As emphasised by McLaren, who refers to the concept of public pedagogy developed by H. A. Giroux, "pedagogy as an oppositional practice and active process of learning is fundamental to the creation of critical citizenship, inclusive democracy, and the demands of the global public sphere" (McLaren, 2014, p. 128). In this context, the activities of XR Poland are aligned with the practices of social movements dedicated to climate politics, grassroots engagement, the education of citizens and the promotion of active civil responsibility for one's own life, the fate of society, and the future of the entire planet. We believe that the activity of the XR movement is an example of public pedagogy, an oppositional practice, and an active process of learning.

3   XR: Genesis, Self-Definition and Structure

The formation of XR was considerably affected by numerous reports on climate change issued by the UN-affiliated Intergovernmental Panel on Climate

Change (Masson-Delmotte et al., 2018) and in particular by the special report *Global Warming of 1.5°C* of 8th October 2018, which had very wide media coverage in Poland. The main point of the report is that, with the global temperature level being now 1°C higher than before the industrial age, its rise by more than 1.5°C will exacerbate destructive climatic developments (droughts, fires, floods, hurricanes) and aggravate their ramifications (biodiversity loss, inaccessibility of potable water, famine), which humans will no longer be able to control. In other words, when the last 'security threshold' – that of 1.5°C – is exceeded, life on the Earth will be annihilated (Masson-Delmotte et al., 2018).

Apple suggests that today, in our postmodern reality, we should focus on creating what he calls decentred unities, i.e., spaces relevant to education and larger social transformations which will help progressive movements find a common platform and serve as sites of shared struggle, without imposing any single understanding of exploitation and domination on the fighting groups (Apple, 2012). As the activities of the XR movement illustrate, the establishment of such decentred units is not a fantasy, but a viable venture. In our research we include the perspective of XR as a global movement established in the UK, but our focus was mostly on XR in Poland, how it was established and what kind of adaptation the activists made to render XR more local. Among our interviews we have spoken with three out of the four people, who initially organise local groups both in Warsaw and Wrocław and mobilise people to make the first performative activities recognised on the streets and in local media and launched XR in Poland. All three interlocutors are simultaneously engaged in other forms of activism within Polish civil society. We recognised the limitation of the adaptation process due to cultural and social reality. We also understand and value the differences in age, background and experiences between the British and Polish co-creators of the XR. While XR activists organise joint actions, they normally function within local groups, most of which are based in particular cities. These groups are divided into thematic sectors, focused on a range of fields, e.g., art, research, or regeneration. The ideas of dispersed leadership and locality are supposed to prevent intra-group tensions bound up with power relations, to support local contacts and to bolster the communal investment of the movement. In 2020, XR Poland went nationwide in some of its activities, such as strategy development, financial control and legal frameworks.

4   XR: Learning (for) Civil Disobedience

In our paper, we rely on the definition of civil disobedience offered by J. Rawls in *A Theory of Justice*, where he says that civil disobedience is "a public, non-violent, conscientious yet political act contrary to law usually done with the aim of bringing about change in the law or policies of the government" (Rawls, 2005, p. 364).

Civil disobedience is thus inseparable from civil actions aimed against the power whose practices have for one reason or another been recognised as morally, politically or socially inadmissible. The injustice of government's policies, the lack of reflection among people wielding power and the pernicious effects of their actions, as perceived or anticipated by the citizens, have been and are impulses behind ventures that deliberately breach the law but are undertaken as an ultimate form of opposition. Civil disobedience seeks to non-violently demonstrate attitudes and articulate demands with full clarity about, and readiness to brave punishment for one's deeds (Arendt, 1972, pp. 51–52). Civil disobedience is not a revolutionary negation of the legal order as such; instead, it exposes the government's harmful approach to the rights of individuals and/or social groups (Blackstone, 1971, p. 5). Civil disobedience is a moral action in the face of immorality condoned or perpetrated by the government. As a practice of social action, civil disobedience is applicable to all political regimes since the category of injustice is politically universal and appears across all systemic realities. Reasons for embracing civil disobedience may vary (ranging from racial segregation and abuse of minority rights, to demanding employee rights, to raising environmental issues), and the forms in which it is enacted are highly diversified (e.g., mass actions or individual actions, happenings or non-performative activities), but its consequences remain the same. Namely, those who break the law must be prepared for punishment. Civil disobedience is dangerous to governments because previously marginalised or niche discourses become broadly activated, while the questioning of governmental actions and decisions (or the lack thereof) affords opportunities for the rise of new leaders or social movements.

To make civil disobedience an important element of the ideas and actions of XR, the movement had first to define its expectations of this tool, to come up with the ways to use it and to teach its activists how to employ it (since for many of them XR was the first step on the way to civil engagement). The use of the socially engaged tool that is civil disobedience in XR represents a form of practising public pedagogy, as understood by Biesta (2018), as it is based on the analysis of social, political, media, social-media and educational discourses and on the launching (and encouraging) of actions for the sake of the general public and on behalf of groups that have not yet perceived or have failed to understand the gravity of the situation (Biesta, 2018). Civil disobedience is also an activity for the sake of the community and finds its educational and political legitimation in pedagogies of resistance, which involve "remedial activities" in the face of local and global oppression (Horton & Freire, 1990; Zańko, 2020, pp. 107–248). Finally, civil disobedience is also an element of biographical learning, as well as of 'self-directed' and 'externally-directed' transformations in certain political, social and personal contexts (Alheit, 2018; Biesta, 2018). These pedagogical categories augment the ideas of civil disobedience with concepts which are appreciated by people who approach their XR participation as an informal educational activity. Besides civil engagement, it also brings about personal change. This non-material educational benefit broadens the perspectives of personal choices, reflections and attitudes. Its social dimension is manifested in educating members, observers, onlookers and readers and in the ways of articulating individual positions. A key factor in civil disobedience consists in the activation of the "political self", which, according to F. Gros,

> contains a principle of universal justice and is above all not simply 'the public image' of oneself as opposed to the internal self. We must stop confusing the public and the external. The public self is our political intimacy. It is, within us, the power of judgment, the capacity to think, the critical faculty. And it is from this point in us that the rejection of consensual self-evidence, social conformity and take-away thought wells up. This resource of the political self, however, remains vain and unproductive if it is not supported by a collective, linked to a group action decided on by many, and the bearer of a project for the future. Without it, movements of disobedience risk at every turn being instrumentalized, recruited and stifled under slogans and changes of leadership. (Gros, 2020, p. 7)

Gros's reflection envisions people morphing into activists who comprehend the power of their voices and mobilise their agency. Such concepts surfaced in the narratives of our interlocutors – the members of XR Poland.

In the XR movement, in pursuit of the movement's goals of climate protection, civil disobedience is considered to be the basic instrument for influencing governments. XR activists firmly believe that it is urgent to muster mass civil involvement by launching concerted information-cum-action campaigns which further the realisation of their demands. E. Chenoweth's '3.5% principle' (Chenoweth, 2020), which is based on the study of citizens' activity, mass participation of the minimum 3.5% of the population and exerting pressure on governments, has been espoused by the movement as one of its principles (About Us, 2020). Besides its aura as morally justified action, civil disobedience is also a spectacular pursuit, especially in societies with low levels of civil activity.

To persuade 3.5% of Poles to undertake work for the sake of the climate and become involved in social actions and civil activities seems a daunting task. If we specify that this means more than one million people, the task seems a veritable mission impossible. The point is that the idea entertained here is one of mass engagement in a society whose social capital is ranked among Europe's lowest and where mutual trust levels are dismally low (Kurowska & Theiss, 2018; Markowska-Przybyła & Ramsey, 2016). Given this, the actions of XR Poland activists are preceded by educational campaigns, the establishment of local sections, the effective management of the social media of local XR groups, the use of internal communication platforms and the solid planning of civil disobedience events. The symbolic power of actions serves as an important tool of identification with the movement and its demands, because every civil disobedience entails potential personal risks to the participant. This compels the witnesses of such acts to reflect on the motivations that drive the activists who put their freedom on the line for the sake of climate. Why do they do this? An activist's narrative pictures this engagement in the following way:

IL_4
[…] because civil disobedience is about people being ready to sacrifice some good that they have for the sake of the common good […]

[…] *bo obywatelskie nieposłuszeństwo jest też o tym, że ludzie są w stanie poświęcić jakieś swoje dobro na rzecz jakiegoś powszechniejszego dobra* […]

By the end of 2020, XR Poland had staged three big civil disobedience events: two in Warsaw and one in Wrocław. The first action in Warsaw took place on 27th September 2019, when the activists stopped the traffic at the De Gaulle Roundabout, one of the city's major junctions (Społeczna Inicjatywa Medialna, 2019); and the second was launched on 7th September 2020, when Świętokrzyska Str., a big inner-city artery, was blocked during the morning rush hours (Szymanderski-Pastryk, 2020). The action in Wrocław, on 24th September 2019, jammed the traffic on the street leading to Wrocław's Lower Silesian Province Office. Blockades at the venues critical for the urban traffic are by no means the only form of XR civil disobedience activities. The activists also often employ 'artivist' instruments, that is, practices in which art – specifically, engaged forms of art linked to everyday and communal life – is used for activist purposes (Glăveanu, 2017). XR activists usually avail themselves of street art strategies and culture jamming devices. For example, in June 2019, they stuck subversive leaflets visually and verbally reminiscent of obituaries on the buildings of Poland's biggest cities, amongst which Wrocław and Warsaw. One of them read: "In loving memory of Poland, 966–2050, who died of global warming, flooding by the Baltic, hunger, drought and wars. Saddened by her passing, we invite you to join the funeral" (Extinction Rebellion, 2019). In September 2019, as part of the Rebellion Week organised by XR, female activists dressed up as Red Widows and accompanied by mourners in red appeared on the streets of Warsaw and in the metropolitan underground. The performative action, which symbolically compelled the witnesses to reflect on the lethal threat of the escalating climate crisis, was commented on by XR activists: "We are part of the picture. We are driven by COMPASSION and our emotion flows from the very depths of our being in the endangered and ignored world. Freely and free. Our specific intent in entering the urban space is to MOVE and IMPRESS" (MSZ, 2019).

These critical pedagogies of performance (Denzin, 2009) had at their core government-targeted demands to launch preventive policies against the climate catastrophe as quickly as possible. The acts of civil disobedience informed by the philosophy of artivism embodied an attempt to re-channel attention toward the climate crisis in ways radically departing from the mainstream narrative. As such, XR actions fully tap into the possibilities offered by civil society within the bounds of the democratic order. When exploring civil disobedience, Gros emphasises that democracy is not just a political system as any other one, but a *critical process* which cuts across all of them and "forces them to be precisely *more democratic*. It is a demand for freedom, equality and solidarity. This demand, which moves disobedience, is critical democracy" (Gros, 2020, p. 140, italics in original).

Following the 2015 parliamentary elections, a coalition government of nationalist-populist parties with anti-civil liberties, anti-EU and anti-climatic political objectives is in power in Poland, who disassembles the democratic mechanisms and institutions. The citizens who contested the Polish government had to recall what instruments could be used in resisting governmental policies. Civil disobedience was one of the items on this list. As observed by the Polish Ombudsman A. Bodnar, "towards the end of 2015, this story made its comeback, the only thing was that it was somewhat unmoored, and it was unclear what this civil disobedience should actually consist in" (Bodnar & Bartosik, 2020, p. 18). Four years later, the XR movement entered the stage, with civil disobedience as a tool which its members had been diligently preparing themselves to employ. Before any action was launched, the XR groups studied here had invested a lot of effort in designing civil disobedience actions, formulating and getting their message across, learning how to act and boosting intra-group belief that this particular form was what made the movement distinct. The narratives below, which were collected before the second of the XR actions, exemplify various contexts shaping attitudes to civil disobedience:

> IL_9
> In our Wrocław group, the story with our actions, with civil disobedience, was also that, I guess, we needed this kind of test, to see what it was all about, whether we were up to it and what the responses would be,

because you often don't know what the police will do, whether anybody will respond to it and what happens later

Z tym naszym działaniem właśnie, jako grupy wrocławskiej, nieposłuszeństwem obywatelskim to tak też było, że chyba była potrzeba takiego sprawdzenia właśnie, jak to u nas jest i czy jesteśmy w stanie, jakie będą reakcje, bo też często nie wiadomo jak się na przykład zachowa policja, czy ktoś na to zareaguje i co dalej się będzie działo.

The possible responses at the two ends of action are an important factor in deciding to resort to civil disobedience. The lack of experience in using this kind of instrument of protest was an important reason behind comprehensively revised preparations for participation in civil disobedience. In the XR movement, such activities associated with informal learning, preparations for events and the cultivation of bonds are referred to as the culture of regeneration (About Us, 2020). The skills of working with people who want to fully exercise their citizen rights but need support are also a trademark of the new activism, in which direct action is only one component of broadly conceived activity, and activists prepare in mutual care for socially and biographically important events.

Preparations for the first organised action of civil disobedience were also associated with efforts for the integration of local XR groups, the development of the communication model and learning to act together, which was in and of itself both a stage in the formation of the Polish structures of the movement and an element of informal learning of being-in-the-group.

IL_6
Firstly, networking, because on paper, there were, *about a dozen groups in Poland declared their existence, let's say 10 to 12,* but in fact *communication* among these groups *was zero,* save Facebook or whatever, and it was completely bland, while we wanted to stage our first civil disobedience event in the autumn, first declarations of rebellion in Poland

Po pierwsze, networking, *ponieważ istniało już na papierze,* ***deklarowało się, relatywnie kilkanaście grup w Polsce, powiedzmy*** *10–12, ale de facto komunikacja była żadna pomiędzy tymi grupami, oprócz tam Facebooka jakiegoś i to było takie nijakie, a na jesień chcieliśmy zrobić pierwsze nieposłuszeństwo obywatelskie, pierwsze deklaracje rebelii w Polsce*

From the perspective of XR activists civil disobedience was as a matter of fact a necessity, given that the standard methods that citizens could use to impact the government had proven to be ineffective. Consequently, XR as a new activist movement has tried to promote a new form of action, as confirmed by our interlocutors' narratives:

IL_7
Sometimes, in introductory meetings, we say that petitioning and other such standard forms of protest didn't work, and that is why Extinction Rebellion appeared and has been using the strategy of civil disobedience, but it's actually not fully true, because, emphatically, if it weren't for these prior movements, well we wouldn't be as effective either

My czasami mówimy, że, na spotkaniach wprowadzających, że te petycje i takie standardowe formy protestu nie działały, dlatego powstała Extinction Rebellion i ona wykorzystuje strategię obywatelskiego nieposłuszeństwa, ale nie jest tak do końca, bo właśnie to też trzeba zaznaczać, że gdyby nie było tamtych ruchów poprzednich, no to my też nie bylibyśmy tak skuteczni

IL_3
And that clicked for me, it simply did, it clicked for me that it was pressure exerted in a peaceable way but categorically, meaning common civil disobedience

No mi to zagrało, po prostu zagrało, zagrało mi to, że jest to presja, że jest to presja wywierana w sposób pokojowy, ale jednak kategoryczny, czyli powszechne nieposłuszeństwo obywatelskie.

IL_9
But I think that in fact what I've just started, that this belief in the effectiveness of this form of opposition is the main impulse to try such things, but also that it may be an opportunity to reformulate this disobedience somewhat; for example, it becomes performative, that when they had these costumes on and dug across this lawn in London, this was also a form of this kind, simply not yet a familiar one

Ale myślę, że tak naprawdę właśnie to co zaczęłam, że ta wiara w skuteczność tej formy oporu to jest główny motor tego, żeby coś takiego próbować, ale też może to jest okazja, żeby to nieposłuszeństwo trochę przeformułować, tak jak na przykład ono się robi takie performatywne, że w jakichś strojach tak jak na przykład ten trawnik przekopywali w Londynie, że to też jest taka forma, tylko nieobeznana do tej pory

These interview excerpts encapsulate the key dimensions of XR in Poland: the regaining of radical tools of social influence due to the energy of the new movement; the openness and mass character of civil change-oriented actions; the radicalisation of citizens' activities and their performativity. Besides the fundamental deliberate transgression of the law and the endorsement of the nonviolence principle, civil disobedience actions launched by XR Poland Activists were meticulously prepared acts which brought the message of the movement into relief in the overall action script and the content presented during the events; the movement's logo was always exposed, sound systems were used to ensure audibility, and the events were widely publicised in social media, which had addressed the issues in advance and thus secured a mass resonance for XR undertakings. The imperative of immediate action against climate catastrophe, which has been the central axis of all the activities launched by the XR movement, echoes Klein's insistence on the weightiness and necessity of such actions:

> The urgency of the climate crisis also gives us something that can be very helpful for getting big things done: a firm, unyielding, science-based deadline. We are, it bears repeating, out of time. We've been kicking the can down the road for so many decades that we are just plain out of road. Which means if we want a shot at avoiding catastrophic Warming, we need to start a grand political and economic transition *right now*. (Klein, 2017, p. 213, original emphasis)

Besides involving collective activities, civil disobedience is always bound up with personal engagement, individual decisions to participate, and doubts prompted by the risk of being arrested, punished or otherwise harassed; at the same time, civil disobedience affords opportunities for reaping non-material benefits, such as self-knowledge and experience. Such reflections were articulated in the narratives of our interlocutor as well:

> IL_1
> So, starting from this assumption, we, as it were, concluded that we were past the option of education, and that we should rather encourage civil disobedience, and, let's say, it was a kind of education, outward-going, so to speak, outreach
>
> *Czyli jakby wychodząc z tego założenia my uznaliśmy, że właśnie opcja edukacji już jest gdzieś tam za nami i raczej powinniśmy namawiać do nieposłuszeństwa obywatelskiego i to był jakiś tam rodzaj edukacji powiedzmy, jakby na zewnątrz, outreach*

IL_2
[…] at the same time, I had a bit of a problem with it, that I wasn't going to be at the frontline of confrontation with the police; well, I simply had no experience of it, and I felt really bad about not being able to initiate some hardcore action, even though I feel brave, but simply to do one thing or another, say, that we're painting squad cars, whatever, just guessing, simply I'm not able to do this. Practically, I feel brave, but on the other hand, gosh, I don't want to do it. So there were such aspects to it. But I tried to take part in these actions, and find a place for myself, and give my support till the very end

[…] jednocześnie też trochę miałem z tym problemu, że ja nie miałem też być może pójść w pierwszej linii konfrontacji z policją, no nie miałem doświadczenia wcześniej i ja się czułem strasznie źle z tym, że ja nie potrafię zainicjować jakiejś hardcorowej akcji, pomimo tego, że się czuję odważny, żeby po prostu zrobić coś tam, że malujemy radiowozy, nie mam pojęcia, tak już teraz strzelając, że nie jestem w stanie, żeby to zrobić. Praktycznie czuję się odważny, a z drugiej strony kurde, no nie chcę tego robić. Więc takie elementy w to wchodziły. Ale starałem się w tych akcjach uczestniczyć i znajdować sobie jakieś miejsce i zawsze właśnie wspierać do samego końca

IL-1
Well, honestly, *the thing that has always fascinated me most was these civil disobedience actions; I've learned a lot in this group*, briefly, we've staged a few cool actions and with really fantastic people, and I've learned a lot there

No i nie ukrywam, **że najbardziej mnie gdzieś tam fascynowały właśnie akcje nieposłuszeństwa obywatelskiego, bardzo dużo się nauczyłem w tej grupie,** *tak pokrótce, kilka akcji udało się fajnych zrobić z naprawdę wspaniałym ludźmi i bardzo dużo się dowiedziałem tam.*

5 XR: A New Formula for a Social Movement?

We may risk a thesis that the main areas of activity of the XR movement identified and described by us embody a new format of social movements. We believe that this new format of social movements is, first of all, related to the process of learning by XR activists from the experience of non-governmental organisations, informal groups, social movements, which were active in Poland and in the world before and after 2000. We mean here civil and animal rights organisations, pacifist and environmental groups, as well as numerous anti-globalist and alter-globalist movements operating in the era of social media. The leaderlessness of the movement postulated by XR activists, the use of social media, the efficient management of electronic communication, the development of an image policy and the creation of own information channels for supporters of the XR movement are just some of the effects of learning, drawing creatively on the achievements of other organisations, groups and social movements operated before them.

From an educational perspective, XR activists themselves engage importantly in a bottom-up process of creating and learning *democracy in action* (Biesta, 2011), which stands in opposition to a passive form of democratic education based on objectifying socialisation. The pedagogies of the XR movement seem to go beyond those rational modes of teaching and learning that can actually reinforce repressive myths by trying to dictate how individuals should think, who they should be and what they should do etc., instead of allowing for the creation of an open discourse of resistance that also takes into account performative, aesthetic, bodily, and emotional dimensions (Burdick & Sandlin, 2013). In our view, the pedagogies of the XR movement are also part of post-humanist thinking about the world, deconstructing the dualistic mind of man, blurring the – essentially violent – opposition created by him: culture – nature, demolishing the misconception that the environment is absolutely subordinated to man (Burdick & Sandlin, 2013).

Secondly, based on knowledge from interviews what is new is the creation of a movement formula that seeks to ensure XR activists' physical and psychological safety – called by XR principles regenerative culture, particularly during actions that draw on ideas of civil disobedience. XR activists attempt to combine mass demands for urgent change in climate policy with attention to the individual aspirations and needs of their members. At the same time, XR's actions can be seen to differentiate the massified global demands of the Movement and make them more real to local, national situations. XR's cultural practices are well grounded in the realities of everyday life.

Third, the XR movement is a movement that actively supports other minorities, oppressed, subjugated groups fighting for their rights in conservative Poland. For example, in 2020, XR activists supported protests by LGBTQ+ communities discriminated against in Poland and supported protests by women opposing stricter anti-abortion laws. During these demonstrations, flags of the XR movement could be seen flying. Solidarity posts by XR activists appeared on social media. Moreover, members of the XR movement, referring to the *know-how of the* movement, supported the protesters by teaching them how to behave when arrested by the police (providing practical information on legal responsibility) and how to deal with the consequences of participating in civil disobedience (providing practical tips on how to reduce stress related to experienced violence and other repercussions of being in a protest).

This multidimensionality of the XR movement allows us to think of it as a new social movement with a glocal orientation, responding with care and responsibility to the needs of its members, supporting the voice of other resistance groups fighting for a more democratic, just world. XR is creating a new quality of social participation that will result in a broader awareness of climate change and, above all, in mass action for micro and macro changes that will reduce environmental degradation and thus increase the chances of survival of our planet.

Note

1 At the request of our interlocutors, we made their statements anonymous. In the chapter, instead of the names of XR activists, we use the abbreviation IL (Interlocutor). The original Polish is given together with an English translation.

References

Alheit, P. (2018). Biographical learning – within the lifelong learning discourse. In K. Illeris (Ed.), *Contemporary Theories of Learning* (pp. 154–165). Routledge.

Ambroziak, A., & Pacewicz, P. (2020, February 21). We are sending 52 reports on 'LGBT freezones' to twin regions of the EU. Terminate the agreement! *OKO.press*. https://oko.press/we-are-sending-52-reports-on-lgbt-free-zones-to-twin-regions-of-the-eu-terminate-the-agreement/

Apple, M. W. (2012). *Can education change society?* Routledge.

Arendt, H. (1972). *Crises of the republic: Lying in politics, civil disobedience, non-violence, thoughts on politics and revolution*. Harcourt Brace Jovanovich.

Biesta, G. (2011). The ignorant citizen: Mouffe, Rancière, and the subject of democratic education. *Studies in Philosophy and Education, 30,* 141–153.

Biesta, G. (2018). Interrupting the politics of learning. In K. Illeris (Ed.), *Contemporary theories of learning* (pp. 243–259). Routledge.

Blackstone, W. T. (1971). The definition of civil disobedience. *Journal of Social Philosophy, 2*(1), 5–8. https://doi.org/10.1111/j.1467-9833.1971.tb00198.x

Bloom, H. (Ed.). (2007). *Henry David Thoreau* (Updated). Bloom's Literary Criticism.

Bodnar, A., & Bartosik, B. (2020). *Obywatel PL*. Wyd. WAM.

Burdick, J., & Sandlin, J. A. (2013). Learning, becoming, and the unknowable: Conceptualizations, mechanisms, and process in public pedagogy literature. *Curriculum Inquiry, 43*(1), 142–177. https://doi.org/10.1111/curi.12001

Cervinkova, H., & Rudnicki, P. (2019). Neoliberalism, neoconservatism, authoritarianism: The politics of public education in Poland. *Journal for Critical Education Policy Studies, 17*(2), 1–23.

Chase S. E. (2005). Narrative inquiry: Multiple lenses, approaches, voices. In N. K. Denzin & Y. S. Lincoln (Eds.), *The Sage handbook of qualitative research.* (3rd ed., pp. 651–680). Sage Publications.

Chenoweth, E. (2020). *Questions, answers, and some cautionary updates regarding the 3.5% rule.* Harvard University. https://carrcenter.hks.harvard.edu/files/cchr/files/CCDP_005.pdf

Denzin, N. K. (2009). A critical performance pedagogy that matters. *Ethnography and Education, 4*(3), 255–270. https://doi.org/10.1080/17457820903170085

Extinction Rebellion. (2019). *Polska 966–2050.*

Glăveanu, V. P. (2017). Art and social change. The role of creativity and wonder. In S. H. Awad & B. Wagoner (Eds.), *Street art of resistance* (pp. 19–37). Palgrave Macmillan.

Goto Gray, S., Raimi, K. T., Wilson, R., & Árvai, J. (2019). Will Millennials save the world? The effect of age and generational differences on environmental concern. *Journal of Environmental Management, 242,* 394–402. https://doi.org/10.1016/j.jenvman.2019.04.071

Gros, F. (2020). *Disobey! A guide to ethical resistance.* Verso Books.

Horton, M., & Freire, P. (1990). *We make the road by walking conversations on education and social change* (B. Bell, J. Gaventa, & J. Peters, Eds.). Temple University Press.

Johnson, C. G. (2011). The urban precariat, neoliberalization, and the soft power of humanitarian design. *Journal of Developing Societies, 27*(3–4), 445–475.

Klein, N. (2017). *No is not enough: Resisting Trump's shock politics and winning the world we need.* Haymarket Books.

Korolczuk, E. (2020). The fight against 'gender' and 'LGBT ideology': New developments in Poland. *European Journal of Politics and Gender, 3*(1), 165–167. https://doi.org/10.1332/251510819X15744244471843

Krastev, I., & Holmes, S. (2020). *The light that failed: Why the West is losing the fight for democracy.* Pegasus Books.

Kurowska, A., & Theiss, M. (2018). Solidarity practices in Poland and their social capital foundations. In C. Lahusen & M. Grasso (Eds.), *Solidarity in Europe: Citizens' responses in times of crisis* (pp. 103–126). Palgrave Macmillan. https://doi.org/10.1007/978-3-319-73335-7_5

Kvale, S. (2007). *Doing interviews.* Sage Publications.

Markowska-Przybyła, U., & Ramsey, D. M. (2016). The association between social capital and membership of organisations amongst Polish students. *Journal of Scientific Papers Economics & Sociology*, *9*(4), 305–321. https://doi.org/10.14254/2071-789X.2016/9-4/19

Masson-Delmotte, V., Panmao, Z., Pörtner, H.-O., Roberts, D., Skea, J., Shukla, P. R., Pirani, A., Moufouma-Okia, W., Péan, C., Pidcock, R., Connors, S., Matthews, J. B. R., Chen, Y., Zhou, X., Gomis, M. I., Lonnoy, E., Maycock, T., Tignor, M., & Waterfield, T. (Eds.). (2018). *Global warming of 1.5°C.* An IPCC special report on the impacts of global warming of 1.5°C above pre-industrial levels and related global greenhouse gas emission pathways, in the context of strengthening the global response to the threat of climate change, sustainable development, and efforts to eradicate poverty. https://www.ipcc.ch/sr15/

McLaren, P. (2014). *Life in schools: An introduction to critical pedagogy in the foundations of education* (6th ed.). Paradigm Publishers.

msz. (2019, September 28). Tydzień Rebelii. Czerwone wdowy i czarni żałobnicy przeszli przez miasto. *Gazeta Wyborcza Warszawa*. https://warszawa.wyborcza.pl/warszawa/5,54420,25246992.html?i=3

Ost, D. (2005). *The defeat of Solidarity: Anger and politics in postcommunist Europe.* Cornell University Press.

Piotrowski, G., & Muszel, M. (2020). "Czarne protesty" jako wydarzenie transformacyjne praktyk obywatelskich działaczek z małych miast. *Civitas. Studia z Filozofii Polityki*, *27*, 131–162. https://doi.org/10.35757/CIV.2020.27.06

Polanska, D. V. (2018). Going against institutionalization: New forms of urban activism in Poland. *Journal of Urban Affairs*, *42*(2), 176–187 https://doi.org/10.1080/07352166.2017.1422982

Potulicka, E., & Rutkowiak, J. (2012). *Neoliberalne uwikłania edukacji*. Impuls.

Rawls, J. (2005). *A theory of justice* (Original ed.). Belknap Press.

Sowa, J. (2015). *Inna Rzeczpospolita jest możliwa! Widma przeszłości, wizje przyszłości.* W.A.B.

Społeczna Inicjatywa Medialna. (2019). *Marsz Klimatyczny i blokada Ronda de Gaulle'a* [Video]. YouTube. https://utn.pl/USJLA

Szymanderski-Pastryk, M. (2020). *Blokada centrum Warszawy przez Extinction Rebellion #Rebelia2020*. [Video]. YouTube. https://utn.pl/oy2of

Thunberg, G. (2019). *No one is too small to make a difference*. Penguin.

Zańko, P. (2020). *Pedagogie oporu*. Impuls.

PART 4

Re-Making Community

CHAPTER 12

Changes in Community Life

Marjorie Mayo

Abstract

This chapter sets out to summarise the effects of the economic, political and social changes that have been impacting most heavily on the most disadvantaged communities in Europe. These effects have been exacerbated by the impacts of the COVID-19 pandemic, since its emergence in 2020. There is evidence of increasing polarisation as a result, with the growth of Far Right extremism, along with evidence of increasingly overt racism, sexism, homophobia and Islamophobia. But there is also contrasting evidence of resistance to Far Right extremism, with examples of community-based solidarity and mutual support, examples that illustrate the contributions of adult learning and popular education, exploring alternative ways forward, based on narratives of hope, not hate.

The chapter concludes that adult learning and popular education are more important than ever in the contemporary context, whatever their inherent limitations, as subsequent chapters go on to demonstrate. Lockdowns have been imposing constraints on face-to-face engagements, but adult educators have been responding in innovative ways, widening participation through digital technologies, reaching new audiences in the process, both locally and beyond. There would seem to be positive lessons here with potentially significant implications for post pandemic times.

Keywords

adult learning – popular education – mutual aid – COVID-19 pandemic – far right populism – disadvantaged communities – neo-liberal globalisation – austerity – social solidarity

1   Introduction: 2008 to Now

Back in 2008, the proceedings of a European Research Conference focused on the 'Local in Global: Adult Learning and Community Development' (Fragoso et al., 2008, 2011). Together these papers made a compelling case for the importance of adult learning, promoting active democratic citizenship, enabling communities to address their concerns at the local level and beyond, in the context of globalisation, pursuing democratic agendas for solidarity and social justice.

That was then. But 2008 was a momentous year, marking a watershed for so many communities across Europe and beyond, internationally. So much has changed – and in so many ways. This chapter sets out to summarise the effects of the economic, political and social changes that have been impacting most heavily on the most disadvantaged communities in our societies.

The first part of this chapter focuses on the impact of the financial crash of 2007–2008. Whilst the financial order survived (with government support for the City of London, in the British case), austerity programmes have been experienced by the rest of us, including those in greatest economic and social need (Farnsworth & Irving, 2015). Neoliberal globalisation had been leading to increasing polarisation, as it was. Austerity policies have been exacerbating the situation still further, since 2008.

Increasing poverty and social deprivation have been the result, with growing fragmentation, as communities have been competing for diminishing supplies of quality jobs and services (Dorling, 2010, 2018). The growth of zero hours contracts has been particularly marked in Britain, as labour markets have been fragmenting in the context of neoliberal austerity. But job insecurity has been experienced more widely internationally, along with increasing fears for the future. Small wonder then that Far Right populist movements have been able to exploit people's anxieties and resentments, blaming outsiders, the 'other', for their situations.

And then came the COVID-19 pandemic, highlighting the problems still further. Communities' responses have differed significantly. The COVID-19 pandemic has been demonstrating the possibilities for more collaborative ways forward. There have been inspiring examples of mutual aid and social solidarity in response to COVID-19. And there have been creative ways of engaging communities, using new technologies to communicate, despite the lockdowns. There are lessons here for the development of more inclusive approaches to adult learning and community development for the future. But there have been less inspiring responses too, (including cases of racist violence against Asians, blamed for allegedly bringing the virus into Britain from China). The pandemic has been highlighting – and exacerbating – existing problems within our societies, with increasing inequalities, yawning gaps in public services and diminishing levels of trust in democratic solutions in the context of 'fake news'. This has been the context for the growth of Far Right populism.

The chapter then moves on to consider experiences of adult learning and popular education in response to these challenges. Popular education sets out to work with communities to explore their anxieties and concerns, unpacking the underlying causes of their problems (Crowther et al, 2005, Freire, 1972, 1996). This approach provides the basis for developing more effective collective strategies for social change, working with communities from the bottom up. This is not about simply giving people the facts, but about enabling them to distinguish between the facts and 'fake news' for themselves, in the context of Far Right populism – taking rational decisions about whether to get vaccinated, for example, rather than succumbing to the myths of the anti-vaxxers. And this is also about taking account of people's emotions, their only too understandable resentments and fears (Hoggett, 2016), as the basis for developing mutual understanding, building less divisive strategies for communities' futures.

There are numerous examples of adult learning and popular education to illustrate these arguments, including examples of informal learning through the arts and sports, such as the UK movement to tackle racism in football, established in recent decades yet sadly still needed.[1] Popular education takes place in a variety of settings, including community-based learning through engaging in mutual support networks (Sitrim & Colectiva Sembrar, 2020). These can provide rich opportunities for collective learning, developing shared strategies for responding to the challenges of COVID-19 – whilst taking account of the limitations, bearing in mind the importance of linking the local with the global, developing wider strategies for the pursuit of social justice.

The chapter concludes that adult learning and popular education are more important than ever in the contemporary context, whatever their inherent limitations, as subsequent chapters go on to demonstrate. Lockdowns have been imposing constraints on face-to-face engagements, but adult educators have been responding in innovative ways, widening participation through digital technologies, reaching new audiences in the process, both locally and beyond. There would seem to be positive lessons here with potentially significant implications for post pandemic times.

2 The Impacts of the Financial Crash of 2007–2008

The causes of the financial crash were rooted in neo-liberal globalisation processes, precipitated by the tensions arising from increasing financialisation. And so were the impacts which were similarly global in their reach. There have been variations across national borders, of course, both in Europe and beyond. But local experiences need to be understood within this global framework.

In Britain, for example, successive governments decided that the financial sector had to be protected, leaving the most vulnerable to bear the costs of the austerity policies that followed. By 2015 the arithmetically average household in the best-off 10% of the income distribution in UK had 17 times more money to live on each year than the arithmetically average household in the poorest tenth of UK society (Dorling, 2018, p. 143). The gap between the richest 1% and the poorest was more startling by far, never mind the gap between the richest 0.1% of the population and the rest. These inequalities have been increasing. And they have been the result of policy choices by governments, choices that have been described in terms of "the symbiotic relationship between austerity and neoliberalism, a fusing of ideology and economics that is both subtle and obvious" that "represents a significant transformative process hiding in plain sight" (Farnsworth & Irving, 2015, pp. 3–4).

The UN Special Rapporteur on extreme poverty and human rights, Philip Alston, visited Britain in 2018, concluding that despite being the world's fifth largest economy with areas of immense wealth, a fifth of the population were living in poverty. "Britain is not just a disgrace" he concluded "but a social calamity and an economic disaster, all rolled into one". This was the result of government policies, driven by ideological commitments "to change the value system, to focus more on individual responsibility, to place major limits on government support", replacing what have been claimed as the British values of compassion with what he described as "a punitive, mean-spirited, and often callous approach apparently designed to instil discipline where it is least useful, to impose a rigid order on the lives of those least capable of coping in today's world, and elevating the goal of enforcing blind compliance over a genuine concern to improve the well-being of those at the lowest levels of British society" (Alston, 2018). Meanwhile "many of the public places and institutions that previously brought communities together, such as libraries, community and recreation centres and public parks have been steadily dismantled or undermined" – never mind the impact on other public services such as education, including adult education and health. And all before the impact of the implementation of Brexit, let alone the impact of COVID-19.

Britain has been an extreme case, then. But the economic, social and political effects of neoliberal austerity policies have been experienced more widely by far. Inequalities have been growing apace, with the most unequal societies experiencing the most destructive consequences. Drawing on data from the UN, the World Bank, the WHO and the US Census, amongst other sources, Wilkinson and Pickett have explored the connections between high levels of inequality and poor social outcomes, on a global scale, leading to shorter, unhealthier and unhappier lives, along with higher levels of violence and lower levels of social solidarity (Wilkinson & Pickett, 2010). And this research was carried out before the full impacts of austerity had been experienced, not to mention the impacts of the COVID-19 pandemic.

Cuts in public services followed just when the need for public services had been increasing, including cuts in educational provision. This would seem more important than ever in the current context. The OECD has recognised the increasing relevance of lifelong learning for broader social purposes, in the context of globalisation and climate change. But more needs to be done, with more emphasis on learning for citizenship (OECD, 2019). This report in fact argued that a healthy democracy relies on the civic knowledge and skills of its citizens, as well as their direct participation in society, and indicated the dangers associated with social media which behave like echo chambers returning people's ideas and beliefs in unaltered form. The report stressed the risks deriving from this that trust in civic institutions may decline and that unrest in society may rise. The report concluded that lifelong learning for active citizenship and democratic processes of social change remained crucial (OECD, 2019).

3 The Growth of Far Right Populism

Meanwhile Far Right populism has been growing apace. So, what do we mean by Far Right populism? Definitions of populism have been and continue to be contested, with varying understandings in different localities and contexts, from Latin America and India to Europe and the USA. Nor do all forms of populism come from the Far Right, although these are the forms that are the focus of this particular chapter. Despite the differences, however, populisms do tend to share a number of common characteristics (Lazaridis et al., 2016). Laclau has summarised these shared features as follows, starting from populisms' tendency to emerge during crises of representation, when formal political processes fail to meet social demands (Laclau, 2005). There are resonances here with the contemporary context, although Laclau himself was writing well before the 2008 recession.

In such contexts, Laclau continued, a section of the community (the 'underdog') may present itself as representing the whole community – the people versus the elite/ the establishment. The British political scientist, Crick, has described populism in similar terms as a "style of politics and rhetoric that seeks to arouse a majority who are, have been or think themselves to be outside the polity, scorned and despised by an educated elite" (Crick, 2002) defining the 'us' of the 'despised' majority against the 'others' such as immigrants, Muslims and African-Americans, to cite some of the most evident examples.

There are numerous illustrations in the contemporary context. Arlie Hochschild's study of Anger and Mourning on the American Right (Hochschild, 2016) provides a case study in point, exploring the feelings of people, especially white people in the southern states of the USA, frustrated by declining incomes and seething with resentment at bearing the brunt of government decisions to bail out the financial elite who they blamed for causing the 2008 crash in the first place. To add insult to injury, these southerners felt that liberal elites despised them for being "ignorant, backward, rednecks, losers" (Hochschild, 2016, p. 23). They were "feeling strangers in their own land, afraid, resentful, displaced and dismissed" by the very people who were doing so much better out of the crisis than they were (Hochschild, 2016 p. 23).

British studies have identified very similar grievances, fuelled by comparable emotions, mistrust of politicians, profound anxieties and comparable feelings of nostalgia. There were expressions of regret for a mythical past when Britain was great, a golden age which was being undermined by immigrants, especially Muslims (Winlow et al., 2017). But what did the so-called liberal elite care? The results of the 2016 referendum on Brexit can be seen in this context, expressing genuine – if misunderstood – grievances amongst a section (but by no means all) of those who voted to leave, exacerbated by powerful emotions of resentment, fear and nostalgia for a mythical golden past.

The British case has its own particular features, including its imperial past. Failure to come to terms with this history has been associated with the specificities of racism, xenophobia and nationalism in this country (Gilroy, 2004), highlighting the importance of decolonising the curriculum, questions that have gained new urgency in the context of Black Lives Matter. Whilst Britain has its own specific challenges to confront, there are significant issues for educationalists to address more widely, in other contexts too, however; how to tackle the underlying causes of communities' problems as well as understanding the emotional effects on people's consciousness?

Before coming onto the social, political and emotional dimensions of the challenges that need to be faced though, a brief summary of the growth of the Far Right itself as this has been taking place in Europe and elsewhere is necessary. Far Right political parties have been gaining ground, even if the trends are not all moving in the same direction. Donald Trump won the US presidential election in 2016 for example, only to lose the following election in 2020, even if by a narrow margin. There is still significant support for the Far Right in the US. The European Parliament has significant groupings of Far Right parties too, some 10% following the elections in 2019, compared with some 5% between 2014 and 2019. These groups have been divided amongst themselves with shifting alliances between them. But they would seem to give expression to widespread feelings of distrust in European institutions and national governments' abilities to tackle the problems that have been arising from the financial crash and austerity. And they provide channels for the expression of racism and xenophobia, especially resentments against Muslim immigrants and asylum seekers.

Whatever the internal contradictions and divisions within the Far Right, then, their impacts have been only too significant. These effects have not been confined to situations in which Far Right politicians have been in power, either, significant as these effects have, of course, been. Their agendas have impacted more widely too, as mainstream parties such as the Conservatives in Britain have shifted to accommodate pressures from the Far Right, as with proposals to tighten immigration controls and constrain civil liberties such as the right to peaceful protest.

4   Ideological Aspects

Populism's theoretical roots have been traced to debates within postmodernist thinking, approaches that became predominant in the last decades of the twentieth century. Questioning more structural approaches, postmodernist critiques of 'grand narratives' such as Marxism have made significant contributions to the social sciences. But these critiques have a potential downside. If there are no grand narratives does this mean that anything goes? Is it all relative? And who needs experts anyway, as a particular politician questioned in Britain in recent years? There is not the space to develop these arguments further here. The point to emphasise is simply this, that this is an ideological context in which so-called 'fake news' can flourish, a 'post truth' era in the making. And this can have literally lethal effects (Mayo, 2020).

The Far Right in the USA has produced some of the more extreme examples of this 'post truth' era. QAnon apparently considers that Democrats are running a massive ring devoted to the abduction, trafficking, torture, sexual abuse and cannibalisation of children as part of a Satanic cult. So far, so looney. But this type of disregard for the facts can be seen as part of a far wider problem. Donald Trump's allegations of fake news to discredit criticism has served to undermine public trust in politicians and in political processes more generally. The same could be said of British Prime Minister Boris Johnson's blatant disregard for the facts during the campaign to persuade voters to leave the European Union, just as he continued to disregard the facts in his initial response to the COVID-19 pandemic.

The effects are only too evident when it comes to the issue of trust in COVID-19 vaccines. Myths have been spread online, including the suggestion that vaccinations implant electronic devices that enable Bill Gates to track our every movement. Such myths have been fuelling the anxieties of anti-vaxxers, with potentially lethal effects in the context of the COVID-19 pandemic.

5 COVID-19's Effects in Summary

COVID-19 has had polarising effects within and between communities. But there have been heroic responses as well. The emergence of mutual aid groups provides one such example (Mayo, 2021; Preston & Firth, 2020). There has been evidence of increasing solidarity within and between communities. And communities have been developing their own understandings, whether through formal or less formally organised initiatives, exploring the causes and consequences of the pandemic, along with the causes and consequences of the inequalities that are being exacerbated as a result.

So how to enable communities to explore the interconnections between the global and the local dimensions of their concerns? How to start from people's immediate issues, taking their anxieties and resentments seriously, working through processes of mutually respectful dialogue? How to take account of people's emotions as well as providing the analytical tools to develop strategies towards more hopeful rather than more hateful futures (Freire, 1996)?

6 Adult Education and Community Development in the Context of the Pandemic

This is precisely where Freirian approaches to popular education have relevance, as has already been suggested, working with communities to explore their anxieties and concerns, unpacking the underlying causes of their problems (Crowther et al., 2005; Freire, 1972, 1996; James & Theriault, 2020). This type of popular education provides the basis for developing more effective collective strategies for social change, not simply giving people the facts, but enabling them to distinguish between the facts and 'fake news' for themselves, in the context of Far Right populism – taking account of people's emotions; their only too understandable resentments and fears (Hoggett, 2016).

Resources for adult education and community development have been affected by austerity in many contexts. Formal participation in adult education in the UK almost halved in the first decades of the twenty-first century (Bhattacharya et al., 2020). But this does not mean that there have been corresponding reductions in adult learning or community organising per se. On the contrary, there have been a range of examples of popular education in practice. Social movements and social movement organisations have been doing it for themselves.

In the British context activists have been educating themselves and others about the issues that have been concerning them from the teach-ins organised by the Occupy movement, through to The World Transformed (TWT) festivals from 2016. Initially organised alongside Labour Party conferences, these events have engaged literally thousands of activists, many, but not all of them young activists, keen to explore a range of economic, social and political issues via a combination of lectures, seminars, workshops and cultural events. This was not about party-political education per se – rather this was about wider processes of popular education for social change. As the programme for the 2018 event (which engaged over 6,000 participants) explained, this was an international as well as a more local event, aiming to create "an open space for collective political education that strengthens our entire movement" (The World Transformed, 2018, p. 2). This was intended to be about education for action. "Together, we are imagining the world we want to live in and planning how to get there" the programme emphasised (p. 2).

This particular TWT festival organised a workshop to share experiences of popular political education. These experiences included a wide range of activities and approaches from local study groups, popular education sessions and events including popular education initiatives targeted at specific communities and groups, such as young Black and Minority Ethnic people. The list made no claim to be comprehensive, but it did provide some indication of the range of activities involved, including popular education via cultural activities and sports. There are so many international examples of popular education via the arts to draw upon here, from street theatre, drawing on the approaches that were pioneered by Boal and others in Brazil (Boal, 1979) through to quilting in Vancouver Island, Canada and fabric arts and crafts in Aotearoa, New Zealand (Clover & Stalker, 2007). The arts and sports have particular relevance in the current context, given their potential for engaging with the emotions, taking account of people's hopes and desires as well as engaging with their resentments and anxieties.

Meanwhile, despite the restrictions that have been imposed by successive lockdowns, innovative approaches have been developing, using new technologies to reach wider audiences both locally and beyond. The necessity to operate online has had its own advantages. As the Archive and Library Manager of the Marx Memorial Library and Workers School has explained (Jump, 2021): "With other heritage organisations and education providers, we faced a new suite of problems. How could we continue to provide access to our collections and education programmes off-site?" (p. 201).

This was a major stimulus as it turned out, speeding up existing plans to develop courses online. And there were immediate benefits. Jump reflected on how "Logistical and financial obstacles surrounding inviting international speakers evaporated" and international audiences grew, as well as national and more local audiences. In the face of adversity, Jump concluded,

> MML has been able to adapt, putting our efforts behind digital innovation. This has involved expanding the reach of our education programmes, making our collections and access to our building possible in new ways and bolstering our membership scheme and related campaigns. (Jump, 2021, p. 203)

None of this is to suggest that the pandemic has been anything other than devastating, however. Some organisations have been better placed to cope than others, with more – or less – access to digital technologies. The special supplementary issue of CONCEPT included a contribution from South Africa on the challenges of redesigning popular education workshops on current issues, socio-political analysis and women's health, via the telephone (von Kotze, 2020). Online learning via the telephone presented very particular challenges, to say the least. Nor does online learning offer comparable opportunities for the promotion of critical dialogues, being less effective, perhaps, than more direct forms of popular education in practice. Not that popular education initiatives offer magic bullet solutions in any case, as will be re-emphasised subsequently. Rather, popular adult education and community development have significant contributions to make towards the development of wider strategies for change, in the context of global recession, austerity, the pandemic and the growth of Far Right populism.

7   Mutual Aid

Austerity has impacted on the provision of resources for community development, just as it has impacted on resources for adult education and lifelong learning. Yet here too, people and communities have been finding ways of coping as best they can. The pandemic may have exacerbated social divisions, with Far Right politicians fanning pre-existing tensions within and between communities. But communities have been developing more positive responses too, as exemplified by the growth of mutual aid groups, both in Britain and beyond, internationally.

There have been examples of social solidarity across a range of contexts in the Middle East, South Asia, Southern Africa, Europe and both North and

South Americas (Sitrin & Colectiva Sembrar, 2020). "Our better angels live just around the block, everywhere", Mike Davis has concluded, teaching us about "the enormous potential for love and resistance in a world threatened by apocalyptic capitalism" (Davis, 2020, back cover). Somewhat ambitious claims when set against the realities of the challenges to be faced? What has been achieved so far, then?

Mutual aid groups have clearly been offering very valuable forms of practical support, for a start. In the British context, this has involved shopping for people who are shielding, for example, picking up prescriptions for people who are sick, sharing information and advice about where and how to get other forms of support and promoting well-being initiatives such as yoga and pilates, online. People have also been providing a listening ear for each other, combatting the sense of isolation that has been affecting so many, during the pandemic lockdowns.

Most importantly too, mutual aid services are being provided on the basis of need – as expressed by the people concerned. There are absolutely no value judgements to be made about who deserves what, in my personal (if extremely limited) experience in Britain. This stands in sharp contrast with more recent public policy discourses, distinguishing the deserving from the undeserving poor, who need to be shaken out of their reliance on benefits. The cruelty of such approaches has been so clearly demonstrated in the UN's Special Rapporteur's report on his visit to investigate extreme poverty and human rights (Alston, 2018). Mutual aid is far closer to the principle of from each according to his ability, to each according to his need – consistent with a more inclusive and essentially more democratic approach.

Whilst mutual aid groups emphasise the importance of mutuality, well-being and community solidarity, this is absolutely not about communities substituting public services, however. On the contrary, in fact. The mutual aid groups with which I am familiar, in London, set out to develop constructive relationships with service providers, aiming to work in partnership with them to co-produce public services in more effective and more democratically accountable ways.

There would seem to be significant learning points here, with elements of popular education in practice, starting from people's immediate needs whilst raising questions about alternative scenarios for the future. Mutual aid groups bring you face to face with so much unmet need, illustrating the appalling extent of food poverty and precarious living, along with the cruelty of the benefits system, just to mention some of the most obvious lessons to be learnt in the British context. Such experiences can raise participants' consciousness, increasing people's awareness of the need for longer term strategies to tackle the underlying causes of poverty, inequality, discrimination and oppression. And mutual aid groups can raise participants' consciousness through their engagement in prefigurative forms of social relationships, testing out alternative ways of living and relating to each other more collectively.

8 Conclusions

This chapter started from the challenges posed by recession, austerity and the COVID-19 pandemic, challenges that impact upon community life in different contexts across the globe. The associated growth of Far Right populism has been exacerbating these challenges, fuelling resentments and fears within and between communities; undermining trust in the context of 'fake news'. Popular adult, community-based education offers no magic bullets in response. On the contrary. But popular adult community-based education does have contributions to make, enabling communities to explore more hopeful ways forward for the future.

Critical thinking would seem to be more necessary than ever in this 'post truth' era, as Sandra Egege's work on teaching critical thinking (Egege, 2020) illustrates. Students need to be able to evaluate competing theories, including conspiracy theories, weighing up the evidence rather than assuming that any one view is as valid as any other. We need to have the tools to engage with climate change deniers for instance, just as we need the tools to engage with anti-vaxxers. And we need to be aware of our own emotional investments in our existing beliefs (as amplified within social media bubbles). Critical thinking should be embedded within curricula, Egege proposes, as well as being taught in its own right. This can be applied to adult learning just as much as to learning in schools, colleges and universities.

Critical thinking has been central to Freirian approaches, as this chapter has also suggested, starting from people's immediate concerns, engaging them in exploring the underlying causes of their problems through processes of mutually respectful dialogue. The effects of the pandemic make this more essential than ever, given the global nature of the challenges that are being posed. There are parallels and interconnections here with the importance of understanding climate change, too, in the context of neoliberal globalisation. Veronique Tadjo's moving tales from the Ebola outbreak in West Africa emphasise precisely these points. The tree's story offers an account of the origins of Ebola from the perspective of nature itself. Human intrusions and depredations of the forest have exposed them to new viruses. This is the result of what the tree describes as the dislocation between humans and nature when "Humans today think they can do whatever they like. They fancy themselves as masters, as architects of nature ... Their voracity is boundless" with disastrous effects for the ecosystem as a result (Tadjo, 2021, p. 10).

Tadjo goes on to reflect on ways of engaging communities, through the "prefect", the public health officer's account. He explains that the outreach teams need to give people detailed information about the illness, its mode of transmission, the risks and the available treatments. But "Science alone is not enough to bring the virus under control", he adds. "We need to reduce the level of ignorance", and most importantly to take account of the tension, the fear (Tadjo, 2021, p. 74). They have to take account of people's emotions, just as they have to understand and take account of local community cultures and practices.

Community responses to the pandemic include comparable opportunities for learning, including learning through engaging in mutual aid and other initiatives to promote social solidarity. People can and do learn very practical lessons about their immediate situations and their community's needs, along with very practical lessons about the inadequacies of public policy responses. There are so many questions to be explored about the underlying causes of people's immediate problems and the ways in which these inter-connect at local, national and international levels.

Communities' engagement in mutual aid and other forms of social solidarity contain wider implications for the future, too. These forms of engagement have been offering experiences of prefigurative forms, sketching out alternative ways of living and relating to each other in more mutually supportive ways. There are other, more hopeful – and more sustainable – possibilities, prefiguring the development of "new societies in the shells of the old" (Preston & Firth, 2020, p. 67).

Note

1 https://www.theredcard.org

References

Alston, P. (2018). *Statement on visit to the United Kingdom, by Professor Phillip Alston, United Nations special rapporteur on extreme poverty and human rights*. Office of the United Nations High Commissioner for Human Rights.

Bhattacharya, A., Corfe, S., & Norman, A. (2020). *(Adult) education, education, education*. Social Market Foundation.

Boal, A. (1979). *Theatre of the oppressed*. Pluto.

Clover, D., & Stalker, J. (Eds.). (2007). *The arts and social justice*. NIACE.

Crick, B. (2002). *Democracy: A very short introduction*. Oxford University Press.

Crowther, J., Galloway, V., & Martin, I. (2005). Introduction: Radicalising intellectual work. In J. Crowther, V. Galloway, & I. Martin (Eds.), *Popular education: Engaging the academy* (pp. 1–7). NIACE.

Davis, M. (2020). Back cover note. In M. Sitrin & Colectiva Sembrar (Eds.), *Pandemic solidarity*. Pluto.

Dorling, D. (2010). *Injustice*. Policy Press.

Dorling, D. (2018). *Peak inequality*. Policy Press.

Egege, S. (2020). *Becoming a critical thinker*. Macmillan.

Farnsworth, K., & Irving, Z. (Eds.). (2015). *Social policy in times of austerity*. Policy Press.

Fragoso, A., Kurantowicz, E., & Lucio-Villegas, E. (Eds.). (2008). *Local in global: Adult learning and community development*. WN DSW.

Fragoso, A., Kurantowicz, E., & Lucio-Villegas, E. (Eds.). (2011). *Between global and local: Adult learning and development*. Peter Lang.

Freire, P. (1972). *Pedagogy of the oppressed*. Penguin.

Freire, P. (1996). *Pedagogy of hope*. Bloomsbury.

Gilroy, P. (2004). *After empire*. Routledge.

Hochschild, A. R. (2016). *Strangers in their own land: Anger and mourning on the American Right*. New Press.

Hoggett, P. (2016). *Politics, identity and emotion*. Routledge.

James, N., & Theriault, V. (2020). Adult education in times of the Covid-19 pandemic: Inequalities, changes, and resilience. *Studies in the Education of Adults, 5*(2), 129–133.

Jump, M. (2021). MML operating in a time of Covid: Challenges and opportunities. *Theory & Struggle. 122*. 200–203. https://doi.org/10.3828/ts.2021.20

Laclau, E. (2005). Populism: What's in a name? In F. Panizza (Ed.), *Populism and the mirror of democracy* (pp. 32–49). Verso.

Lazaridis, G., Campani, G., & Benviste, A. (Eds.). (2016). *The rise of the far right in Europe*. Palgrave Macmillan.

Mayo, M. (2020). *Community-based learning and social movements*. Policy Press.

Mayo, M. (2021). Covid-19 and mutual aid: Prefigurative approaches to caring? *Theory and Struggle, 122*(1), 80–91. https://doi.org/10.3828/ts.2021.9

OECD (2019). *OECD skills outlook 2019*. https://doi.org/10.1787/df80bc12-en

Preston, J., & Firth, R. (2020). *Coronavirus, class and mutual aid in the United Kingdom*. Palgrave Macmillan.

Sitrim, M., & Colectiva Sembrar (Eds.). (2020). *Pandemic solidarity*. Pluto.

Tadjo, V. (2021). *In the company of men*. Small Axes; Hope Road.

The World Transformed. (2018). *The world transformed programme*. https://theworldtransformed.org/

von Kotze, A. (2020). Community education in times of Covid-19. *Concept, 11*(Supplement), 1–3. http://concept.lib.ed.ac.uk/article/view/4376

Wilkinson, R., & Pickett, K. (2010). *The spirit level*. Penguin Group.

Winlow, S., Hall, S., & Treadwell, J. (2017). *The rise of the far right*. Policy Press.

CHAPTER 13

Learning to Make (and Remake) Society
Social Mediation and Mediators' Learning Biographies

Rob Evans

Abstract

Mediation and the culture associated with it, characterized by the respect towards the other, focusing on dialogue, the enhancement of citizenship, the importance given to individuals, and to the development of their skills in the process of change, constitute an important factor in any process of 're-sewing' social ties under threat of rupture or loss. In a European project, encounters with social mediators took place in biographical-narrative interviews, in which individuals engaged in dialogic interaction co-create meaningful life stories. The detail of the interview talk documents significantly how professional trajectories are defined, and how this is affected by group belonging, ethnic or cultural discourses, as well as gender, age, professional and educational relationships, and so on. The biographical narratives which will be discussed in this chapter will try to show that they can offer insight into the learning processes that move individuals to work in vulnerable communities, and that the creation of a common space of experience – a space of learning in diversity – can be heard as it emerges in talk. The work of social mediators is seen as an important contribution to the making and remaking of solidarity and inclusivity in communities.

Keywords

social mediation – intercultural diversity – inclusion – learning biography – biographicity – adult learning – COVID-19 pandemic – dialogue

1   Introduction

Mediation and the culture associated with it, constitute an important factor in any process of remaking social ties under threat of rupture or loss. In a European project, encounters with social mediators took place in biographical-narrative interviews. The biographical narratives which will be discussed in this chapter try to show that they can offer insight into the learning processes that move individuals to work in vulnerable communities, and that the creation of a common space of experience – a space of learning in diversity – can be heard as it emerges in talk. The work of social mediators is seen as an important contribution to the making and remaking of solidarity and inclusivity in communities.

Before the COVID-19 pandemic broke into the lives of communities and much attention was shifted towards the health and conditions of vulnerable sections of our societies everywhere – the old and unwell, the isolated and the institutionalized, those in precarious employment and those struggling in insufficient living space to raise children alone, the young and the very young – globally concerns about the 'bonds of society' seemed focused on little more than 'catching up' after the World Financial Crisis of 2008–2009, patching up deficiencies and finding ways to limit the effects of migration. Thus, a representative report of 2019 from the Bertelsmann Stiftung for the EU and OECD (Hellmann et al., 2019) diagnosed the problems of 2019 thus:

> While the Social Justice Index shows a slight but ongoing upward trend since economic recovery began in 2014, the overall score remains below the pre-crisis level. In addition, there are still striking discrepancies with regard to available opportunities to participate in society in the 41 countries surveyed. (p. 6)

The authors of the report found that on average, very little had been done to advance social inclusion and non-discrimination in the years before. Further:

> Populist governments are also responsible in many cases for discrimination against migrants, refugees, Muslims or other religious minorities, ethnic minorities, and supporters of the LGBTQ community. According to reports by our country experts in Austria, Italy, Hungary and Poland in particular, discrimination against these groups has continued to grow. (Hellmann et al., 2019, p. 17)

Particularly since the dramatic waves of migration to the EU and US in the period after 2015, the problems of migration, work, education, diversity, and intercultural communication – and essentially of the challenge of finding some kind of *'vivencia'* (see Lucio-Villegas in this volume) as an answer to these problems worldwide – made the potential contribution of mediation and particularly *social mediation* towards the promotion of an open, inclusive, safe and peaceful civil society more relevant than ever. What is, then, social mediation and what did it offer both for the pre-pandemic world, and the world that may yet emerge from the pandemic?

I shall employ here at the outset the definition of social mediation formulated by one of the mediators interviewed for this research project. Social mediation lays claim to the definition 'social', according to Makasy (2019) because

> it sees the individual (as a system of values) and society (representing norms, values, rules) in a relationship of interdependence. This signifies that the bond that unites these two poles must be maintained for the sake of the equilibrium between the two parties and in this way society is maintained. Essentially it is about permitting each individual to find and have a place in society in its widest sense and by respecting human dignity. The aim of this is to make it possible for all to live well and create a healthy society in which it is good to live. It's about complementarity where the self, the other, us and society contribute in a kind of co-responsibility. But that is not always easy. One method for working, furthering and fixing this bond for the future is mediation which is at the heart of the daily practice of mediators. The mediator is the support, the tool that makes mediation possible in any given social context. (p. 5, author's translation)

Mediation and the culture associated with it, characterised by respect towards the Other, focusing on dialogue, the enhancement of citizenship, the importance given to individuals and to the development of their skills in the process of change, can constitute an important factor, therefore, in 're-sewing' social ties that may be guaranteed by law but which are under attack from discrimination, economic inequality, and are undermined by struggles among the most vulnerable in societies for scarce social resources.

By way of illustration of the urgency of the situation, a report published by the European Anti-Poverty Network (EAPN, 2020) pointed out the results of structural inequality in the distribution and redistribution of income and wealth after one year of COVID: they found that the pandemic was "widening the gap between richer and poorer countries, and regions, particularly urban/rural, and deprived neighbourhoods"; further they saw precarious workers as among the most hard-hit victims of the pandemic; women and minorities were seen to be over-represented in badly-paid essential jobs in retail, health and social services; inequalities in health, lack of affordable housing, unequal provision of education and lifelong learning opportunities were reported; finally, everywhere social services were overstretched and underfunded (EAPN, 2020, pp. 3–5).

In this context, social mediation represents a form of that dialogue central to the making of communities and society elaborated theoretically by Freire (Freire, 2020) and others and discussed elsewhere in this volume.[1]

In a European ERASMUS+ project,[2] social mediators took part in qualitative biographical-narrative interviews. Using extracts from biographical narratives I collected in Barcelona (2017) and Paris (2019) which will be discussed below I will try to show that they can offer insight into the learning processes that move individuals to undertake frequently difficult work in vulnerable communities, and that the creation of a common space of experience – a space of learning in diversity – can be heard as it emerges in talk (Evans, 2019). The work of social mediators is seen as an important contribution to the making and remaking of solidarity and inclusivity in communities.

2   Social Mediation

It is common to cite the Créteil declaration of 2000 as the foundation stone for the development of forms of social mediation in Europe (Bartolone, 2000). 42 experts there drew up a document which sought to define and establish basic principles. Amongst the most important principles of social mediation were its contribution to the empowerment and autonomy of citizens; the creation and repair of social bonds; the resolution of conflict and the use of peaceful means to foster citizenship and the exercise of citizens' rights; the role of a neutral third party as interlocutor between citizens and the state to enable disadvantaged and vulnerable sections of society to attain their rights and for the "proper fulfilment of the role of public services" to be guaranteed. Likewise the "respect of the rights of citizens and consumers" were, among other demands, to be fulfilled by an agreement between the state and civil authorities and citizens (Bartolone, 2000, pp. 127–128). The corporatist elements of the Créteil document are unabashed and the attempt to achieve a social deal in order to defuse growing tensions in multi ethnic communities was, and remains, transparent *and* ambivalent (see for example the very mixed aims of EFUS, 2021).

Since Créteil – and indeed since the setting up of the European Forum for Urban Security just mentioned in 1987 – many different forms of mediation have been developed and among them different realisations from country to country of social mediation. Certainly, in Europe practices vary considerably (for a relatively recent roundup see Almeida et al., 2015). Research about social mediation practices worldwide and the collection of resources for study and training are coordinated, for example, by the *Observatoire des Médiations* at the University of Lyons in France by Jean-Pierre Bonafe-Schmidt (Medit, 2021) and comparative studies of practice around the EU and in projects have been published (for example Almeida, 2016a, 2016b; Almeida et al., 2015; Silva, 2016; Silva et al., 2016, 2017, 2019).

As Almeida (2016a) points out, various forms of mediation have emerged in Europe and

> Each country has adopted mediation as an alternative mode of conflict/dispute resolution and as a form of social regulation, with a dual function, latent and manifest, 'to make society' and 'to regulate conflicts'. (p. 41)

Thus, social mediation "does society", she goes on to say

> as it creates social bonds grounded in cultural and historical representations of society, but it is also an alternative method of conflict resolution, a way that allows its transformation, relying on a voluntary commitment defined and assumed between the parties. (Almeida, 2016a, p. 42)

This form of social mediation, strongly represented and active in Southern and francophone Europe is active in schools, the community, in environmental initiatives, in public transport, the judiciary process and prisons, in health systems, and importantly in intercultural and multicultural social work. Mediators involved in the EU project around which this chapter is framed were working, for example, with refugees from Syria via a humanitarian corridor in Trapani, Sicily, with Roma communities, amongst others, in Madrid, migrants from the Maghreb and West Africa in Seville, in 'priority' communities and in public transport and citizen aid in Limoges, Pierrefitte, and Saint Quentin, France, in family mediation in Brussels, and with refugees in Saxony-Anhalt in Germany, to name only some of their areas of work.

The pandemic hit the work of social mediators hard. While the lockdowns of various severities immediately rendered routine face-to-face operations impossible, there was, as everywhere else, a marked growth in the use of digital communication, with all its concomitant inequalities. Ben Mrad and Demaret state that electronic conferencing became, in fact, mediators' main instrument for interventions (Ben Mrad & Demaret, 2021, p. 1). In this connection, Moisan (2021) draws out the peculiar ironies of the lockdown situations created in response to the COVID-19 pandemic:

> This new context represents a powerful revaluation for social mediation. Social mediation is no more than 40 years of age and it has the task to create or repair social bonds in response to requirements of the state or

the health authorities. Lockdown is like a huge wave that subsiding carries away with it the whole substance of social life in communities: the schools and the bonds they create for children, parents and the institutions that remain closed down; social centres and every space for cultural, sports or leisure activities are deserted; teams of social workers are gone; all religious activities are suspended. All the 'essentials' which the state usually provides excluded, everything that makes up the salt of everyday relations. In a sense, this is the moment of truth for social mediation. (p. 25, author's translation)

Moisan cites two examples from France where the rules of social distancing and lockdown signified that the work of maintaining contact with civil society and guaranteeing assistance and solidarity where most desperately needed fell entirely onto the social mediators employed by the respective local administrations. Where practically every normal form of citizen's advice, family counselling, family-school communication, or maintaining contact with the elderly, sick and solitary was shut down (or limited for reasons of hygiene to 'window-counselling'[3]), the teams of day and night mediators took on many new urgent tasks. The examples from Limoges and Saint Quentin (Moisan, 2021, p. 27) are eloquent testimony for this transformation and promotion of the fields in which social mediators work to re-make society. While Moisan pointedly employs the metaphor of the breakers and their undertow, elsewhere in this volume we are shown how the pandemic has created its own social 'wake' in the form of thousands of volunteers, local initiatives, community interventions. The unforeseen might of the pandemic 'wave' pushed these actors into dialogue and cooperation. The durability of these new social bonds have yet to manage the transition at some point to some kind of 'normality'. The following pages will seek to answer the question: what drives the social mediator in her work? What, by extension, drives, and has to drive the remaking of communities?

3   The Project and Interview Data

The CReE-A project (*Création d'un espace européen-Arlekin*) had as its objective the creation of a professional community for social mediation in Europe. A European consortium involving 7 national partners, which included organisations for mediation and training, universities, cities, individual experts for mediation theory and praxis, as well as representatives from national as well as European politics, worked together to establish a structured interchange between the theory and practice of European mediation. One objective of the project was to identify common practices of social mediation, and to promote awareness and knowledge of these practices (CreE-A, 2021; Silva et al., 2017, p. 67).

The most obviously important feature of the project was the Tour d'Europe, a journey of experiential learning modelled on the journeyman traditions of European artisans. Each year practitioner mediators (or professionals from mediation-near practices) were sent from country to country around the 7 participating countries on a "journey of immersion in the realities of mediators' work", participating reflexively in a "journey through Europe, during which each participant knew and shared biographical and professional experiences, as a mediator with other Practitioner-Mediators of different countries" (Silva et al., 2017, p. 75). Each participant brought with them prior practitioner experience and knowledge, and each was confronted in their period of immersion with fellow mediators who received them and provided them with a learning space in which different practices could be compared and confronted, and in which diverse learning biographies interacted and knowledge, both formal and tacit, could be exchanged.

During the seminars of the project in Barcelona and Paris, 10 participants (7 practitioner mediators and 3 expert mediators) were interviewed about their experience during the Tour d' Europe as they lived it during their immersion in the host country (Evans, 2019). The encounters with the participant-mediators took place in unstructured, biographical interviews. The detail of the interview talk can document how meaning-making takes place, and how this is affected by group belonging, ethnic or cultural discourses (Pavlenko, 2007), as well as gender, age, professional and educational relationships, and so on. The interview is sensitive to language resources and as such it was only logical to conduct the interviews in the languages of the participants themselves, in the case of those presented here, French. Where extracts from the interviews are discussed, however briefly, the discussion always relates to the French language original. A rough English translation of each extract is provided for orientation purposes only. A simple explanatory key to the few transcript signs used here is given in the endnotes.[4] The arguments for a 'stripped language' interview transcript and a 'low-inference' approach to the utterances of interviewees are implicit in the following and have been extensively discussed elsewhere (see Evans, 2020, pp. 383–387; 2021, p. 45).

There are, of course, a number of different approaches to the biographic interview in particular and narratives centred on life-stories. In the following the discursive-biographic interview, which focuses on languaged meaning-making in the interactive discourse of biographical narratives is employed. Other areas of biography and life history research must necessarily be excluded from this short discussion, though their theoretical and empirical value is not in question (Bertaux, 2005; Evans, 2008; González Monteagudo, 2011; Merrill & West, 2009; Pineau & Le Grand, 2007; Schütze, 1976).

4 Using Biographical Interviews to Understand the Mediator

Research interview respondents participating in diverse life worlds, such as the mediators interviewed in Barcelona and Paris, provide insight in interviews into the significance of critical change processes for their individual and collective learning. In so doing, they can be heard building own discourses of learning, in which acceptance of, and resistance to, the dominant discourses of institutions and civil society is laid down in the interdiscursive layering of interaction with (a) the own told narrative, (b) with the researcher agenda and (c) in the all-important dialogue with those significant others whose voices and narratives give expression to the complexity and transacted meanings of individual and group learning contexts. The mediator brings to their work and to their talk a personal history, a family history, a history of learning and a history of life-choices, to name but a handful of the critical steps in the development of individual practice.

Butoyi (name changed), the mediator whose talk will be considered first, provides evidence of this element of the life history. Asked to talk about her education and choice to study law, Butoyi replies that

> Extract 1 BUTOYI
> j'ai choisi les études en fait → je fais le droit parce que je (...) je (...) j'ai cherché des études (xxx) parce que j'ai envie d'aider mon prochain (.) envie de venir en aide des autres et je me suis demandée (.) uhm (.) quelles études est-ce que je peux faire pour aider les autres
>
> *I chose to study in fact I did law because I I I looked for courses because I wanted to help other people wanted to be a help to others and I wondered uhm what can I study to help others*

She thinks. Her speech is marked by hedging and self-repair and then formulates a strong first-person claim, employing heavy repetition ("envie d'aider"; "venir en aide"; "pour aider"). She continues:

> Extract 2 BUTOYI
> et (...) uhm (...) j'ai aussi (EpD) → j'ai aussi réalisé que les uhh (1.) dans les relations juridiques quand une personne a besoin de demander quelque chose (.) → (ESp) je sais que j'ai droit par example à telle aide uhm mais

→ je ne sais pas comment demander parce que (.) voilà quoi faire pour demander → j'ai demandé mais on m'a refusé le droit c'est intéressant parce que → je vais apprendre justement (…) comment (xxx) des aides comment réclamer des droits uhh c'est comme ça je me suis lancée un peu j'ai eu un peu cette rêve (.) voilà! de la → JUSTICE! et des choses faites correctement

and uhm I also realised that the uhh in legal matters when a person needs to ask something like I know like for example I have a right to this assistance uhm but I don't know how to ask because right what should you do to ask I asked but they refused my right that's interesting because I'm going to learn specifically how legal aid how to ask for one's rights uhh it's like that I kind of threw myself I half had this sort of dream you know about justice and about things being done correctly

Butoyi slips in her narrative into the guise and voice of an anonymous Other. Butoyi's knowledge claim is given a voice from 'off-stage' (ESp), a voice in the first person, an immediate claim of veracity and urgency. This use of the embedded speech of an unknown other (see Goffman, 1981) serves to justify Butoyi's standpoint. Emphatic prosodic language, harnessing energy and volume, is framed thus by heightened fiction-like detail and consciously sober rhetoric.

Butoyi's family background plays a role in the values she expresses. Her grandfather was a school director in Burundi. The experience of immigration, of arriving in Belgium, was not without significant difficulties.

Extract 3 BUTOYI
on arrivait en Belgique avec maman et mes soeurs uhh mon père était déjà ici on quittait tous les conforts qu'on avait là-bas pour venire en Belgique … il était difficile au début uh (.) donc uhh il fallait s'adapter

The arrival in Belgium with my mother and my sisters uhh my father was already here it meant leaving behind all the comforts back home to come to Belgium … it was difficult at the start uh (.) well uhh you had to adapt

Under the pressure of the new, foreign environment in Belgium, "on a dû readapter ici, refaire les études" (it was necessary to adapt, study from scratch). In these remarks, the repeated use of the impersonal pronoun is noticeable. This allows the speaker to recede into the background and the generalised experience of her family is proposed and is foregrounded. The epistemic narrative is thus generalised.

A significantly more emotive, personal account of adapting to life in France and the direct experience of racism and exclusion is given by another mediator, Liesse (name changed). Daughter of a mixed-race couple in Madagascar facing discrimination in their home community, Liesse's mother continued her studies, leaving Liesse herself behind in the country, where she grew up with her grandmother and her grandfather who was a schoolteacher. Aged 11, Liesse was taken to France by her mother who had meanwhile re-married. The details in her account of this supremely painful period of her life are revealing. She finds in the depths of France a new step-father – "mais un agriculteur", "but a farmer". The significance for her in telling this – the enigmatic use of "but" is open-ended – projected for the listener perhaps, this can really only be guessed at. The so common reluctance to provide the details of the location of this French farmer reflect the initial idea that the information is perhaps useless, given the sheer obscurity and unimportance of the place for others who have no acquaintance with the place. Upon further questioning, Liesse added that they lived in the Gers region, to the West of Toulouse. As such, this is a fittingly stark frame for Liesse's biographical trajectory and already pregnant with meanings for her future development.

> Extract 4 LIESSE
> j'ai quitté ma grand-mère de Madagascar en fait pour venir en France c'était très dur parce que je ne parlais pas très bien le français pas du tout alors moi mais je parlais le Malgache le Malgache et le Créole voilà et du coup quand je suis arrivé ici c'était difficile parce que ma mère du coup elle s'est remariée avec un français mais un agriculteur qui abitait dans la France vraiment profonde dans le sud ça s'appelle en effet c'est dans le département du Gers agriculteur et tout et c'était très dur petit village je ne parlais pas français et en plus il y a aucun noir dans le village ... il y avait une école il y avait une école où j'étais très très mal très très mal passée j'ai vraiment souvenirs douloureux de l'école de l'école primaire

> *I left my grandmother from Madagascar to come to France it was really hard because I didn't speak French well at all because then I spoke Malagasy Malagasy and Creole right so and then when I arrived here it was difficult because my mother had just remarried a Frenchman but a farmer who lived in the really deep France in the south it's called in fact it's in the Department Gers a farmer and everything and it was very hard a little village I didn't speak French and as well there's no Black person in the village ... there was a school there was a school where I was I had a really bad really really bad time I have really painful memories of the school of the primary school*

LEARNING TO MAKE (AND REMAKE) SOCIETY 215

The extent of the alienation Liesse experienced as the only Black child in a school of La France profonde is expressed meticulously by using list-like description, hammer-like repetition of key phrases, repetition, too, of key words ("tout, tout, tout"). Liesse establishes an unassailable position on this experience of discrimination and finds a core of pride in the assertion, as so often in her talk, of her highly intimate bond with her country of origin.

> Extract 5 LIESSE
> j'avais beaucoup de moquerie parce que je étais celle qui venait de loin qui ne parlait pas français qui avait des habitudes alimentaires différentes qui avait des habitudes vestimentaires différentes j'étais j'avais des habits de Madagascar en fait j'avais les habits très colorés très je les voulais c'est ce que je connaissais c'est ce que je connaissais j'ai rémarqué on se moquait de moi en fait ça m'attristait c'est que du coup tout ce que j'étais ma culture tout tout tout je considérerais comme quelque chose de négatif parce que c'est ce qu'on m'a renvoyé c'était négative j'ai cru c'était negatif j'ai changé j'ai changé ma manière de faire j'ai changé ma manière de m'habiller
>
> *I was made fun of a lot because I was that one that came from far away who didn't speak French who ate different food wore different clothes I was I had clothes from Madagascar yeah I had really colourful clothes really I wanted them it was what I knew it was what I knew I could see they were laughing at me that made me sad so just like that what I was my culture everything everything everything I thought it was all negative because that's what was communicated to me it was negative I changed I changed my way of doing things my way of dressing*

In the following extract, Liesse reopens the painful chapter of her school life and concludes the whole devastating story with four times "nul, nul, nul, nul". It seems superfluous to underline that this drastic expression of pain and distress must be stronger than the ability to shape the narrative otherwise, in a less candid way. Her candour is inescapable, because it is unerasable.

> Extract 6 LIESSE
> en Madagascar avec mes amis, en plus, j'avais ma famille j'avais où me considérer comme un (xxx) on me disait que c'était positif et d'un seul coup en fait j'ai vu que tout ce qui était negatif et du coup je me considérais nul nul nul nul
>
> *in Madagascar with my friends and more I had my family I had a place where I was seen as a (xxx) I was told everything was positive and then just*

like that in fact I saw that everything was negative and straightaway I saw myself as zero zero zero zero

Asked whether there had been open racism in the behaviour of teachers, she confirmed that there had:

Extract 7 LIESSE
alors moi jetais jeune je l'ai crue je l'ai crue parce que je me suis dit (Esp)
→ comment se fait-il que elle me crit tous les jours alors qu'elle sait que je ne parle pas français uhh ce quel elle faisait je le sentais vraiment comme une humiliation mais pour moi c'est comme si elle faisait exprès pour m'humilier à chaque fois et jetais humiliée jetais humiliée

well I was young I thought it was I thought it was because I said to myself how come she shouts at me every day after all she knows I don't speak French uhh what she did I felt really as humiliation but for me it is as if she did it precisely to humiliate me each time I was humiliated I was humiliated

The repetition, once again, makes the underlying significance of the related experience more than obvious, but must be seen too as other-oriented talk aimed at specifying the interpretation to be made and understood, and at the same time offering a shared glimpse of Liesse's emotional reaction: suffering, not anger, a passive response, not active resistance. She underlines with great generosity, however, that what she took for open racism may have been an expression of serious illness on the part of the teacher in question, who was later treated for severe depression.

Liesse was constrained to finish school in an agricultural college because of her overall examination results and experienced the 2 years spent in the same rural environment, learning something that she was not interested in, among conservative teenagers who had chosen this path, as a costly waste of time that would nevertheless finally give her the chance to study. During this time, she was faced with open mobbing.

Extract 8 LIESSE
du coup mais les 2 années c'est très très très très dur très très dur parce que d'une part ça ne m'interessait pas de l'âge de 16 jusqu'à 18 ans c'était très dur parce que je n'aimais pas ce que je faisais ça ne m'intéressait pas mais encore le racisme le racisme parce que en fait presque c'était c'était vraiment ma première expérience avec le racisme parce que tous les jours quand je venais à l'école il faisaient vraiment des images sur le tableau avant que les enseignants arrivaient ils faisaient des mots

right but the 2 years it's very very very very bad very very bad because on the one hand it didn't interest me at all from 16 to 18 it was very hard because I didn't like what I was doing it didn't interest me but there was also racism racism because in fact it was almost it was really my first experience of racism because every day when I came to school they really drew pictures on the blackboard before the teachers arrived they wrote words

The mobbing in the college was open and extremely personal and Liesse recounts that she reported nothing of this at home – it is important to note that her mother is the only point of reference in the family in this account – because of the value the family always placed in learning and because she wished to hide this institutional failure from a mother who had to be only a housewife (Liesse's significant prosodic lengthening of the word *seu:::lement/on:::ly* is indicated by successive colons) because her own diploma was not recognised in France:

Extract 9 LIESSE
avec mon langue avec mes tresses et tout j'avais les cheveux longues et maman on faisait tout le temps des tresses et j'aimais exprès parce que ça me fait rappeler le pays et uhh pendant des ans c'était dur dans cette cette expérience et que j'en parlait pas à ma mère je n'en parlais pas à ma mère parce que elle travaillait très dur elle mettait d'ailleurs elle était seu:::lement femme femme de ménage parce que son diplôme n'était pas accepté et je ne parlais pas parce que je savais qu'elle travaillait dur

with my language with my dreadlocks and everything I had long hair and maman we always wore locks and I really loved them because that reminded me of my country and uhh for some years it was hard in this this experience and because I didn't speak about it to my mother didn't speak about it to my mother because she worked very hard she put she was anyway on:::ly a house house wife because her degree wasn't recognised and I didn't speak because I knew she had to work hard

Interestingly, Liesse tells how her younger sister resisted discrimination and insult, talking back because – she later revealed to her older sister – she could not bear the weight of shame at being different, an immigrant. A central element in this different emotive response to discrimination would seem to be in their respective relationships to the homeland, Madagascar. While Liesse, feeling different, foreign, Black tied this to her origins and kept her origins vividly alive inside her while she changed outwardly to conform to white French society, her sister effectively refused her origins, developing no significant rapport to the Malagasy past of her family. They also came to inhabit wholly different worlds in France.

5   Biographical Resources and Everyday Frames of Experience in the Life History

The biographical method therefore allows us to ask how change in people's environments is recognised subjectively by individuals, and how such change influences learning in life/work/learning situations.

When someone begins to tell their life story, as Liesse and Butoyi are doing, talking about places, times and events connected to each other, Daniel Bertaux argues that "there is a life-history as soon as someone tells someone else, whether it is a researcher or not, any episode from their lived experience", because the discursive account takes on a form which is relatively spontaneous and dialogical (Bertaux, 2005, pp. 36, 38; author's translation).

Liesse, having attempted through university studies in Sociology to in some way contribute to the family tradition of learning, decided to break off her studies and found employment on a government funded project of assistance for families facing problems of school absenteeism. This first encounter with mediation aroused her interest ("ça peut être intéressant"), recalling obviously problems she herself knew well. Similarly, work later on with Roma communities during the Degree towards the profession of mediateure éducative/school mediator brought her into contact with school absenteeism again, as well as all the problems facing newly arrived immigrants, their ignorance of the social system, the stigmatism they faced in society. All areas of experience familiar to her.

After the Licence (Bachelor) she needed a State Diploma as the former is not recognised for the social services. This brought her to the post as médiatrice de la rue (street worker). Asked about these first experiences in a 'priority' neighbourhood in Limoges, she replied:

> Extract 10 LIESSE
> une expérience vraiment très riche c'était très riche ... on a vraiment des rapports humains on aide on discute en directe mais il manque le côté aider concrètement suivre
>
> *a really rich experience very rich it was very rich ... you have real human relationships you help you discuss directly but the side of really concrete help was missing following up*

To be able to help more, Liesse applied for and got the job she still has, working as a médiatrice en journée. The experiences in the community challenge her theoretical knowledge and even more so herself as a member of the community in dialogue with others. Could she work and act as a 'correct human being' on the streets?

> Extract 11 LIESSE
> ce depend des moments des situations tu pouvais rencontrer tellement différentes situations il y avait moments quand j'étais correcte moi-même souvent dans la rue les personnes ne renvoient pas leur colère il y avait des moments où je devais travailler sur mon comportement correct je devais travailler mon comportement pour un autre perce qu'on rencontre tellement de situations qui font sortir de nous-mêmes souvent dans la rue les personnes les personnes ne renvoient leur souffrance frustration colère et parfois je pense olala une fois je me suis enervée mais vraiment enervée pendant une intervention et c'était un échec c'était un échec

> *that depends on the moments the situations you could come across such different situations there are moments when I was correct myself often in the streets the people don't hold back their anger there are moments where I had to work on my correct behaviour I had to work on my behaviour to another because you meet situations that make us come out often on the street people people don't hold back their suffering frustration anger and sometimes I think o God once I got really irritated but really irritated during an intervention I failed the task I failed*

6 'Biographicity', Agency and Biographical Reflexivity

To be able to develop in talk a more coherent own narrative – in language terms to 'translate' oneself – it is crucial to have access to learning spaces within which biographical resources can be acquired and deployed, and which, in turn, determine how experience and common sense are interpreted. These resources we can think of as the individual sum or distillation of many different learning processes. They are the result of the individual meaning given to experience which produces subjective forms of knowledge. This knowledge in its turn is the basis of new cultural and social structures of experience. This social practice of accessing (and constructing) life-wide biographical resources – 'biographicity' in Peter Alheit's words (2018) – enables and shapes temporal and continually emerging and changing context-bound reflexivity in order to meet the everyday requirements of an individually steered life-course. As Alheit points out: "This biographical structure virtually constitutes the individuality of the self. It can be understood to be a temporally layered, individual configuration consisting of social experiences – including, of course, embodied and emotional sentiments" (Alheit, 2018, p. 14).

Gaston Pineau similarly underlines the essence of knowing how to live ("pouvoir-savoir vivre") and the difficulties involved for everyone in being agentic and in carrying forward the project of their lives. He states: "Every being is a cogito, but at the same time crafting themselves, forming themselves only as well as they can" (Pineau, 1996, p. 78).

A biographic approach, then, which examines agentic identity as a resource drawn upon to make sense of learning experiences and, more simply, as Pineau suggests, in order to survive in the world (1996, p. 78) draws our attention as researchers and educational practitioners to what is taking place at the frontiers between lived life and reflected life, or "biocognitive frontiers" in Pineau's words (1996, p. 78).

> Extract 12 BUTOYI
> la mediation c'est le (EpD) → savoir-vivre (2.0) avant d'être une technique intuitive où il y a des professionels des choses comme le creea[5] c'est aussi une chose intuit– uhh un savoir-vivre du quotidien
>
> *mediation is savoir vivre before it becomes an intuitive technique where you have professionals in things like at creea there's also something intuit– uhh a savoir vivre for the everyday*

Butoyi expresses here an idea very close to the notion of biographic learning employed by Gaston Pineau. 'Doing being' a 'foreigner', a woman, a man takes places at the level of the 'everyday', while biographical otherness, gender or class, for instance, must be conceived in a 'lifetime' sense. Liesse also takes a broad view of her contribution and that of others to her who, she underlines, have given her much. Asked how she sees herself she replies "aujourd'hui je me considère comme une être humaine correcte" (today I think of myself as a human being who acts correctly) and pressed to account for this, she affirms, too, in words dominated by epistemic discourse and formed in a carefully constructed avowal which conveys her theory of recognition and echoes Pineau's notion of crafting herself in response to experiences made with others:

> Extract 13 LIESSE
> je me trouve quand même correcte et la question c'est pourquoi pourquoi (EpD) → je pense parce que je fais attention je fais attention à l'autre je

fais attention à l'autre voilà pourquoi la question parce que (EpD) → je pense que je fais attention à l'autre concrètement comme j'aurais voulu qu'on fasse attention à moi je pense

I think I am pretty correct and the question is why why I think because I pay attention I pay attention to others I pay attention to the other just as I would have liked them to pay attention to me I think

Liesse accounts for this position because "je le sais que trop bien ce que c'est que de se sentir mal je sais ce que c'est malheureusement la souffrance", she says, "I know only too well what it is to feel bad I know unfortunately what suffering is". Being a mediator, intervening in moments of conflict between strangers, people from entirely other life contexts, linguistic practices, behavioural uses – sharpens the process of producing agency at the borders of the everyday and the lifetime. Thus, as Silva et al. (2016, p. 94) observe, the biographical construction of the mediator is both an act and a reflective process. As life developments continue in each new turn of the lived life, Bettina Dausien suggests that "new experiences are made which the subject is required to integrate in already existing self and world-constructions, and as a result these are confirmed and stabilised (reproduction) or alternatively they must be 're-written' (transformation)" (Dausien, 1996, p. 574; author's translation).

Butoyi recounts the difficulties experienced in her immersion phase of experience with experienced mediators, dealing with families and their daily problems of paying gas and electricity bills, keeping their flats, difficulties in understanding and being understood. The emotions are difficult to manage, but this is a path she has taken, an activity she has begun to try to be successful in. There are limits, however.

Extract 14 BUTOYI
la mediation c'est dur (.) c'est DUR hahah ahh oui c'est beacoup de travail sur soi et un peu comme uhh tous les conflits en (xxx) en mediation il y a conflits qui sont réglés tout seuls alors conflits qui sont tellement difficiles que la médiatrice ne va pas à les résoudre et aussi ça depend des personnes (1.0) uhh à qui on propose une mediation il y a une certaine personne qui dit (ESp) → je vais essayer pourquoi pas ça va marcher des autres personnes qui restent braquées jusqu'à la fin on arrivera à rien (EpD) → je pense aussi que tout le monde n'est pas fait pour la médiation

mediation is hard it's hard hahah ahh yes it's a lot of work on yourself and a bit like uhh all conflicts in (xxx) in mediation there are conflicts which are settled by themselves then there are conflicts that are so difficult that the mediator can't solve them and that also depends on people uhh some people you propose a mediation to there is someone certain person who says (ESp) I'll try why not that will work and others who stay stuck till the end and get nowhere (EpD) I think too that not everyone is made for mediation

The biography is, then, constructed over life-time horizons and draws upon resources of experience, laid down in 'layers' or 'strata' which represent 'reserves of sense or meaning' (Dausien, 1996, pp. 576–577). The biographical interview, allowing the telling of the changing life history, opens up a space, however, for reflection. Thus, both Liesse and Butoyi relate in similar fashion the shock of their first encounter with mediation practices in the field. They express doubts and acknowledge that mediation represents a challenge. Their narratives show moments of biographical experience in connection with the practice as a mediator that can be seen as a theory of an event (see Capps & Ochs, 1995, pp. 15–16). The research context provides in fact a kind of 'stage' upon which biographical agency is related, 're-written' (metaphorically speaking), contextualised and re-constructed.

Liesse's relationship to the challenges of social mediation is openly troubled. In her words we can almost hear her searching for an own coherence in the face of the difficulties posed by the human suffering or human aggression that she encounters in her work. Repetition, the prosodically telling resort to phatic reaction (tongue clicking), the shifting of her discourse from third person generalisation to first person admissions, admissions, in fact, communicate a sense of a loss of agency, a loss of certainty that troubles her. It speaks volumes for Liesse's candour once again that she voices this sense of unease in the interview encounter.

Extract 15 LIESSE
La colère c'est (…) (Pro) → (tss) c'est la difficolté du travail médiatrice parce que il y a des situations (…) on peut pas rester aahh on peu pas rester neutre on peut pas rester sans rien dire on a le devoir de s'exprimer certes il faut savoir parler mais je ne dis pas que la colère et l'expression de la colère soient légitimes mais (xxx) cette colère est humaine aussi elle est humaine (xxx) d'être équilibrée mais moi il y a des moments que je n'y arrive pas il y a des moments c'est trop dur c'est pas possible je n'y arrive pas

There's this anger (…) (clicks tongue) it's the difficulty of the mediator's work because there are situations … you can't stay ahh you can't stay neutral you can't just not say anything you have a duty to express yourself sure you should know how to talk but I'm not saying anger and expressing anger are ok but (xxx) that anger is human as well it is human (xxx) being fair but I there are moments I just can't there are moments it's too hard it's not possible I can't

Butoyi, by contrast, draws a more reassuring conclusion from the fray:

> Extract 16 BUTOYI
> donc la mediation permet ça (1.0) prendre du récul uhh ne plus être DANS LE CONFLIT? mais faire un bond en arrière pour l'observer et réfléchir sans le mettre en question
>
> *so mediation allows that ... to step back uhh not be in the conflict but step back to observe and reflect without questioning*

Butoyi is able to draw the conclusion from the experience she has made in the community of practice represented by the period of time shared with the mediators participating with her in the CreE-A project, that she can in fact already see that she has a place in the field of social mediation.

> Extract 17 BUTOYI
> moi je (.) cette année de spécialisation que j'ai faite et même surtout le projet creea m'a premise de comprendre que VOILÀ au depart (.) au depart je me suis dit (Esp) → que je suis pas capable moi à résoudre les conflits des gens NON ça semblait impossible mais quand même être médiatrice c'est une place que je (1.0) peux prendre
>
> *I this year of training that I've done and even more than anything else the creea project have helped me to see that there at the start at the start I said to myself that me I wasn't capable of resolving people's conflicts no that seemed impossible but in the end being a mediator is a thing that I can do*

She has come to understand that: "On doit se sentir capable", "you have to feel capable".

Liesse recognises, too, that the potential of mediation is what counts. Her thoughts are hesitant and cautious, but the essential position is clear. She believes in mediation as a means of giving every single person a space for contact and dialogue, which she translates here as "each can be a friend to the other".

> Extract 18 LIESSE
> même s'il y a moments de doute quand on a changé de:: de:: direction et plus ça et il y a eu ces moments la médiation comme élement en fait pour que chacun puisse être copain

even if there are moments of doubt when the direction has been changed and stuff like that and there are other moments mediation is like an element in fact there so that everyone can be a friend to everyone else

7 Social Mediation Making Community

Teams of social mediators across Europe found themselves confronted with a classic state of anomie when lockdowns were decided on and social distancing was imposed in every sphere of life. Practitioners of contact in 'normally' functioning civil societies, active as neutral third parties in re-making social bonds between vulnerable and invisible sections of society with the institutions of that society charged with guaranteeing services, aid and social justice, the social mediator was in many places confronted with a fundamental challenge as the pandemic wrong-footed the institutions and exposed the vulnerable to a disorienting social vacuum.

Moisan illustrates how very diverse organisations of social mediation across Europe responded to this anomalous situation. He cites the reports of these organisations in regular zoom-meetings of the CreE-A network during 2020 and after (Moisan, 2021). The organisation Mosaïco in Turin, Cepaim in Spain, the mediators of the cities of Nantes, Saint Quentin and Limoges in France, found themselves filling the void left by the wave of the pandemic. "In general, this central position taken up by social mediators, the only organisations in direct contact with the population, led them to become a platform for contacts to the local institutions" (p. 27). Moisan concludes that, while the crisis may have merely stretched the capacities of social mediators more than usual, yet in a way similar to their usual way of working, their capacity to fill the space left by the institutions and their ability to maintain contact with the most vulnerable and largely invisible underlines the potential to respond where community is breaking down and to intervene with initiatives capable of re-knitting broken bonds (p. 30).

The narrative of the mediators Liesse and Butoyi are heard speaking at a significant moment for their development. Butoyi is immersed in new experiences of work, learning, social interaction, close personal and intellectual or emotional relationships. Liesse, significantly more experienced at the point in which she spoke to me, is reflecting critically on her anything but linear trajectory from her youth to this point in her professional development. Liesse lives, and is living, through turbulent and challenging situations of social dialogue with people for whom the bonds of civil society are, at best, fragile. Her personal and professional life trajectory would seem to provide her with the qualities that social mediation can demand. Helena Neves Almeida suggests, in fact, that mediation presupposes knowledge, experience and professional abilities with the potential to transform personal, interindividual, social and community relationships, and to construct a more cohesive, peaceful, just and inclusive society (Almeida, 2016b, p. 31). This means serious work on themselves and their ability to work together with others under physically and emotionally difficult situations, coping with the adversity of social injustice and the diversity of their civil society co-actors. Silva et al. (2016) call this work with good reason a labour of (self)-reconstruction and co-construction in action and interaction with others (p. 94).

This brief discussion of extracts from the interview talk of two mediators offers a glimpse, however incomplete, of the local construction in talk of a narrative of biographical learning that is audibly cautious, yet already explicit in the framing of new knowledge and new agency. Drawing on rich and varied biographical resources, both can be heard as they reflect on the path they have chosen, as they reassess the road already travelled – including setbacks and doubts – and as they process what they believe they have learnt. In their respective narratives they map out a space of learning in diversity – a space where, in Liesse's words, "everyone can be a friend to everyone else", a space from which they make their contribution to the making and re-making of solidarity and inclusivity in communities.

Notes

1 See for example the chapters by Lima, Lucio-Villegas and Caride et al.
2 The 3-year (2017–2019) ERASMUS+ project CreE.A Construction d'un espace européen de la Médiation sociale pour l'inclusion EACEA, N° 580448-EPP-1-2016-1-FR-EPPKA3-IPI-SOC-IN.
3 As in the case of social workers and mediator-near services of Caritas in the city of Magdeburg, for example (private communication, Amidou Traoré).
4 (xxx) = unintelligible passage or word;
   (.) short pause, hesitation, hedging;
   (ESp) = embedded speech, the speech of others;
   (EpD) = epistemic discourse, knowing, understanding, theorising;
   CAPITALS = emphasis, louder speech;
   ::: = drawled speech, emphasis;
   (PRO) = prosodic speech, e.g. tongue clicking.
5 She is referring to the meetings of the CreE-A project.

References

Alheit, P. (2018). The concept of "biographicity" as background concept of lifelong learning. *Dyskursy mlodych andragogow, 19*, 9–22.

Almeida, H. N. (2016a). Analytical dimensions of mediation. Reflexive contribution on school mediation in Portugal. *Journal of Education, Psychology and Social Sciences*, *4*(1), 39–46.

Almeida, H. N. (2016b). Sustentabilidade da mediacao social. Debates e desafios atuais. In A. M. C. Silva, M. d. L. Carvalho, & L. R. Oliveira (Eds.), *Sustentabilidade da Mediacao Social: Processos e Práticas* (pp. 13–33). CECS.

Almeida, H. N., Pinto Albuquerque, C., & Cruz Santos, C. (Eds.). (2015). *Social and community mediation in Europe: Experiences and models*. Simoes & Linhares.

Bartolone, C. (2000). *New ways of conflict resolution in everyday life: Social mediation*. Les editions de la DIV.

Ben Mrad, F., & Demaret, P. (2021). Médiations et innovation. *La Lettre des Médiations*, *11*(2021), 1–2. https://www.observatoiredesmediations.org/Asset/Source/refBibliography_ID-155_No-01.pdf

Bertaux, D. (2005). *L'enquête et ses méthodes. Le récit de vie* (2nd ed.). Armand Colin.

Capps, L., & Ochs, E. (1995). *Constructing panic: The discourse of agoraphobia*. Harvard University Press.

CreE-A. (2021). *Création d'un espace européen de la médiation sociale – Arlekin*. https://www.cree-a.eu/en/home/

Dausien, B. (1996). *Biographie und Geschlecht*. Leske + Budrich.

EAPN. (2020). *Supercharging poverty. 2020 Poverty watch report*. EAPN.

EFUS. (2021). *European forum for urban security*. https://efus.eu/

Evans, R. (2008). L'entretien auto/biographique et les paroles. L'analyse du langage employé dans les entretiens discursifs-narratifs. In J. G. Monteagudo (Ed.), *Approches non-francophones des histoires de vie en Europe* (Vol. 55, pp. 193–222). Université de Paris VIII.

Evans, R. (2019). Learning biographies in a European space for social mediation [Vol. Especial Comunicação intercultural e mediação nas sociedades contemporâneas]. *Comunicação e Sociedade*, 71–88. https://doi.org/http://dx.doi.org/10.17231/comsoc.0(2019).3061

Evans, R. (2020). Examining a Kazakh student's biographical narrative and the discourses she lives by. In H. Wright & M. Høyen (Eds.). *Discourses we live by Narratives of educational and social endeavour* (pp. 383–402). Open Book Publishers. https://doi.org/https://doi.org/10.11647/OBP.0203

Evans, R. (2021). Biographical interviews and the micro-context of biographicity: Closely listening for meaning, learning and voice. In A. Bainbridge, L. Formenti, & L. West (Eds.). *Discourses, dialogue and diversity in biographical research. An ecology of life and learning* (pp. 39–52). Brill Sense.

Freire, P. (2020). *Pedagogia do oprimido* (75th ed.). Paz & Terra.

Goffman, E. (1981). *Forms of talk*. Blackwell.

González Monteagudo, J. (Ed.). (2011). *Les histoires de vie en Espagne. Entre formation, identité et mémoire*. L'Harmattan.

Hellmann, T., Schmidt, P., & Heller, S. M. (2019). *EU and OECD social justice index 2019*.
Makasy, C. (2019). *La Connaissance et la compréhension de la médiation pour favoriser la reconnaissance du métier et la legitimité du médiateur ou de la médiatrice*. CREEA.
Medit. (2021). *Observatoire des Mediations*. https://www.observatoiredesmediations.org/
Merrill, B., & West, L. (2009). *Using biographical methods in social research*. Sage.
Moisan, A. (2021). La médiation sociale face à la "distanciation" des liens sociaux. *La Lettre des Médiations, 11*, 24–30. https://www.observatoiredesmediations.org/Asset/Source/refBibliography_ID-155_No-01.pdf
Pavlenko, A. (2007). Autobiographic narratives as data in applied linguistics. *Applied Linguistics, 28*(2), 163–188.
Pineau, G. (1996). Les histoires de vie comme art formateur de l'existence. *Pratiques de formations/analyses, 31*(Janvier 1996), 65–80.
Pineau, G., & Le Grand, J.-L. (2007). *Les histoires de vie* (4th ed.). Presses Universitaires de France. (Original work published 1993)
Schütze, F. (1976). Zur Hervorlockung und Analyse von Erzählungen thematisch relevanter Geschichten im Rahmen soziologischer Feldforschung. In Arbeitsgruppe Bielefelder Soziologen (Ed.), *Kommunikative Sozialforschung* (pp. 159–261). Wilhelm Fink Verlag.
Silva, A. M. C. (2016). Formacao, investigacao e praticas de mediacao para a inclusao social (MIS) em Portugal. In A. M. C. Silva, M. d. L. Carvalho, & L. R. Oliveira (Eds.), *Sustentabilidade da mediacao social: Processos e práticas* (pp. 35–51). CECS.
Silva, A. M. C., Cabecinhas, R., & Evans, R. (Eds.). (2019). *Comunicação intercultural e mediação nas sociedades contemporâneas*. CECS. www.revistacomsoc.pt
Silva, A. M. C., Carvalho, M. d. L., & Aparicio, M. (2016). Formacao, profissionalizacao e identidade dos mediadores socais. In A. M. C. Silva, M. d. L. Carvalho, & L. R. Oliveira (Eds.), *Sustentabilidade da mediacao social: Processos e práticas* (pp. 93–104). CECS.
Silva, A. M. C., Carvalho, M. d. L., Moisan, A., & Fortecöef, C. (2017). Arlekin: A collaborative action-research-training project without frontiers. *International Research Journal of Human Resources and Social Sciences, 4*(3), 66–87.

CHAPTER 14

Social Pedagogy and Community Networks
Global Coexistence in Pandemic Times

José Antonio Caride, Rita Gradaílle and Laura Varela Crespo

Abstract

During the 1990s, the report for UNESCO by the International Commission on Education for the Twenty-First Century, led by Jacques Delors (1996), identified some of the principal tensions between the global and the local, the universal and the particular. In its proposals, "learning to live together" was one of the four basic pillars of contemporary education along with "learning to be", "learning to do", and "learning to learn".

Returning to the community entails activating lessons and learning that continue throughout life, from early childhood to old age. And with them, possibilities for educating and being educated that transcend the curriculum and academic programmes, referring to social pedagogy and its identities from the end of the last century to the present day The return to community solidarities acquires news meanings for knowledge and social action-intervention.

Keywords

community development – social pedagogy – globalised society – human rights – community networks – community action – equal opportunities

1   Responding to the Crisis, Looking to the Future: New Opportunities for Living Together in Times of the Pandemic

In the late 1990s on the eve of a new millennium, a report for UNESCO by the Commission on Education for the Twenty-First Century led by Jacques Delors (1996), identified some of the main challenges that would have to be overcome for humankind to make progress with the ideals that uphold democracy, tolerance, mutual understanding, peace, liberty, social justice, the fight against poverty, and the preservation of a healthy and inhabitable environment. All of them, in one way or another, contain tensions that for decades have harmed or inhibited full respect for people's dignity, their rights and the rights of life in all its diversity: between the global and the local, the universal and the individual, haves and have-nots, tradition and modernity, the long-term and the short-term, the spiritual and the material, the market economy and a society of markets.

To overcome these tensions without ignoring the risks inherent to the socio-environmental crises that threaten the survival of a wounded planet (Delibes & Delibes de Castro, 2006), the report stressed the importance of putting education at the service of economic and social development, of people and peoples. Although the suffering caused by a coronavirus pandemic like the current one could not have been anticipated, the model of a society that reconciles knowledge with experience and lifelong teaching and learning would base its proposals and options for improving the future of humankind and the world on four fundamental pillars: "learning to learn", "learning to do", "learning to be" and "learning to live together". A task that later reports (UNESCO, 2015, 2016), identified as part of the need to rethink education as a common good, linking its practices and achievements to ecological and human rights, the rights of the planet and of people.

The approaches in this report are similar to those that Edgar Morin would carry over to his "seven complex lessons in education for the future" (2011, authors' translation), or that Zygmunt Bauman had previously connected to "the challenges of education in liquid modernity" (2009, authors' translation) and they confront the growing uncertainties and complexities of the globalised and accelerated society in which we find ourselves: reuniting what is divided, bringing people together, and strengthening democracies by ensuring public policies are dedicated to social well-being, the values of citizenship, living together at a global level, and development on a human scale (Max-Neff, 1994). As this challenge has broad pedagogical and social implication, it should be met through actions that are consistent with their realities, not just making it a priority but also offering an alternative to the inherited models, with a substantial turn in the processes of change and transformation, both nearby and distant (Caride et al., 2007).

Environmental breakdown is far more than a diagnosis by followers of the ideas of deep ecology who analyse and/or propose what to do to save the planet (Riechmann, 2019; Rifkin, 2019; Wallance-Wells, 2019), and it obliges us to explore – consciously and self-critically – the meaning of our own actions. And also, the meanings of the words we use to read the world, ensuring its survival and reproduction. For several years now, many of these options have made global-local relationships into a central theme. With these options, new ways of relating and communicating with one another have been suggested, not without difficulties, proposing a radical turn in our values, attitudes and behaviour. Education, and all educations, will be decisive: inside and outside school, we must "take the risk of learning together, against the obligations of time itself" (Garcés, 2020, p. 17, authors' translation).

As a form of scientific, academic and professional knowledge that seeks to foster society's educational role at the same time as developing the socialising possibilities of education, social pedagogy – and, consequently, what we choose to call social education – can and must contribute decisively to this becoming reality in different contexts and concrete situations. The educational practices it promotes must be directed towards strengthening the social fabric of the community and the internal resources of the territory, as well as improving and strengthening the capacities of people who live there: a forward-looking education that does not contradict itself in its critical-reflexive goals or in its liberatory and/or transformative practices (Caride, 2005).

This is how Paul Natorp pictured it, albeit with a rather idealistic vision, in the preface he wrote for the Spanish edition of his Sozialpädagogik, associating social pedagogy with "education that is done by the community and makes the community, because its aim is not just the individual" (Natorp, 1913, p. 8, authors' translation). It cannot and must not be forgotten that local communities are an important point of reference in the everyday construction of citizens' civic values, rights and duties, prolonging the formative work of schools and families beyond the school curriculum and family coexistence. Consequently, a forward-looking social pedagogy enables processes of social inclusion and cohesion, as well as of democratic culture to unfold, and these are reflected in the broadest sense of being a citizen above and beyond solely individual interests. With this perspective, educating people to live with others, requires rethinking the cultural and social links in which people construct not only their individual subjectivity but also their belonging in the world. As Gimeno Sacristán observes, "social being means forming part of the networks that connect us to one another" (2001, p. 20, authors' translation), going beyond the immediate – spatially and temporally – to travel through the scenes of life in all of its diversity.

Given that the COVID-19 pandemic was an inescapable context-circumstance, with all of the fears (health, economic, cultural, etc.) it created, we will base our contribution on the theories, experiences and initiatives of an education done in, for and with society. The everyday and communal mission of social pedagogy-education cannot and must not close borders but instead open them (Caride, 2005; Melendro et al., 2018; Petrus, 1997; Pérez Serrano, 2003; Úcar, 2016).

2   Educating and Educating Ourselves Beyond Limits, Between the Global and the Local

Although it may seem obvious, the global refers to the interdependencies encouraged by globalisation: an expression with semantic tracks that are broad, complex and to some extent enigmatic, alluding to processes, phenomena, realities and so on that relate to social, economic, commercial, employment, cultural, political, health, educational, environmental, demographic, etc. relations that have effects on our everyday lives that we are still discovering. The local, the exemplar of the other extreme, refers to the proximities of the geographies – rural, urban, etc. – that embrace people in the landscapes traced by their streets, squares, districts, villages, cities, etc., reflecting who they are as a neighbourhood, community or 'municipality', this last term being a basic structure in the territorial and administrative organisation of a country so that it can autonomously manage its common interests.

As Borja and Castells (1998) showed years ago, the advent of a society where the space of flows is superimposed on that of places results in one of its principal paradoxes being that while feelings of local belonging are reinforced, the processes of globalisation that shrink spatial-temporal coordinates in a society woven by 'social' and 'virtual' networks are at the same time strengthened. Understanding and managing how these two realities combine without weakening citizens' rights has – for several decades – been one of the main challenges for development policies, supposedly guided since the late 1980s by principles that must guarantee their 'sustainability' (CMMAD, 1987). This is a concept that will displease very few and please almost everyone (Bifani, 1999), when it is argued that no economic growth justifies environmental damage or exhausting the resources that maintain life, causing uprooting of the human condition, perpetuating extremes of poverty and wealth, emotional detachment and social exclusion (Dias de Carvalho, 2016).

In this context, the return to community solidarities (Marinis et al., 2010) acquires new meanings for knowledge, social action-intervention, and 'sustainable development' (CMMAD, 1987). And inevitably, the threats inherent to climate change or, in recent months, the COVID-19 pandemic. A cruel and intense pedagogy, as Boaventura de Sousa Santos has called it (2020) that reveals the biological, ethical and social sicknesses of a model of civilisation that appears to be exhausted. Given that the expectations raised by the *Millennium Development Goals* (2000–2015) have been frustrated, as has the sustainability promised by the *2030 Agenda* in the *Millennium Development Goals* (MDGs), we find ourselves in uncharted waters. Not just because of the uncertainties, risks or vulnerabilities predicted decades ago in works by authors such as Beck (1992),

Giddens (1999), Bauman (2000) and many others, which allude to the risks of globalised society, imbalances in the world and the liquidity of contemporary modernity. Neither the repeated paradigmatic allusions – both theoretical and reflexive – to environmental chaos and complexity, nor the conclusive empirical demonstrations of the limits of growth and global change have been enough to convince political decision makers, economic powers, social actors and the general public that another end of the world is possible (Diamond, 2005; Riechmann, 2019; Servigne et al., 2018).

COVID-19 is exacerbating ongoing geopolitical and social challenges, requiring the adoption of innovative and collaborative focuses by a tired and fractured society. Although environmental risks, especially those resulting from climate change, continue to occupy a very important place, the struggle against the pandemic has become the main priority almost everywhere in the world. The fragility of our societies requires this because the effects of COVID-19 on employment, human relations, the digital divide, processes of inclusion and exclusion and so on can further increase poverty and inequality. Consequently, where problems are experienced, action is vital in order to find answers to them; in the spaces where personal relations weave life in common, re-establishing the central role of citizens and active solidarity in a network society are vital, too. And, with this, the value of deciding, of valuing each person's initiatives in processes of social change, the assertion that we can do it. Even though these actions have not always followed a sufficiently well-defined model of socio-educational action-intervention or have fulfilled all the expectations placed in them (Civís et al., 2007), they still offer an opportunity to improve learning, educate ourselves in society, increase options for knowledge, and achieve a fairer, more inclusive and supportive coexistence.

Far from closing in on themselves, territorially and humanly, communities have an obligation – as both a need and a challenge – to fling themselves into the world, recognising the interdependencies that characterise social, educational, cultural, and ecological processes and their impact on the construction of a desirable life, stimulating and consolidating shared responsibilities. For Díez and Rodríguez changing course not only involves deconstructing the dominant discourses, "at the same time stopping some practices that negatively affect humankind as a whole, but also linking this analysis and this praxis to the common sense of many people by offering concrete alternatives that give hope and show that another world is really possible ..." (2018, p. 290, authors' translation) through our practices, through our examples, because future generations need referents that will save humankind and the planet for us.

A few months after the World Health Organisation (WHO) recognised that the illness caused by a coronavirus (COVID-19, a name chosen to avoid stigmatising a geographical location, animal, person or social group) had developed into a pandemic, the 'Ideas' supplement of the Spanish newspaper *El País* ('El Futuro', 2020), asked 60 experts and thinkers about what the keys to the new era should be, and their words contained ideas that differ greatly in nature and scope. These included: "recovering the link between generations" (Hartmut Rosa), "organising a more modest life" (Slavoj Zizek), "returning to the dream of the tribe" (Gabriela Wiener); "protecting the earth, air and water" (Saskia Sassen); "restructuring public and private debt" (Yanis Varoufakis); "moving towards a politics of the common good" (Michael J. Sandel); "building a new pact between generations" (Daniel Innerarity); "discovering the human side of connectivity" (Ethan Zuckerman); "a warning to the sapiens" (Pepe Mujica); "urgency in freeing minds" (Aminata Traoré); "tomorrow is for the ordinary people" (Christophe Guilluy). We will stop here, but these quotes do not exhaust the reflections and proposals.

At the same time that their diagnoses and predictions reached us, in addition to the ones that were constantly spread through all of the media (radio, television, press, etc.), a growing number of people and communities organised themselves in their everyday lives in their homes, towns and villages, neighbourhoods and cities. We will briefly consider some of the initiatives they promoted as new forms of communal action, displaying their great potential for confronting the uncomfortable truths of the crisis of civilisation that has affected us for decades.

3 New Forms of Communal Action in Pandemic Times: Solidarity Networks and Mutual Support Groups

In globalised societies, the basic foundations of the common good that acted as a collective insurance against individual misfortune have become weakened, accentuating processes that exclude large sections of the population and/or make them vulnerable, at both the personal and collective levels. Loss of resources and chronic forms of poverty including financial and material poverty have now been joined by other circumstances (relational, affective, emotional, etc.). These circumstances can be situational or structural and are exacerbated by the marks left, for example, on the dynamics of the family, neighbourhood, or employment by lockdowns. However, without being as generalised as could be hoped, the pandemic has also resulted in the appearance and consolidation of community initiatives and/or solidarity networks (Bauman, 2017), which everything seems to suggest could remain in place for years.

The community networks we refer to are collaborative structures intended to manage the communal problem of COVID-19. In most cases their strengths lie in their inclusivity (as they involve various sectors, different professions and a wide variety of social groups) and flexibility (as they provide multiple options for involvement and cooperation). In the case of Spain, as set out in a report prepared by the Spanish Ministry of Health (Ministerio de Sanidad, 2020), these networks have made it possible to meet specific needs of a variety of types resulting from the pandemic: transmitting information, identifying emerging problems in a changing context, emotional support, care for dependent people and groups, coordinating resources and programmes to care for health and welfare, preventing contagion, collaborating on treatments, etc.

Reorganising the patterns of care in Spain's mediterranean welfare model is one of the main challenges for its social policies, going beyond the families (and especially women) that have traditionally taken care of this task. As Zuñiga and Arrieta note, "the current model of social organisation of care, based on unpaid work by women with little participation by social services and a growing privatisation of household employment, paints a complicated picture" (2021, p. 65, authors' translation).

Victoria Camps (2021) states that a paradigm change is needed, balancing reason and emotions, putting care – and the ethics of care – in a special place, because there is a right to be cared for and a duty to care, without exceptions: it affects everyone, and these responsibilities must be accepted individually and collectively. The pandemic has demonstrated the growing need to give the care system a more equitable distribution that includes the community sphere, given the lack of response from public services. Advocating for the community as an agent for care will create an effective democratic framework that calls on civic responsibility and active participation in the place where one lives (Martínez Buján & Vega, 2021); a declaration of intentions that has taken shape in valuable experiences at the toughest moments in the pandemic.

Situating ourselves in the Spanish context, we will present some examples of community action led by members of the public in the context of the pandemic. These form a point of reference for solidarity, collaboration and mutual help, acting as measures of collective responsibility in the face of new (and old) social hazards. A set of initiatives that allow us to reaffirm, in full agreement with Zubero, "that the community still enjoys excellent health among ordinary people" (2016, p. 50, authors' translation).

Networks of solidarity and mutual support groups have developed in places where there was a prior social fabric and organised citizen collectives, but also in settings where they had not previously flourished. Among the social support or mutual aid networks, it is worth noting various initiatives that have had a notable presence in contexts of nearness, for example: neighbourhood support networks to cover basic needs and provide care (for children, the elderly, the unwell, etc.).

In many districts and neighbourhoods, support networks appeared as an emergency measure given the lack of cover for people's basic needs. The lack of response by an overwhelmed social services system meant that many people – especially workers in the informal economy and other groups in vulnerable situations (single mothers, the elderly, migrants with an irregular administrative status, etc.) – found themselves without the resources to cover their basic needs for food, housing, etc. This lack of a guarantee of a basic minimum for subsistence meant that residents in these areas offered help and collaboration, for example, in the form of food banks, mutual emergency funds, and basic shopping. Special attention was also paid to physical and psychological care, providing help for older people, people with disabilities and people in positions of dependence, owing to the social isolation and unwanted solitude forced on them.

Initiatives flourished – some run by private individuals – that focussed on guaranteeing access to culture, fostering reading and continuing education. They were, in a way, little 'pedagogical missions'[1] that developed in these neighbourhoods.

3.1 *The Experience of "Somos tribu"*

The "Somos tribu" (We are a Tribe) initiative[2] developed in the Puente de Vallecas district (Madrid) from the start of confinement at home on 14 March 2020, when a state of alarm was declared throughout all of Spain. The first step was the creation of a WhatsApp group, which filled up in a few hours. People joined this to offer help by running errands for vulnerable people, dog walking, or providing any other type of support that was needed. Pharmacies, supermarkets, and other places in the neighbourhoods hung up sheets with the telephone numbers of individuals who were offering help and a safety protocol was developed.

From late March, a great demand for food developed since many residents of the Puente de Vallecas district worked in the informal economy (at markets, cleaning, etc.) and did not have employment contracts or any financial cover as they could not go out to work. Consequently, food banks were created (one in each neighbourhood), guaranteeing a basic weekly basket for the families that used them. These had the support of social centres such as La Villana and La Brecha, the La Horizontal cultural association, the Atalaya social centre and the neighbourhood associations of Puente de Vallecas.

Mutual emergency funds were also created to collect money and provide cover for people and families that could not afford the basic costs of food, rent, etc. In addition, specific groups were set up to provide support for mothers, creativity, employment support, etc., and these are in late 2021 still working.

3.2 Shared Culture: Reinvented Neighbourhood Libraries

Many initiatives relating to community support and fostering reading as a means of supporting personal and social development were put in place from the first days of lockdown. These also acted as an element of social support and a strategy to encourage continuous learning. Examples of these include experiences such as the following:

- Sharing books with neighbours: Writers and other people with an interest in reading who had small – or large – libraries at home made their books available to their neighbours. Among them, the writer Jorge Carrión decided to become the librarian for his building, leaving the books his neighbours had requested from him via WhatsApp at their doors. In La Coruña, the writer and university lecturer Héctor Pose made "his library available to his neighbours during lockdown" (La Voz de Galicia, 6 April 2020, authors' translation), so that they could immerse themselves in the wonderful world of literature. Like them, other people and groups encouraged delivering book loans to people's homes and book swaps, thus democratising access to culture during quarantines.
- Librarians facing unwanted solitude: Initiatives such as that of the librarian Lluís Agustí made it possible for reading to become an antidote to unwanted solitude. On 19 March he offered on Twitter to read novels, short stories and poetry over the phone for free to facilitate access to culture while at the same time carrying out important social support work. He selected three pieces to read or recite in Spanish, Catalan, French or Portuguese. For months he read to an average of three people a day, and sometimes eight or nine. Almost all of the people who took him up on this offer were women aged between 30 and 90, and almost all of the requests were for poetry, along with a few short stories and some essays and non-fiction texts.
- Libraries reinvented: Municipal libraries, as amenities that are close to citizens, had to reinvent themselves after having to close their doors because they were not an essential service. For example, the municipal library in Utrera (Seville) along with Civil Protection developed a project called "Más libros: menos virus" (More books: less virus) in which volunteers from civil protection took books to the homes of the people who requested them. Many municipal libraries as well as the central libraries of Spain's autonomous regions and university libraries also opened up access to part of their collections.

3.3 Virtual Communities: Solidarity Interactions Online

Technologically mediated community initiatives are new ways of living (together) and relating to one another and they have great potential for people who actively participate in them. However, the limitations on access and use that particularly affect vulnerable groups (people without income, the elderly, etc.) should not be discounted, and reducing the digital gap remains one of the challenges of the moment. Even so, their benefits have been evident in this crisis, connecting people despite social distancing and forming links in the intangible spaces and times of the internet.

Among others, we believe that "*Frena la curva. JuntXs somos más Fuertes*" (Slow the curve: we're stronger together) is worth noting. The citizen platform "Frena la curva" (FLC) started development on 12 March 2020 with the aim of listing and connecting the citizen initiatives that were starting to appear in Spain in response to the coronavirus crisis. The team from the Aragon regional government's Laboratorio de Gobierno Abierto (Open Government Laboratory) started thinking about the need for a digital tool that would channel the wave of solidarity expected given the spread of the virus. Subsequently, groups of volunteers, companies and social organisations joined the initiative. The online platform was launched on 14 March and acquired a nationwide reach.

Technology was put at the service of solidarity, becoming the largest repository of public innovations in Spanish. This is a platform where volunteers, entrepreneurs, activists, social organisations, crafters and public open innovation laboratories cooperate to channel and organise social energy and civic resilience in the face of the pandemic, giving a response by society that complements that of the government and that of the existing public services (www.frenalacurva.net). The following indicators of the impact of this experience stand out: listing more than 900 initiatives in the citizen innovation guide; replication of the platform in 22 countries; more than 140 common challenge projects; 28,000 face masks donated; 300,000 visits (Spain) to the map of citizen initiatives, etc.

4 For a Pedagogy of Opportunities with a Social and Civic Commitment

The community initiatives that developed spontaneously in districts and neighbourhoods complemented – and sometimes substituted – the work of a social services system that was nearing collapse. Ensuring greater public involvement is essential at present – and will continue to be so in the post-COVID era – to offer sustainable responses with communal participation, in line with the complexity of common challenges. When the biological immunity needed to overcome this health crisis will have been achieved, it will be necessary to consider social immunity and its impacts on people's everyday lives, connecting public initiatives with active participation by citizens. In this context, social pedagogy could help "make access channels possible that help people and accompany them – in person and/or virtually – as they progress towards social and communal inclusion" (Úcar, 2012, p. 11, authors' translation).

In our current pedagogical and social coordinates, it should be noted that the pandemic has involved new ways of making communities and has revitalised experiences that already had a long history of collaboration in local communities. Given their importance and involvement in the search for collective responses to the public health crisis, it is important to recognise the community networks created in neighbourhoods and districts, which emerged in strength during the lockdowns, and also the virtual communities whose role in generating and maintaining social ties beyond physical boundaries was fundamental. If the pandemic can be regarded as a "total social fact" (Ramonet, 2020, authors' translation) that has shaken social relations as a whole and involved all agents, institutions and values, it has also entailed a system of shared obligations and responsibilities, put at the service of the common good (Subirats & Rendueles, 2016).

On foundations of joint responsibility, Marco Marchioni (1997) more than two decades ago recalled that the organised community is the most important resource and is "a contribution to strengthening democracy, to revitalising it, to its ability to be a living thing in the body of society and not a purely formal element" (p. 549, authors' translation). Change, commitment and participation must go hand-in-hand in this process, seeking an equitable relationship between the public and the communal, since we need a broad vision of social protection that emerges from collective participation and supports our co-existence, beyond our individual interests (Martínez Buján, 2020).

Adverse situations, such as those caused by the COVID-19 pandemic, require a social pedagogy that criticises inequalities and is committed to development that is more just, more inclusive and more human, as communities have to work on their vulnerabilities seeking alternatives to the discrimination, exclusion and suffering that all crises cause. The pandemic has revealed an urgent need to implement shared efforts where community action and public intervention create alliances for the common good, promoting dialogue and a community focus when tackling the social challenges it has posed.

Notes

1 See Lucio-Villegas in Chapter 2 on this point.
2 https://somostribuvk.com

References

Bauman, Z. (2000). *Liquid modernity*. Polity Press.
Bauman, Z. (2009). *Los retos de la educación en la modernidad líquida*. Gedisa.
Bauman, Z. (2017). *Tiempos líquidos: Vivir en una época de incertidumbre*. Tusquets.
Beck, U. (1992). *Risk society: Towards a new modernity*. Sage.
Bifani, P. (1999). *Medio ambiente y desarrollo sostenible* (4th revised and updated edition). IEPALA.
Borja, J., & Castells, M. (1998). *Local y global: La gestión de las ciudades en la era de la información*. Taurus.
Camps, V. (2021). *Tiempo de cuidados: Otra forma de estar en el mundo*. Arpa.
Caride, J. A. (2005). *Las fronteras de la pedagogía social: Perspectivas científica e histórica*. Gedisa.
Caride, J. A., Freitas, O., & Vargas, G. (2007). *Educação e desenvolvimento comunitário local: Perspectivas pedagógicas e sociais da sustentabilidade*. Profedições.
Civís, M., Longás, E., Longás, J., & Riera, J. (2007). Educación, territorio y desarrollo comunitario. Prácticas emergentes. Educació Social. *Revista d'Intervención Socioeducativa, 36*, 13–25.
CMMAD. (1987). *Nuestro futuro común*. Alianza Editorial.
Delibes, M., & Delibes de Castro, M. (2006). *La tierra herida: ¿qué mundo heredarán nuestros hijos?* Destino.
Delors, J. (1996). *Learning: The treasure within: Report to UNESCO of the international commission on education for the twenty-first century*. http://hdl.voced.edu.au/10707/114597
Diamond, J. (2005). *Colapso: Por qué unas sociedades perduran y otras desaparecen*. Debate.
Dias de Carvalho, A. (2016). *Acerca del exilio de la condición humana: Desafíos para la educación y el trabajo social*. Editorial Magisterio.
Díez, E. J., & Rodríguez, J. R. (2018). *La 'polis' secuestrada: Propuestas para una ciudad educadora*. Ediciones Trea.
El futuro después del coronavirus. (2020, May 4). *El País, suplemento ideas, 259*. https://elpais.com/especiales/2020/coronavirus-covid-19/predicciones/
Frena la curva. (2021). *Frenalacurva*. Retrieved September 9, 2021, from https://frenalacurva.net/
Garcés, M. (2020). *Escuela de aprendices*. Galaxia Gutenberg.
Giddens, A. (1999). *Runaway world: How globalization is reshaping our lives*. Profile.
Gimeno Sacristán, J. (2001). *Educar y convivir en la cultura global. Las exigencias de la ciudadanía*. Morata.
Marchioni, M. (1997). *Planificación social y organización de la comunidad. Alternativas avanzadas a la crisis*. Editorial Popular.

Marinis, P. de, Gatti, G., & Irazuzta, I. (Eds.). (2010). *La comunidad como pretexto: En torno al (re)surgimiento de las solidaridades comunitarias*. Anthropos-Universidad Autónoma Metropolitana.

Martínez Buján, R. (2020). El paradigma de los comunes y la protección social pública como claves hacia el bienestar. *Cuaderno de Relaciones Laborales, 38*(2), 289–304.

Martínez Buján, R., & Vega, C. (2021). El ámbito comunitario en la organización social el cuidado. *Revista Española de Sociología, 30*(2), a25. https://doi.org/10.22325/fes/res.2021.25

Max-Neff, M. (1994). *Desarrollo a escala humana: Conceptos, aplicaciones y algunas reflexiones*. Icaria.

Melendro, M., de Juanas, A., & Rodríguez, A. E. (2018). *Pedagogía social: Retos y escenarios para la acción socioeducativa*. UNED.

Ministerio de Sanidad. (2020, April 30). *Redes comunitarias en la crisis de Covid-19*. https://www.mscbs.gob.es/profesionales/saludPublica/prevPromocion/Estrategia/docs/ImplementacionLocal/Redes_comunitarias_en_la_crisis_de_COVID-19.pdf

Morin, E. (2011). *Los siete saberes necesarios para la educación del futuro*. Paidós.

Natorp, P. (1913). *Pedagogía Social: Teoría de la educación de la voluntad sobre la base de la comunidad*. Ediciones de La Lectura. (Original work published 1899)

Pérez Serrano, G. (2003). *Pedagogía social, educación social: Construcción científica e intervención práctica*. Narcea.

Petrus, A. (Ed.). (1997). *Pedagogía social*. Ariel.

Pose, H. (2020, April 6). *Hai moito libros que nos poden axudar a asimilar o que está pasando*. La Voz de Galicia.

Ramonet, I. (2020, May 4). *La pandemia y el sistema mundo*. https://www.aesed.com/es/la-pandemia-y-el-sistema-mundo

Riechmann, J. (2019). *Otro fin del mundo es posible, decían los compañeros: Sobre transiciones ecosociales, colapsos y la imposibilidad de lo necesario*. MRA Ediciones.

Rifkin, J. (2019). *El Green New Deal global: El colapso de la civilización del combustible fósil y la transición a una nueva era económica para salvar el planeta*. Paidós.

Servigne, P., Stevens, R., & Chapelle, G. (2018). *Une autre fin du monde est posible: Vivre l'effondrement (et pas seulement y survivre)*. Seuil.

Sousa Santos, B. (2020). *La cruel pedagogía del virus*. Akal.

Subirats, J., & Rendueles, C. (2016). *Los (bienes) comunes. ¿Oportunidad o espejismo?* Icaria.

Úcar, X. (2012). Prólogo: Entre comunidades y redes. In I. Peña-López & F. Balagué (Eds.), *Acción comunitaria en la red* (pp. 9–13). Graó.

Úcar, X. (2016). *Pedagogías de lo social*. UOC.

UNESCO. (2015). *Rethinking education: Towards a global common good?* https://unevoc.unesco.org/e-forum/RethinkingEducation.pdf

UNESCO. (2016). *Education 2030: Incheon declaration and framework for action for the implementation of sustainable development goal 4*. https://unesdoc.unesco.org/ark:/48223/pf0000245656

Wallance-Wells, D. (2019). *The uninhabitable Earth: Life after warming*. Tim Duggan Books.

Zubero, I. (2016). El papel de la comunidad en la exclusión social. In T. Morata (Ed.), *Pedagogía Social comunitaria y exclusión social* (pp. 47–73). Editorial Popular.

Zuñiga, M., & Arrieta, F. (2021). Analizando la función de la comunidad en el sistema de organización social de los cuidados en Euskadi. *Zerbitzuan, 74*, 65–82. https://doi.org/10.5569/1134-7147.74.04

CHAPTER 15

Communities and Adult Learning in the Making and Remade

Rob Evans, Ewa Kurantowicz and Emilio Lucio-Villegas

1   We Fall Down and We Get Up Again

Looking back in order to look forward is always timely, we can assume, yet it seems particularly fitting – and urgently so – as we move into the third year of the COVID-19 era. The fact is, the arguments we researchers in adult education and learning as a professional or social community were unpacking at the start of 2020 when this particular project got underway have been, to say the least, remixed and re-set as we try to react to the enormous challenge posed by every form of post-COVID projection. The possible outcomes of the war raging in Ukraine as these lines are being written are entirely incalculable and, both locally and globally, are doubtless set to re-define practically all givens from the time 'before'.

Yet, to remain with the issues that dominated the writing of this volume, and in full consciousness of the sheer unfathomable suffering the COVID-19 pandemic has already brought and seems set to inflict for time to come, we see some things in public discussion and political discourse that are tentatively positive emerging from the stress tests social and welfare systems, education systems, law portfolios on sexual and gender equalities, equal pay, minimal pay, migration and asylum, the future of health and care systems, and so on and so on, have been subjected to. Tentatively positive, it must be stressed. Ignoring for a moment, if we can, the ignorance of populism's refusals to recognise the gravity of the situation, the fanfares for the easy solutions of 'smart' and 'home'-working, the dreams of solving global warming by everyone simply staying at home (including the children and the basic abolition of the institution called school), ignoring all this for a moment, if we can, the pairing of COVID with the global climate crisis has reset the agenda brutally but lucidly for alternative ways ahead for individuals, communities, local lives and global destinies and the possible contribution that learning and living together can make towards a more just, more meaningful interpretation of the possibilities of learning lives. As Lepore et al. write in their chapter: "All forms of inequalities hitherto hidden within countries and across the globe have become visible

© ROB EVANS, EWA KURANTOWICZ AND EMILIO LUCIO-VILLEGAS, 2022
DOI:10.1163/9789004518032_016
This is an open access chapter distributed under the terms of the CC BY-NC 4.0 License.

and have been exacerbated. As calls for 'build back better' are being heard, it is important not to lose sight of 'build back equal', too". It is in this light, that we wish to close this book with thoughts that have been encouraged by the readings collected here.

2   Challenging the Discourses of Utility and 'Useful Knowledge'

Most of the chapters in this volume directly challenge mainstream discourses of utility operating in education, in social life broadly and that serve in the defence of established, 'unquestionable' epistemologies and ontologies. Lima's critique (Chapter 1) of neo-liberal and liberal social thinking is grounded in a thorough re-appraisal of the concept of dialogue. Dialogical action aims to create and strengthen cultures of openness, democracy and participation, favouring sustainable development. This dovetails with Lucio-Villegas' proposal (Chapter 2) to reconsider deschooling as an alternative to the much-vaunted 'tools' for life or empty 'qualificationism'. A critique of mainstream lifelong learning demands that we look further than providing merely the "tailored services" that a recent irreproachably positive UNICEF document promises in the post-COVID period to meet the "learning, health, and psychosocial wellbeing" (Giannini et al., 2021) of children and young people, and instead marry learning with a culture of openness and dialogue. This is clearly the argument developed in turn by Zoletto (Chapter 3) and Noworolnik-Mastalska (Chapter 4), in connection with the learning chances, full inclusion and recognition of migrant workers, in the first case, or the difficulties under the dead weight of mainstream learning discourses in Europe to create meaningful frameworks for experiencing and learning citizenship for European youth, in the second.

3   New Knowledge, New Society

It would seem that despite the accumulation of experience over decades of struggles for rights and freedoms and the tireless campaigning for gender equality, for the recognition of Indigenous peoples' rights, for free and equal access to learning and health, and despite the sheer crushing evidence of anthropogenic global climate change, the very real achievements in some places remain still fragile goods. A real, critical practice of inclusion; the respect in practice for the rights of the socially vulnerable; a palpable readiness of society to engage with otherness and learn to embrace a re-drawing of histories, a real remaking of knowledge in order to remake communities of people and societies – all of this remains to be defended where achieved, or remains yet to be put together, in gruelling piecework threatened at every step. The promises and real hopes, to give just one example, that the notion of vital services to community and society in the pandemic would see a re-evaluation of women's employment with better recruitment, pay and conditions resulting, have (unsurprisingly) already been dashed in at least one major European economy as this is written (Marzano, 2021).

Research aimed at creating and promoting positive social justice outcomes, aimed at reducing inequality, improving the lives of the very people at the grassroots in communities actually involved in the knowledge production process – as research partnerships between universities and communities try to do (Chapter 5) – is one forceful demonstration of what can be tried and achieved. The creativity and courage involved in building up women's and gender museums (Chapter 6) show very starkly, too, how feminist pedagogies impact with dramatic and unsettling force in central debates to question presences and absences in mainstream pedagogies of lifelong learning. Through such pedagogical practices the world is presented, seen and known differently and adult educators are provided with platforms to incite discussion and unsettle stagnant discourses in ways that can "change the imagination of change".

This new knowledge for a new society involves above all stressing difference. The most common reactionary response to social problems, however, has always been to exclude and defame. Countering this, the kind of creative andragogy Jocey Quinn argues for (Chapter 7) stretches the usual frameworks of neoliberal *and* radical discourses which, she says, tend to glide over the relational nature of the world we live in. This creative andragogy can, however, offer visions of more than human and more than social mutuality. What does this entail? This posthuman vision of the person not as autonomous, but as connected across multiple forms of matter, people living and acting in and with the whole non-human environment, with objects, spaces, living creatures and the materiality of what makes up virtuality, provides a new way forward for social learning as it demands from us a radically different way of understanding ourselves and our relationship to others, to community and the world. A way forward that can remake the rift between human actions and the natural world, for instance.

4   Social Learning, the Meaning of Activism

It was inevitable that in looking back to look forward we would have to examine what can be done, and how, by whom, and under what circumstances. To change things, people as individuals and in groups must become active. Clearly, activism has continued and has evolved as global concerns have increasingly entered our lives, no longer at the pace of the evening news or the latest edition of the local newspaper, but relentlessly, second by second in our pockets, handbags, or through our eternal tweets and streams. The evolution of activism, activism to change society for the better, then, is our topic, the activism of the street and the activism of the social media. But more fundamentally, the activism in people's lives and their motives and motivations.

Ligus shows us (Chapter 8) how ideas, values, symbols, collective images, collective beliefs and opinions, accumulated over a long period, as well as commonly shared experience derived from various ideologies of the modern and postmodern worlds have become sources of local ideologies used in constructing a social and/or cultural programme for the members of a migrant community to learn in a community and re-shape their understanding of 21st century localism. Individual and collective experience in intergenerational transmission is constantly reinterpreted, providing a rich source of knowledge, often recovered in the process of social dialogue and informal learning. The potential for transformation in the intergenerational transmission of knowledge, coupled with an opening up to the knowledge of all groups and communities living together in pluricultural societies, can only be guessed at. An idea of how influential such community-based experience can be is discernible in the research Pilch Ortega describes (Chapter 9). Social learning after an earthquake in Mexico is brutally characterised by the struggle to survive but also by social solidarity. The consequences that such crises have for people's lives and the resulting collaborative social practices that can emerge from these crises show in the concrete case presented that, in wake of the natural disaster, social rules and power relationships were questioned by the people. New-found social reflexivity enabled people to analyse their circumstances in order to overcome established power regimes and to create new social practises which respond more adequately to their needs.

Social reflexivity and the decision to act upon newly won understanding or conviction are intensely biographical phenomena. This can be seen vividly in the chapters contributed by Bilon-Piórko (Chapter 10) and Gontarska et al. (Chapter 11) in the testimonies of the activists the authors interviewed. Straddling as these two studies do very different periods of recent Polish history, they help us to see both what motivated these people to become active, what probably keeps them going, and what, too, is able to stall them. Above all, we can see how the transformation of civil society through activism works back on activism in its turn to transform modes and practices, but also the individual and group narratives of why they (want to) do it. The older, lifelong activist *Krzysztof* that Bilon-Piórko introduces us to is moved by a predictable list of 'triggers': sensitivity to social issues, individual personality-related motives, a strong sense of agency, curiosity about the world, aspiration to do something good for the world and a sense of self-fulfilment and personal satisfaction. Nothing unusual in this list. Yet it should be remembered that these internal and external triggers were 'primed' by the war and occupation and were pulled by over 40 years of one-party rule in Poland. The marriage of civil activism with party membership was clearly a life filled with selfless educative campaigns and good works. Which inevitably collapsed in on itself long before the system itself collapsed and led to the withdrawal from commitment the author describes. The misfit between *Krzysztof's* pedagogy of social possibility from 'before' and the new times of post-communist Poland in which the activist *Ewa* sees needs and possibilities for change and enters 'new' movements with 'new' languages of activism underlines how much discourses of action and learning are embodied experiences, causing distress as well as euphoria. The mainly younger activists of the Extinction Rebellion movement are, in the view of Gontarska et al. significantly more the owners and creators of their pedagogy of direct action and civil disobedience. Clearly, they enjoy greater intellectual and organisational autonomy as a result of their activism in the age of social media. The interviews with them reveal their sense of having acquired more radical tools of social influence; they unfold their activism in a simultaneously highly personalised milieu of like minds and in open, mass forms of co-ordinated national and international action; the performativity of their campaigns corresponds to the high sense of self-awareness they cultivate; finally, and significantly, the individual decisions of these younger activists to participate in the movement to halt global warming is lived as an opportunity for self-knowledge and as a source of informal learning.

The activists like Krzysztof, even Ewa, may seem by comparison a little staid, and the XR activists may in turn seem inward-oriented and somewhat narcissistic, yet the testimonies of these activists, taken together over a period of substantial social upheaval and change, trace the real possibility of moving from a pedagogy of indignation alone to a pedagogy of hope in Freirean terms.

5   The Social Pedagogy of Remaking Community

Democratic processes of participation and activism certainly reinforce practices of mutual aid and other forms of social solidarity and in the widest sense action for change always transports blueprints for a future, for the future. The last three chapters of this volume in similar ways sketch in forms of engagement that offer the shapes of things that can come and speak of prefigurative forms of *vivencia*, of those alternative ways of living together and relating to each other in more mutually supportive ways. Mayo is confident of her words when she writes (Chapter 12) that there are "other, more hopeful – and more sustainable – possibilities, prefiguring the development of new societies in the shells of the old". This is echoed directly and presciently in the words already reported of a French-Madagascan social mediator interviewed by Evans (Chapter 13) who speaks of the possibility of creating through dialogue and solidarity a space where "*everyone can be a friend to everyone else*", a space in which community is put back together.

Finally, metaphorically putting the lid on the arguments pieced together by the other contributors, the authors Caride, Gradaílle and Varela Crespo (Chapter 14) state the really urgently obvious, namely that this pandemic has involved new ways of making communities, and that is certainly a reason for increased interest and confidence, but more saliently it has revitalised experiences that already had a long history of collaboration in local communities. And it has redirected our attention to the community networks created in neighbourhoods and districts. The authors argue that we must recognise their importance and their involvement in the search for collective responses to the public health crisis, which emerged in strength and almost without being called upon to do so during the lockdowns. The virtual communities, too, whose role, they rightly say, "in generating and maintaining social ties beyond physical boundaries was fundamental". The pandemic took social relations as a whole by surprise; it challenged every social organisation and questioned institutions and values, but it has engendered, too, new ways of communicating, of sharing and of dialoguing. It has made us aware of what we already knew and did; it also made us aware of new ways to do and be. That is something.

6 When All Is Said and Done

The necessary adjustments to the text and successive re-writings and re-thinkings as events toppled one over another: COP26 in Glasgow (UKCOP26.org, 2021) and the protests of the young everywhere; the fourth wave of COVID-19 (which was deepening daily as these lines were first written and has since been overtaken by a fifth and possibly a sixth); organised deployment of migrants on the borders of the EU for the purposes of political destabilisation and as bargaining chips in a 'hybrid' war' – all of these were an essential part of the 'soundtrack' accompanying this book from the start, as it is for all socially committed research. And all of these have nevertheless been since pushed aside by the seemingly unimaginable: the unleashing of war on the European continent in February 2022.

The book is almost finished – at the start of Spring 2022 – and the pandemic still affects our daily life and our ways of organising every type of social process. This influence on social and relational life is dramatic and has prevented many people from leading the social lives they did prior to the pandemic. Mental illness, too, in the forms of depression or anxiety, among others, have increased, including amongst the very young (WHO, 2021). The trauma of war and flight for millions in Europe must now be added to this account. But though this is a problem everywhere, on each continent for very many the dramatic 'normality' of conquering every day the basic minimum income necessary to carry on compounds the impact of COVID in everyday life.

Nevertheless, we want to maintain hope. And this hope is based on practices and projects such as some of those this book presents. The self-organisation of people and communities, the act of solidarity, the building of knowledge based on the people and useful for them seems to be the way to implement shared efforts where community action and public intervention create alliances for the common good, promoting dialogue and a community focus when tackling the social challenges that arise.

Looking at the history of our network, we also see how topics in the areas we have discussed over the years change and how concepts, theories and ideas evolve. In our network, we have recognised that a focus on community (in research and educational life) is necessary in order to continue to look at and research adult education with an interest led by clear commitment. Perhaps this approach, too, will soon be slipping away, transforming, changing?

But we are right now still building and re-building our research consciousness and reflecting on the role of researchers in communities. The ethical dimensions of our presence in the communities we study becomes more and more a crucial question. All the more so, as many themes important to community learning will continue to recur and emerge as hermeneutical research challenges. The response of communities in the face of natural disaster and political inequality, for example, is spelt out eloquently by Pilch Ortega in this volume (Chapter 9). Quite possibly the next most pressing research challenge will be situated on this ethical-methodological plane regarding how we as societies face the experience of the destruction and associated atrocities caused by catastrophes like the Russian invasion of Ukraine and how we will study the processes of adaptation and trauma of local communities, the communities of migrants and refugees and their roles in theatres of dramatic conflict at the margins and at the centres of our societies.

The big picture out in the world is currently anything but encouraging. The pandemic is still paramount everywhere. A war in Europe, staggering numbers of refugees and the social disruption they represent, new political, cultural and economic iron curtains falling everywhere demand actions from us and reflection on our contribution to a new possible *vivencia*. This is only complicated by the continuing civil and military conflicts that globally deny on a daily basis the most meagre forms of dignified co-existence between people and peoples. Afghanistan, the Lebanon, Yemen, Mali, Myanmar are some of the better-known sites of suffering and stalemate, where education chances and learning are closed down or regimented under doctrinaire regimes, and whole generations are deprived of their basic human right to learn, and are often forced into hiding, exile and emigration. Emigration, flight, the plight of migrants and refugees on 'our' borders, on all borders, from Bangladesh to Poland to Spain and Italy and Mexico, and their place in sad statistics of sunken dinghies, in the barbed wire camps of Lesbos and Texas, the tent cities of Dunkirk and Kakuma are the content of our newsflashes and the ammunition for racist and chauvinist politics. But these facts of our rolling news desks, long before the pictures from Kiev or Kharkiv filled the screens, have long been, too, the cause of fear and uncertainty about the future and therefore a cause of frustration and apathy for many. They ask: what can be done, where is it all heading?

Having taken the time to look back in order to look forward, one thing is patently clear to us: patience and unrelenting determination to go forward for change remains urgently necessary. To close, we answer with conviction that there *are* visible and palpable grounds for confidence, but even more abundant grounds for action, and action that *can* and *does* bring about change.

The notion of "pedagogies of possibility" (Manicom & Walters, 2012) serves very well as a possible vision that can accommodate the desire and the need to contribute to the kind of change the authors of this volume argue for in their different ways. Pedagogies of possibility suggest firstly "a grounded and pragmatic assessment of what is feasible, given the parameters of place, time, and resources" (p. 3). The chapters of this book have sketched in such parameters. Holding high hope and the commitment to our ethical-methodological responsibilities as researchers we embrace the second significance of pedagogies of possibility: a commitment to "that which is yet to be imagined, that which might become thinkable and actionable when prevailing relations of power are made visible, when understandings shake loose from normative perspectives and generate new knowledge and possibilities for engagement" (Manicom & Walters, 2012, pp. 3–4).

When all is said and done, that would be something.

References

Giannini, S., Jenkins, R., & Saavedra, J. (2021). *Mission: Recovering education in 2021.* https://www.unicef.org/media/98861/file/Mission%20:%20Recovering%20Education%20in%202021.pdf

Manicom, L., & Walters, S. (2012). Introduction: Feminist popular education. In L. Manicom & S. Walters (Eds.), *Feminist popular education in transnational debates: Building pedagogies of possibility* (pp. 1–23). Palgrave Macmillan.

Marzano, M. (2021, December 4). La crescita e l'occupazione. Non è una ripresa per donne. *la Repubblica.*

UKCOP26.org. (2021). *UN climate change conference 2021.* https://ukcop26.org/

WHO. (2021). *New storybook to help children stay hopeful during COVID-19.* https://www.who.int/news/item/24-09-2021-new-storybook-to-help-children-stay-hopeful-during-covid-19

Index

activism
    and acting communities   157
    and advocacy   162
    and coping mechanisms   157
    and group dynamics   167
    and significance of social commitment   160
    and the costs of activism   158
    and trademarks of new activism   180
    and value systems   164
    as a critical response to existing realities   171
    as an embodied practice   168
    as central core of the biography   159
    bringing justice to the margins   162
    feminist activism central to women's museums   102
    'high profile' and 'everyday' activism   162
    in the age of socia media   246
    'pulsating activism'   157
    triggers for activism   157
adult education
    affected by austerity policies   198
    afflicted by vanguardist utilitarianism   32
    and communities   1
    and community capacity-building   80
    and Freire's ideas   47
    and pitfalls in European projects   66
    and social justice   80
    and social problems   1
    and the COVID-19 pandemic   198
    and work with communities   167
    ensuring it is future-oriented   117
    feminist adult education   100
    formal participation halved   198
    impact of austerity on resources   200
    learning in communities   3
    need to play a role in decolonisation   116
    neglected within education policy   111
    nostalgia as a trap   117
    popular adult education and community development   200
    shaped by visions of flexibility and mobility   79
    transdisciplinary and boundary-breaking   116

adult learning
    and community development   3
    and community generation   118
    and critical thinking   202
    and employability   20
    and human rights   20
    and popular education   193
    and work with communities   10
    as a liberating force   33
    as a site of resistance   8, 120
    facing new challenges   20
    for interdependent communities   118
    inclusive approaches to   192
    incompatible with monocultural agendas   20
    promoting active citizenship   191
    the future of   115
    the instrumentalisation of   29
agency   96, 113, 154, 163, 164, 177, 219, 221, 222, 225, 246
    agency of things and posthuman theory   113
    and neo-liberalism   115
    and self-empowerment   151
    as factor of exclusion   115
    limited by dominant discourses   147
andragogy
    as theory and didactics   8
    corporeal and creative andragogy   119
    of inclusion   8

biographical identity
    concept developed by Schütze and Strauss   132
biographical-narrative interview   158
biography   133
    and collective learning processes   147
Bourdieu, Pierre
    and reproduction of hegemony   40
    social crisis and doxic assumptions   147
    the logics of the field   148
    transformative potential of social crises   143
Braidotti, Rosa   113

CBPR (Community-Based Participatory Research)
  and acquiring CBPR capabilities 86
  and high interest in CBPR training 86
  building research capacity in the global South 81
  global survey on teaching and learning CBPR 85–86
  improving teaching and training in CBPR 86–88
  in major global research projects 81
  privileging the experiential knowledge of community 81
citizenship
  active citizenship and participation 66
  and everyday life experiences 66
  and learning civic competences 64
  as an everyday learning practice 66
  as learning outcome 65
  citizenship education focused on people's rights *see Misiones Pedagógicas*
  education driven by neoliberal LLL discourse 74
  in European policy documents 65
  in need of critical reflection in Europe 73
  increasing the relevance of citizenship education 74
  lack of critical global perspective in EU 66
civil disobedience 175–176
  acquiring self knowledge and experience 182
  and critical democracy 179
  transgression and nonviolence 182
  XR and activists' safety 184
  XR and the 'culture of regeneration' 180
Collectivo Chiquitraca 152
communities
  and collectives memories and identities 128
  and creating 'cultural synthesis' 33, *see also* Freire, Paolo
  and creation of mutual aid 200
  and framing disaster biographically 144
  and potential role of migrants 56
  and the obligation to act 232
  as acting communities 157
  as point of reference of civic values 230
  as privileged spaces 1
  changed through knowledge transformation 111
  competing for diminishing resources 192
  confronted with natural disasters 143
  engaging creatively with COVID-19 192
  exchange of knowledge with universities 84
  in the excluded North 'subaltern' communities 81
  polarising effects of COVID-19 198
community
  and experiential knowledge of members 81
  and knowledge creation 84
  and knowledge curation 91
  and the more than human 116
  as a bounded entity 117
  as a 'doing' 118
  as a privileged space for learning 41
  as a 'verb' not a 'noun' 118
  as act of social mutuality 116
  as alternative to school education 40
  as an agent for care 234
  as foundation of knowledge 41
  as platform for mutual learning 88
  as process and practice 118
  as source of change 79
  community education
    impact of austerity policies 71
    promotion of democracy and citizenship 20
    social dynamics of diversity 29
  community engagement with HEIs 88
  community learning
    under precarious conditions 143
    connected to academic work 85
    gender community mapping 105
    learning processes 128
    more than solely social 116
    multiform community 116
    negated by competitive individualisation 25
    neighbourhood networks and COVID-19 238
    re-making community
      via decolonisation and sustainability 116
    responses to COVID-19 pandemic 203

INDEX

support for practitioners   87
too little focus on how it works   117
corporeality of learning   119
COVID-19 pandemic   1, 6, 11, 12, 13, 31, 80, 81, 90, 206, 209
cultural synthesis   33
CURP (Community-University Research Partnership)   81–83

dementia
　and intergenerational learning   118
　and non-humanistic ways of being   116
　and the post-verbal   113
　categorised as outside the category human   113
　co-production of knowledge   115
　corporeality of learning   119
　disruption of ontological hierarchies   116
　marginalisation in communities   111
　neglected by lifelong learning debates   112
　ontological and epistemological issues not addressed   111
　re-making community   120
dialogue
　and educational processes in Freire   39
　and museum-theatre collaboration for community building   106
　and participatory research   44
　and social mediation   219
　as a guarantee of communication and cooperation   44, see also Freire, Paolo
　as a methodology   39
　as an encounter between human beings   44, see also Freire, Paolo
　as main methodology   39, see also Freire, Paolo
　between cultures and subcultures   20
　building relationships between people   45
　democratic dialogue and conviviality   4
　dialogue and dialogic learning   4, see also Freire, Paolo
　respecting issues and emotions   198
　social dialogue and collective experience   138
　social dialogue and informal learning   9
　social dialogue with fragile populations   224
　with significant others   212

diversity
　cultural and linguistic diversity   53
　cultural diversity   20, 28
　diversity and ambivalence   60
　diversity in languages   59
　diversity of cultural resources   138
　diversity of knowledge   84
　diversity of learning contexts   66
　diversity of urban cultures   58
　loss of biodiversity   175
　migration diversity   57
　sexual and ethnic diversity   48
　urban diversity   52

ecology
　deep ecology   229
empowerment
　a principle of social mediation   208
　and collective agency   154
　of women and girls   100
epistemicide   7, 80
ethnographic
　field investigation   148
　use of observation   113
ethnographic research   172
Extinction Rebellion (XR)   172–174
　and 'artivist' instruments of protest   178
　and new forms of activism   171
　individual and collective counter-hegemonic practice   174

Fals Borda, Orlando   3, 5, 41, 42, 43, 80
far right populism
　distrust in institutions and governments   197
feminism
　as a critical vision and positioning   100
　vilified as a term   100
feminist
　education to (re)historicise herstory   96
　feminist historical consciousness   106
　feminist imaginary   106
　feminist new materialists   113
　feminist pedagogies   244
　feminist public interventions   105
　historical consciousness   96
　intercultural understanding   104
　museologists   101
　pedagogical work for socio-gender justice   96

representations of history and
society   97
Freire, Paolo
    against pedagogism   32
    and 'cultural invasion'   21
    and his Christian faith   39
    and process of 'mythologising the
        world'   27
    and the 'absolutisation of ignorance'   32
    and the acritical nature of clichés   27
    and 'true' non-oligarchic organisation   21
    approach to permanent education   22
    banking concept of education and deficit
        theory   26
    critique of technocratic view of
        learning   23
    education as a process of
        humanisation   21–25
    Education as the Practice of Freedom
        (1967)   20
    Pedagogy of Freedom (1996)   23
    Pedagogy of the Oppressed (1968)   4, 20,
        21, 22, 27, 32, 33, 37
Frena la curva   237

Gelpi, Ettore   31, 33
    and a new world order of education   56
    and educational contexts in
        transition   53
    and learning from below   55
    and 'life culture'   55
    and similarities with Abdelmalek
        Sayad   57
    building on resources of population   60
    concept of culture   55–56
    dialectical approach to educational
        thought   54
    education as training   30
    folk culture and mass culture   56
    researching culture and education
        54–55
    studying cultures and traditions of
        migrants   58
global
    anthropogenic climate change   243
    climate crisis   11, 174, 242
    educational policy discussion   4
    global flows   52
    global interdependencies   231

global learning market   23
global mainstream   2
global overview of engaged research   7
global public sphere   174
global race for talent   27
global recession, austerity and
    pandemic   200
global reconstruction of education and
    development   66
global South   81, 89
global warming   242
globalised supply chains   6
globalist movements   184
global-local relationships   229
globally-connected communities   2
incomprehension of global context
    for citizenship and learning   6
Next Gen global study   89
post-national and global activism   9
survey on CURPs   *see* CURP
XR as global movement   172
grounded theory   148

Illich, Ivan   32, 33
    deschooling society   40–41
    Deschooling Society (1971)   40
    learning webs   41
    replacing school with community   41
    school as transmitter of hegemonic
        knowledge   42
Indigenous
    genocide of Indigenous peoples   7
    indigenous ways of knowing   116
    recognition of Indigenous rights   243
interviews
    and biographical processes of
        learning   131
    and generative themes   47
    and open questioning   173
    and risk of re-traumatisation   148
    coding with Atlas.ti   173
    data analysis with Atlas.ti   174
    empirically linked to videos   149
    language, transcripts and
        analysis   159
    online interviews   173
    unstructured biographical
        interviews   211–212
    with families and carers   113

INDEX   255

knowledge
    as collective societal endeavour   84
    as negative epistemic consequences   96
    as tool for action   80
    CBPR knowledge products   *see* CBPR
    civic knowledge and skills of
        citizens   195
    co-constructing action-oriented
        knowledge   81
    co-creation of knowledge   *see* CURP
    colonial and hegemonic knowledge   40
    created in multiple forms   80
    democratic knowledge partnerships   82
    denigration of experiential
        knowledge   41
    diversity of knowledge   85
    Euro-centric knowledge and
        epistemicide   80
    'givers of knowledge'   96
    hierarchies of knowledge   116
    knowledge claim   213
    knowledge democracy   42
    knowledge production   80
    knowledge to bring about
        change   100
    knowledge workers   89
    knowledge-building capacity within
        communities   81
    lifeless knowledge   41
    local and intergenerational
        knowledge   129
    memory knowledge   130
    mobilisation and dissemination   90
    of the narrative subject   129
    produced in educational acts   44
    radical knowledge transformation   111
    regaining lost community
        knowledge   130
    remaking knowledge   243
    socialising knowledge   48
    subjective knowledge and
        biographicity   219
    transferring knowledge from school to
        community   41
knowledge creation   6, 80, 81, 82, 84

LGBTQ
    LGBTQ+ communities in Poland   184
    stories of LGBTQI2+ communities   99

memory
    complex interrelation of individual and
        collective memory   153
    cultural and communicative
        memory   138
Misiones Pedagógicas   45–46

narrative-biographical interview   148, 154
*National Festival of Theatre Against Gender
    Violence*   106
neoliberal globalisation
    and austerity policies   12
    and climate change   202
    and increasing polarisation   192
    and populism   11

participatory research   41–43
    and Fals-Borda   42
    and Kurt Lewin   41
    and Matja-Liisa Swantz   41
    and popular science   42
    and Rodolfo Stavenhagen   42
    and vivencia   43
    community-based participatory research
        (CBPR)   81
    creating knowledge from experience   39
pedagogy   246
    and citizenship   66
    and COVID-19   231
    as an oppositional practice   174
    Critical Pedagogy   20
    neoliberal pedagogy   32
    of direct action   246
    of entrepreneuralism and
        competition   20
    of liberation   21
    of social possibility   246
    of the oppressed   21
    pedagogy shaping gendered epistemic
        injustice   95
    political pedagogy   21
    public pedagogy and XR   174
    radical-democratic pedagogy   22
PhEmaterialism   113
populism   22, 195, 197
    and trust in COVID-19 vaccines   197
    far right populism   192, 193
    the growth of far right populism   195–198
    theoretical roots   197

posthuman
    vision of the person 115
posthuman theory 113
posthumanism
    and the agentic assemblage 113
    tendency to utopian thinking 113

qualificationism
    and neo-liberal skills regimes 4
    as cultural invasion 25
    as 'tools for life' 243

re-making community 79, 114, 132
    forms of vivencia 247

Sayad, Abdelmalek 57
    Le phénomène migratoire (1981) *see* Gelpi, Ettore
sequential analysis 159, *see also* narrative-biographical interview
social media
    and data collection 148
    as 'bubbles' of existing beliefs 202
    as echo chambers of disinformation 195
    as research materials 172
    effective management of social media for activism 178
social mediation
    a definition 207
    and "re-sewing" social ties 13
    and COVID-19 209
    and creation of social bonds 209
    and professional qualities 224
    as a form of dialogue 208
    different national forms 208
    identifying common practices 211
    making community 224
    principles of 208
    research into 208
    responses across Europe to COVID-19 224
social pedagogy 12, 14, 230, 238, 246
    as education making the community 230
    as social education 230
    committed to justice and development 238
    creating access channels to inclusion 238
    enabling inclusion and cohesion 230
    opening borders 230
sociographicity
    biographical and social learning 147
    social modes of learning 148
solidarity
    and dialogue 247
    and digital technology 237
    and social learning 66
    and social mediation 208
    building solidarity in community learning processes 151
    in a network society 232
    in response to COVID-19 192
    inequality and low social solidarity 194
    mutual aid and community solidarity 201
    networks and the pandemic 233
Solnit, Rebecca 95, 104
Somos tribu 235
Sousa Santos, Boaventura de 80, 231

Tadjo, Veronique
    In the Company of Men (2021) 12, 202–203
The Social and Historical Memory Workshop 46–47
The World Transformed (TWT) *Festival* 199
transcorporeality
    of the human and more than human 116

virtual communities
    and COVID-19 238
    and new forms of dialogue 247
    and technologically mediated community initiatives 236
    maintaining social ties 13
Vivencia 43

Walters, Shirley 1, 6, 20, 80, 102, 249
Williams, Raymond 55–56
    culture as a whole way of life 55
women's and gender museums 96–100
women's museums
    and artefiction 102
    and struggle for justice 96
    as virtual spaces 98
    construction of the feminine 97
    decolonisation and re-historicisation 101
    education as central mandate 100
    feminist adult education 100

gender central to activities 98
Iranian Women's Movement Museum
 (IRWMM) 104
KØN Gender Museum 99
Musée de la Femme 99
Museo de la Mujer 105
preserving women's cultures 97
primary audience 99
sources of feminist imaginary 106
Swedish Museum of Women's
 History 103
WAM Tokyo 103
Women's Museum in Bonn 104
Women's Museum in Merano 98
WWHRM Korea 103–104
Zambian Women's History Museum 100

XR *see* Extinction Rebellion

Zanier, Leonardo 53–54, 58–60
 adult education and vocational
  training 59
 and language training of migrant
  workers 59
 and processes of acculturation 59
 and resources of whole communities
  60
 and social integration of
  migrants 59
 and transnational factors of
  migration 60
 La lingua degli emigrati
  (1977) 59

Printed in the United States
by Baker & Taylor Publisher Services